Dr. C   I0014055

DBMS - Database Management System

Dr. Ch. Seetha Ram

DBMS - Database Management System

Support for large amount of data

VDM Verlag Dr. Müller

Impressum/Imprint (nur für Deutschland/ only for Germany)

Bibliografische Information der Deutschen Nationalbibliothek: Die Deutsche Nationalbibliothek verzeichnet diese Publikation in der Deutschen Nationalbibliografie; detaillierte bibliografische Daten sind im Internet über http://dnb.d-nb.de abrufbar.

Alle in diesem Buch genannten Marken und Produktnamen unterliegen warenzeichen-, marken- oder patentrechtlichem Schutz bzw. sind Warenzeichen oder eingetragene Warenzeichen der jeweiligen Inhaber. Die Wiedergabe von Marken, Produktnamen, Gebrauchsnamen, Handelsnamen, Warenbezeichnungen u.s.w. in diesem Werk berechtigt auch ohne besondere Kennzeichnung nicht zu der Annahme, dass solche Namen im Sinne der Warenzeichen- und Markenschutzgesetzgebung als frei zu betrachten wären und daher von jedermann benutzt werden dürften.

Coverbild: www.ingimage.com

Verlag: VDM Verlag Dr. Müller GmbH & Co. KG
Dudweiler Landstr. 99, 66123 Saarbrücken, Deutschland
Telefon +49 681 9100-698, Telefax +49 681 9100-988
Email: info@vdm-verlag.de

Herstellung in Deutschland:
Schaltungsdienst Lange o.H.G., Berlin
Books on Demand GmbH, Norderstedt
Reha GmbH, Saarbrücken
Amazon Distribution GmbH, Leipzig
ISBN: 978-3-639-35429-4

Imprint (only for USA, GB)

Bibliographic information published by the Deutsche Nationalbibliothek: The Deutsche Nationalbibliothek lists this publication in the Deutsche Nationalbibliografie; detailed bibliographic data are available in the Internet at http://dnb.d-nb.de.

Any brand names and product names mentioned in this book are subject to trademark, brand or patent protection and are trademarks or registered trademarks of their respective holders. The use of brand names, product names, common names, trade names, product descriptions etc. even without a particular marking in this works is in no way to be construed to mean that such names may be regarded as unrestricted in respect of trademark and brand protection legislation and could thus be used by anyone.

Cover image: www.ingimage.com

Publisher: VDM Verlag Dr. Müller GmbH & Co. KG
Dudweiler Landstr. 99, 66123 Saarbrücken, Germany
Phone +49 681 9100-698, Fax +49 681 9100-988
Email: info@vdm-publishing.com

Printed in the U.S.A.
Printed in the U.K. by (see last page)
ISBN: 978-3-639-35429-4

DBMS

CONTENTS

1. INTRODUCTION TO RDBMS

- ❑ What is DBMS?
- ❑ Data Models
- ❑ Relational database management system (RDBMS)
- ❑ Relational Algebra
- ❑ Structured Query Language (SQL)

2. INTRODUCTION TO ORACLE 15-

- ❑ What is Oracle?
- ❑ Oracle database server
- ❑ Oracle Instance
- ❑ What is personal oracle?

- Starting Database
- Starting SQL*Plus
- Summary

Exercises

3.GETTING STARTED WITH ORACLE8*I*

- Creating a table
- Data types
- Displaying table definition using DESCRIBE
- Inserting rows into a table
- Selecting rows from a table
- Editing SQL buffer
- Summary

Exercises

4. Creating sample TABLES

- What is a constraint?
- Types of constraints?
- Sample tables
- Creating integrity constraints
- Creating example table
- Inserting sample data
- Summary
- Exercises

5. Changing Structure and Data

- Altering the structure of a table
- Dropping a table
- Manipulating data
- Transaction
- Locking
- Read Consistency
- Summary

    Exercises

6. Arithmetic and Date functions

- What is a function?
- Types of functions
- Arithmetic functions
- Dual table
- Date arithmetic
- Date functions
- Summary
- Exercises

7. String, Conversion, and Miscellaneous functions

- String functions
- Conversion functions
- Miscellaneous functions

9. JOINING TABLES

- Joining tables

- Self-join
- Outer Join

SET Operators

10. VIEWS

- What is a view?
- Why we need a view?
- Creating and using a view
- Simplifying query using view
- Presenting data in different forms
- Isolating application from changes in definition of table
- Changing base table through view
- Updatable join views
- Dropping a view

11. SUBQUERIES

- What is a subquery?
- Multiple Subqueries
- Nested subquery
- Using subquery in DML commands
- Correlated subquery
- EXISTS, NOT EXISTS, ANY and ALL operators

12. INDEXING, CLUSTERING, SEQUENCE AND PSEUDO COLUMNS

- What is an index

- Why to use an index
- Creating an index
- When Oracle does not use index
- Clustering
- Sequence
- Pseudo columns

13. SECURITY

- Users and privileges
- Object privileges
- Granting object privileges
- Using synonyms
- Revoking object privileges
- System privileges
- Using roles
- ALTER USER command
- Data dictionary views

14. REPORT GENERATION USING SQL*PLUS commands

- What is a report?
- Sample report xy
- Report script
- Break command
- Compute command
- Column command
- Ttitle and Btitle commands

- ❏ Spool command
- ❏ Clear command
- ❏ System variables
- ❏ Displaying information using SHOW command

15. INTRODUCTION TO PL/SQL

- ❏ What is PL/SQL?
- ❏ PL/SQL engine
- ❏ Features of PL/SQL
- ❏ Advantages of PL/SQL
- ❏ PL/SQL Block
- ❏ Writing first PL/SQL block
- ❏ Nested blocks
- ❏ Scope and visibility of variables
- ❏ Labeling the block
- ❏ Assignment Operator
- ❏ Displaying output from PL/SQL

16. CONTROL STRUCTURES

- ❏ IF statement
- ❏ Loop...End Loop
- ❏ Exit command
- ❏ While Loop
- ❏ For loop
- ❏ Goto statement

17. EXCEPTION HANDLING

- What is an exception?
- How to handle exceptions?
- Predefined exceptions
- When NO_DATA_FOUND exception is not raised?
- User-defined exception
- Reraising an exception
- Associating an exception With An Oracle Error
- Exception propagation
- When is a PL/SQL block successful or failure?

18. CURSOR HANDLING

- What is a cursor?
- When do we need explicit cursor?
- Handling explicit cursor
- Cursor FOR loop
- Sample program
- Implicit cursor
- Cursor attributes
- Input arguments to cursor
- FOR UPDATE and CURRENT OF clauses

19. PROCEDURES, FUNCTIONS and packages

- What is a stored procedure?
- Advantages of stored procedures
- Creating a stored procedure
- Creating a stored function
- Recompiling

- Types of parameters
- Parameter modes
- NCOPY compiler hints
- RAISE_APPLICATION_ERROR procedure
- Packages

20. DATABASE TRIGGERS

- What is a database trigger?
- Types of Triggers
- Creating a database trigger
- Correlation names
- Instead-of triggers
- Knowing which command fired the trigger
- Enabling and disabling trigger
- Dropping a trigger

21. LOBs

- Introduction
- LOB Data types
- Defining and Manipulating LOBs
- DBMS_LOB Package

22. OBJECT TYPES

- Introduction to object types
- Creating object type and object
- Using object type
- Creating methods

- Accessing objects using SQL

- Object Type Dependencies

- Object Tables

- Using objects in PL/SQL

- MAP and ORDER MEMBER functions

23. VARRAY AND NESTED TABLE

- What is a collection?

- What is a VARRAY?

- Using VARRAY

- Nested Table

- Using DML commands with Nested Table

- Collection methods

24. Native Dynamic SQL
- What is dynamic SQL?

- Why do we need dynamic SQL?

- An Example of Dynamic SQL

- Execute Immediate Statement

- Using Placeholders

- Execute a Query Dynamically

- Executing multi-row query dynamically

- Dynamic PL/SQL Blocks

1. INTRODUCTION TO RDBMS

- What is DBMS?

- Data Models

- Relational database management system (RDBMS)

- Relational Algebra

- Structured query language (SQL)

What Is DBMS?

Data is one of the most important assets of a company. It is very important to make sure data is stored and maintained accurately and quickly. DBMS (**Data**base **M**anagement **S**ystem) is a system that is used to store and manage data. A DBMS is a set of programs that is used to store and manipulation data. Manipulation of data include the following:

- Adding new data, for example adding details of new student.

- Deleting unwanted data, for example deleting the details of students who have completed course.

- Changing existing data, for example modifying the fee paid by the student.

A DBMS provides various functions like data security, data integrity, data sharing, data concurrence, data independence, data recovery etc. However, all database management systems that are now available in the market like Sybase, Oracle, and MS-Access do not provide the same set of functions, though all are meant for data management. Database managements systems like Oracle, DB2 are more powerful and meant for bigger companies. Whereas, database management systems like MS-Access are meant for small companies. So one has to choose the DBMS depending upon the requirement.

Features of DBMS

The following are main features offered by DBMS. Apart from these features different database management systems may offer different features. For instance, Oracle is increasing being fine-tuned to be the database for Internet applications. This may not be found in other database management systems. These are the general features of database management systems. Each DBMS has its own way of implementing it. A DBMS may have more features the features discussed here and may also enhance these features.

Support for large amount of data

Each DBMS is designed to support large amount of data. They provide special ways and means to store and manipulate large amount of data. Companies are trying to store more and more amount of data. Some of this data will have to be online (available every time). In most of the cases the amount of data that can be stored is not actually constrained by DBSM and instead constrained by the availability of the hardware. For example, Oracle can store terabytes of data.

Data sharing, concurrency and locking

DBSM also allows data to be shared by two or more users. The same data can be accessed by multiple users at the same time – data concurrency. However when same data is being manipulated at the same time by multiple users certain problems arise. To avoid these problems, DBMS locks data that is being manipulated to avoid two users from modifying the same data at the same time.

The locking mechanism is transparent and automatic. Neither we have to inform to DBMS about locking nor we need to know how and when DBMS is locking the data. However, as a programmer, if we can know intricacies of locking mechanism used by DBMS, we will be better programmers.

Data Security

While DBMS allowing data to be shared, it also ensures that data in only accessed by authorized users. DBMS provides features needed to implement security at the enterprise level. By default, the data of a user cannot be accessed by other users unless the owner gives explicit permissions to other users to do so.

Data Integrity

Maintaining integrity of the data is an import process. If data loses integrity, it becomes unusable and garbage. DBMS provides means to implement rules to maintain integrity of the data. Once we specify which rules are to be implemented, then DBMS can make sure that these rules are implemented always. Three integrity rules (discussed later in this chapter) – domain, entity and referential are always supported by DBMS.

Fault tolerance and recovery

DBMS provides great deal of fault tolerance. They continue to run in spite of errors, if possible, allowing users to rectify the mistake in the mean time.

DBSM also allows recovery in the event of failure. For instance, if data on the disk is completely lost due to disk failure then also data can be recovered to the point of failure if proper back up of the data is available.

Support for Languages

DBMS supports a data access and manipulation language. The most widely used data access language for RDBMS (relational database management systems) is SQL. We will discuss more about RDBMS and SQL later in this chapter. DBMS implementation of SQL will be compliant with SQL standards set by ANSI. Apart from supporting a non-procedural language like SQL to access and manipulate data DBMS now a days also provides a procedural language for data processing. Oracle supports PL/SQL and SQL Server provides T-SQL.

Entity and Attribute

An entity is any object that is stored in the database. Each entity is associated with a collection of attributes. For example, if you take a data of a training institute, student is an entity as we store information about each student in the database. Each student is associated with certain values such as roll number, name, course etc., which are called as attributes of the entity.

There will be relationship among entities. The relationship between entities may be one-to-one, one-to-many or many-to-many. If you take entities student, batch and subject, the following are the possible relationships. There is one-to-one relationship between batch and subject. One batch is associated with only one subject. Three is one-to-many relationship between batch and student entities. One batch may contain many students. There is many-to-many relationship between student and subject entities. A single student may take many subjects and a single subject may be taken by multiple students.

Data Models

Data model is a way of storing and retrieving the data. There are three different data models. Data models differ in the way they allow users to view and manipulate relationships between entities. Each has its own way of storing the data. The following are the three different data models:

❏ Hierarchical

❏ Network

❏ Relational

❏

Hierarchical

In this model, data is stored in the form of a tree. The data is represented by parent-child relation ship. Each tree contains a single root record and one or more subordinate records. For example, each batch is root and students of the batch will be subordinates.

This model supports only one-to-many relationship between entities.

This was used in IBM's Information *management system,* IMS.

Network

Data is stored along with pointers, which specify the relationship between entities. This was used in Honeywell's *Integrated Data Store*, IDS. This model is complex. It is difficult to understand both the way data is stored and the way data is manipulated. It is capable of supporting many-to-many relationship between entities, which hierarchical model doesn't.

Relational

This stores data in the form of a table. Table is a collection of rows and columns. We will discuss more about relational model in the next second.

Relational Database Management System (RDBMS)

A DBMS that is based on *relational model* is called as RDBMS. Relation model is most successful mode of all three models. Designed by E.F. Codd, relational model is based on the theory of sets and relations of mathematics. Relational model represents data in the form a table. A table is a two dimensional array containing rows and columns. Each row contains data related to an entity such as a student. Each column contains the data related to a single attribute of the entity such as student name. One of the reasons behind the success of relational model is its simplicity. It is easy to understand the data and easy to manipulate. Another important advantage with relational model, compared with remaining two models is, it doesn't bind data with relationship between data item. Instead it allows you to have dynamic relationship between entities using the values of the columns. Almost all Database systems that are sold in the market, now- a-days, have either complete or partial implementation of relational model.

Figure 1 shows how data is represented in relational model and what are the terms used to refer to various components of a table. The following are the terms used in relational model.

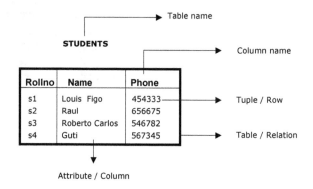

Figure 1: A table in relational model.

Tuple / Row

A single row in the table is called as tuple. Each row represents the data of a single entity.

Attribute / Column

A column stores an attribute of the entity. For example, if details of students are stored then student name is an attribute; course is another attribute and so on.

Column Name

Each column in the table is given a name. This name is used to refer to value in the column.

Table Name

Each table is given a name. This is used to refer to the table. The name depicts the content of the table. The following are two other terms, primary key and foreign key, that are very important in relational model.

Primary Key

A table contains the data related entities. If you take STUDETNS table, it contains data related to students. For each student there will be one row in the table. Each student's data in the table must be uniquely identified. In order to identify each entity uniquely in the table, we use a column in the table. That column, which is used to uniquely identify entities (students) in the table is called as primary key.

In case of STUDENTS table (see figure 1) we can use ROLLNO as the primary key as it in not duplicated.

So a primary key can be defined as a **set of columns used to uniquely identify rows of a table.**

Some other examples for primary keys are account number in bank, product code of products, employee number of an employee.

Composite Primary Key

In some tables a single column cannot be used to uniquely identify entities (rows). In that case we have to use two or more columns to uniquely identify rows of the table. When a primary key contains two or more columns it is called as composite primary key.

In figure 2, we have PAYMENTS table, which contains the details of payments made by the students. Each row in the table contains roll number of the student, payment date and amount paid. Neither of the columns can uniquely identify rows. So we have to combine ROLLNO and DP to uniquely identify rows in the table. As primary key is consisting of two columns it is called as composite primary key.

Figure 2: Composite Primary Key

PAYMENTS

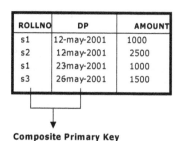

ROLLNO	DP	AMOUNT
s1	12-may-2001	1000
s2	12may-2001	2500
s1	23may-2001	1000
s3	26may-2001	1500

Composite Primary Key

Foreign Key

In relational model, we often store data in different tables and put them together to get complete information. For example, in PAYMENTS table we have only ROLLNO of the student. To get remaining information about the student we have to use STUDETNS table. Roll number in PAYMENTS table can be used to obtain remaining information about the student. The relationship

STUDENTS

ROLLNO	NAME	PHONE
s1	Louis Figo	454333
s2	Raul	656675
s3	Roberto Carlos	546782
s4	Guti	567345

PAYMENTS

ROLLNO	DP	AMOUNT
s1	12-may-2001	1000
s2	12-may-2001	2500
s1	23-may-2001	1500
s2	23-may-2001	1000

Foreign Key

between entities student and payment is one-to-many. One student may make payment for many times. As we already have ROLLNO column in PAYMENTS table, it is possible to join with STUDENTS table and get information about parent entity (student). Roll number column of PAYMENTS table is called as *foreign key* as it is used to join PAYMENTS table with STUDENTS table. So foreign key is the key on the many side of the relationship. ROLLNO column of PAYMENTS table must derive its values from ROLLNO column of STUDENTS table. When a child table contains a row that doesn't refer to a corresponding parent key, it is called as orphan record. We must not have orphan records, as they are result of lack of data integrity.

Figure 3: Foreign Key

Integrity Rules

Data integrity is to be maintained at any cost. If data loses integrity it becomes garbage. So every effort is to be made to ensure data integrity is maintained. The following are the main integrity rules that are to be followed.

Domain integrity

Data is said to contain domain integrity when the value of a column is derived from the domain. Domain is the collection of potential values. For example, column date of joining must be a valid date. All valid dates form one domain. If the value of date of joining is an invalid date, then it is said to violate domain integrity.

Entity integrity

This specifies that all values in primary key must be not null and unique. Each entity that is stored in the table must be uniquely identified. Every table must contain a primary key and primary key must be not null and unique.

Referential Integrity

This specifies that a foreign key must be either null or must have a value that is derived from corresponding parent key. For example, if we have a table called BATCHES, then ROLLNO column of the table will be referencing ROLLNO column of STUDENTS table. All the values of ROLLNO column of BATCHES table must be derived from ROLLNO column of STUDENTS table. This is because of the fact that no student who is not part of STUDENTS table can join a batch

Relational Algebra

A set of operators used to perform operations on tables is called as **relational algebra**. Operators in relational algebra take one or more tables as parameters and produce one table as the result.

The following are operators in relational algebra:

- Union
- Intersect
- Difference or minus
- Project
- Select
- Join

Union

This takes two tables and returns all rows that are belonging to either first or second table (or both). See figure 4.

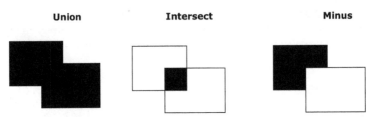

Figure 4: Union, Intersect and Minus

Intersect

This takes two tables and returns all rows that are belonging to first and second table. See figure 4.

Difference or Minus

This takes two tables and returns all rows that exist in the first table and not in the second table. See figure 4.

Project

Takes a single table and returns the vertical subset of the table. See figure 1.5.

Select

Takes a single table and returns a horizontal subset of the table. That means it returns only those rows that satisfy the condition. See figure 1.5.

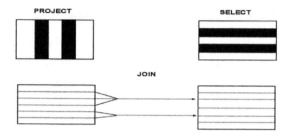

Figure 5: Project, Select and Join

Join

Rows of two table are combined based on the given column(s) values. The tables being joined must have a common column. See figure 5.

Note: See chapter 3, for SELECT and PROJECT, chapter 9 for JOIN, UNION, INTERSECT and MINUS.

Structured Query Language (SQL)

Almost all relational database management systems use SQL (Structured Query Language) for data manipulation and retrieval. SQL is the standard language for relational database systems. SQL is a non-procedural language, where you need to concentrate on what you want, not on how you get it. Put it in other way, you need not be concerned with procedural details.

SQL Commands are divided into four categories, depending upon what they do.

- DDL (Data Definition Language)
- DML (Data Manipulation Language)
- DCL (Data Control Language)
- Query (Retrieving data)

DDL commands are used to define the data. For example, CREATE TABLE.

DML commands such as, INSERT and DELETE are used to manipulate data.

DCL commands are used to control access to data. For example, GRANT.

Query is used to retrieve data using SELECT.

DML and Query are also collectively called as DML. And DDL and DCL are called as DDL.

Data processing Methods

Data that is stored is processed in three different ways. Processing data means retrieving data and deriving information from data. Depending upon where it is done and how it is done, there are three methods.

- ❑ Centralized data processing
- ❑ De-centralized data processing
- ❑ Distributed data processing

❑

Centralized data processing

In this method the entire data is stored in one place and processed there itself. Mainframe is best example for this kind of processing. The entire data is stored and processed on mainframe. All programs, invoked from clients (dumb terminals), are executed on the mainframe and data is also stored in mainframe.

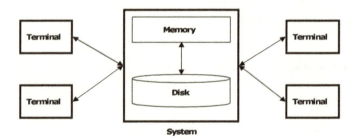

22

Figure 6: Centralized data processing.

As you can see in figure 6, all terminals are attached to mainframe. Terminals do not have any processing ability. They take input from users and send output to users.

Decentralized data processing

In this data is processed at various places. A typical example is each department containing its own system for its own data processing needs. See figure 7, for an example of decentralized data processing. Each department stores data related to itself and runs all programs that process its data. But the biggest drawback of this type of data processing is that data is to be duplicated. As common data is to be stored in each machine, it is called as *redundancy*. This redundancy will cause data inconsistency. That means the data stored by two departments will not agree with each other.

Data in this mode is duplicated, as there is no means to store common data in one place and access from all machines.

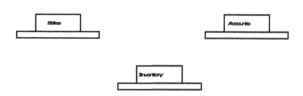

Figure 7: Decentralized Data Processing.

Distributed Data Processing (Client/Server)

In this data processing method, data process is distributed between client and server. Server takes care of managing data. Client interacts with user. For example, if you assume a process where we need to draw a graph to show the number of students in a given month for each subject, the following steps will take place:

Figure 8: Distributed data processing.

1. First, client interacts with user and takes input (month name) from user and then passes it to server.

2. Server then will query the database to get data related to the month, which is sent to server, and will send data back to client.

3. The client will then use the data retrieved from database to draw a graph.

If you look at the above process, the client and server are equally participating in the process. That is the reason this type of data processing is called as distributed. The process is evenly distributed between client and server. Client is a program written in one of the font-end tools such as Visual basic or Delphi. Server is a database management system such as Oracle, SQL Server etc. The language used to send commands from client to server is SQL (see figure 8). This is also called as two-tier client/server architecture. In this we have only two tiers (layers) one is server and another is client. The following is an example of 3-tier client server, where client interacts with user on one side and interacts with application server on another side. Application, which processes and validates data, takes the request from client and sends the request in the language understood by database server. Application servers are generally object oriented. They expose a set of object, whose methods are to be invoked by client to perform the required operation. Application server takes some burden from database server and some burden from client.

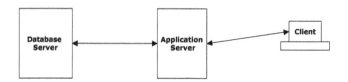

Figure 9: 3-tier client-server architecture.

In 3-tier client/server architecture, database server and application server may reside on different machines or on the same machine. Since the advent of web application we are also seeing more than 3-tiers, which is called as n-tier architecture. For example, the following is the sequence in a typical web application.

1. Client- web browser, sends request to web server.

2. Web server executes the request page, which may be an ASP or JSP.

3. ASP or JSP will access application server.

4. Application server then will access database server.

Summary

A DBMS is used to store and manipulate data. A DBMS based on relational model is RDBMS. Primary key is used for unique identification of rows and foreign key to join tables. Relational algebra is a collection of operators used to operate on tables. We will see how to practically use these operators in later chapter. SQL is a language commonly used in RDBMS to store and retrieve data. In my opinion, SQL is one of the most important languages if you are dealing with an RDBMS because total data access is done using SQL.

Exercises

1. _____ Designed relational model.

2. Data models are _____, _____ and _____.

3. Composite primary key is _____.

25

4. A row is otherwise known as _____.

5. How many tables does SELECT operator take? _____.

6. _____ is an example for an RDBMS.

7. SQL command used to create table belongs to _____ category.

8. _____ is the key used to join a child table with parent table.

9. _____ is the standard language for RDBMS.

10. Client/server architecture is an example of _____ data processing method.

11. Centralized database is used in both _____ and _____ data processing methods.

12. What is a domain? _____

2. INTRODUCTION TO ORACLE

- ❑ What is Oracle?
- ❑ Oracle database server
- ❑ Oracle Instance
- ❑ What is personal oracle?
- ❑ Starting Database
- ❑ Starting SQL*Plus
- ❑ Summary
- ❑ Exercises

What is Oracle?

Oracle is the name of the database management system that comes from Oracle Corporation. Oracle9i is the latest product released by Oracle Corporation. Unlike Oracle8i, which is only a database management system, Oracle9i is a collection of following software:

- Oracle9i Application Server – Oracle9iAS

- Oracle9i Database Server – Oracle9iDB

- Oracle9i Developer Suite – Oracle9iDS

In simple words Oracle9i is a platform and not a simple database management system.

Oracle9iDB is the database management system that is used to store and access data. Oracle is by far the most widely used relational database management system (RDBMS). Oracle Corporation is second largest software company next to Microsoft. Oracle Corporation has been targeting Internet programming with the caption - software powers the internet. This book is about Oracle Database Server. It doesn't discuss about other products in Oracle9i. Oracle Corporation is also into Enterprise Resource Planning (ERP). It has Oracle Applications that includes Oracle Financials etc.

Oracle Database Server

Oracle database server is one of the databases that are widely used in client/server computing as back-end. Front-end programs that are written using application development tools such as Visual basic access Oracle and submit SQL commands for execution. Oracle8i onwards oracle is trying to provide extra facilities that are required to be an internet database.

Figure 1: Oracle Server as Server in Client/Server computing model.

Oracle8i provides special features to support various types of data that is to be stored in web sites. Oracle supports both OLTP (online transaction processing) applications as well data warehouse applications, which contain a very large database (VLDB).   One of the biggest advantages of Oracle has been its presence on around 100 different platforms. Oracle is quite scalable, which means it can scale up and down very easily as the requirements change. Oracle also provides Java Virtual Machine (JVM) as part of database. This enables oracle to run java programs. In fact, starting from Oracle8i, oracle can run programs written either in PL/SQL or Java.

Oracle Instance

Oracle instance is a collection of memory structures and processed that are used to manage oracle database. Each oracle database is to be accessed by one or more Oracle instances. If two or more instances are accessing the same database, it is called as parallel server architecture. In order to start using an oracle database, we must first start Oracle instance. Oracle instance will them open the database and make it available to users. It is beyond the scope of this book to discuss what Oracle instance actually contains. Please read "Oracle Concepts" manual for complete information about oracle instance. In nutshell every oracle installation contains at least one Oracle Instance and one oracle database.

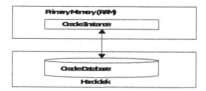

Figure 2: Oracle Instance and Oracle Database.

What Is Personal Oracle?

Personal Oracle is one of the flavors of Oracle. This is not a product that is used by production system (systems where real data is stored). This is more like a learning tool. It runs on desktop PCs. In personal oracle, oracle instance, oracle database and client application all run on the same machine (see figure 3). Whereas in Oracle database server, only oracle instance and database reside on the server and client applications run on clients.

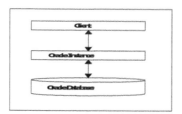

Figure 3: Personal Oracle.

It is also possible to develop an applications using Personal Oracle on you desktop/laptop and deploy them in a client/server environment.

Starting up Database

Before we access oracle database, we must start oracle database. Starting up oracle database means starting oracle instance and associating oracle instance with an oracle database so that oracle instance can access the database. The process is very length and complicated. Several steps are involved in it. But fortunately we do not have to know all that happens when a database starts.

We just need to select an option or two to startup database. Generally you do not have to startup database in case of Oracle Server running on Windows NT/Windows 2000 as oracle server automatically starts in this case. However, if you ever have to start oracle database on Windows NT/Windows 2000, follow the steps given below:

♦ Start services program using **Administrative Tools** -> **Service** in Windows/2000 or **Control Panel** -> **Service** on Windows NT.

♦ If service ***OracleServiceOracle8i*** has not yet started, click on it with right button and select **start** option from popup menu.

The exact name of the service depends on the name you have given to oracle instance at the time of installing it.

Note: Starting and shutting down the database is the job of Database Administrator. As this books assumes that you are an application developer, it doesn't get into those details.

Starting up database in Personal Oracle

Unlike Oracle Server in Personal Oracle, Oracle Instance doesn't start on its own. The Oracle Instance must be explicitly started. The following are the steps to start oracle on Personal Oracle:

♦ Select **start database** option in **Personal Oracle8i for windows** menu.

♦ When a dialog box is displayed wait until the message *Oracle Instance Started* appears.

♦ Click on **Close** button to close the dialog box.

Starting SQL*PLUS

Sql*plus is a tool that comes along with Oracle. It is used to issue SQL and SQL*PLUS commands. It provides command line interface through which we can enter SQL and SQL*PLUS command.

To start SQL*PLUS, take the steps given below:

- Select **start->programs->Oracle - Oracle8i.**

   Oracle8i is the name of the instance. It may be different on your system.

- Then select **Application Development -> SQL Plus**.

- When **Log On** dialog box is displayed, enter *username*, *password* and *Host string*. Use tab key to move from one field to another. For more information about each of these fields, see next section.

- Click on **OK**.

- If the information supplied is valid then you enter into Oracle and SQL*PLUS will display **SQL>** prompt.

Username, Password and Host String

Oracle is a multi-user database. Whoever is access the database must log on to database. To log on we have to supply username and password. When the given username and password are recognized by Oracle, it will allow us to access data. A user can access only the data that belongs to his/her and not the data of others. However, it is possible for a user to grant privileges to others so that other can access his/her data. Creation of users and management of overall security is the responsibility of Database Administrator (DBA). DBA is the person who makes sure that database is functioning smoothly. He is responsible for operations such as taking backup of the database, recovering the database in the event of failure, fine tuning database to get best performance. So, if you want to have a new account under your name, please consult administrator of your database.

Username & Password

Every user who wants to access oracle database must have an account in the database. These accounts are created by DBA. Each account is associated with username and password. Oracle comes with a set of predefined accounts. The following are the usernames and passwords of these accounts.

Username	Password
system	manager
sys	change_on_install
Scott	tiger
Demo	demo

Note: when you enter into oracle using either **system** or **sys** then you become DBA. That means you get special privileges to perform major operations such as creating users etc.

Host String

Host string is a name that is used to access oracle server that is running on a different machine from client. This is required only when you are trying to access oracle server that is not on the current machine. That means, you never need to use host string for Personal Oracle as client and oracle always run on the same machine in Personal Oracle. Host string is required when you are trying to connect to Oracle Server running on remote machine. Host string is actually called as **net service name**. Net service name is a name that is stored in TNSNAMES.ORA file on the client to provide the following information.

Host	Name of the machine or IP address of the machine on which oracle server is running.
Instance name	Name of the Oracle Instance running on the remote machine.

Port Number   Port number of the listener, a program that takes requests from clients. Port number is an integer that uniquely identifies the program on the server.

How to enter SQL statements?

SQL*PLUS allow to types of command to entered at the prompt - SQL and SQL*PLUS.

SQL commands include commands of ANSI/ISO SQL and extra commands added to ANSI SQL by oracle.

The following are the rules to be followed while entering SQL commands.

◆ An SQL statement may be entered in multiple lines.

◆ It is not possible to break a word across lines.

◆ SQL statement must be terminated by semicolon (;).

The following is an example of SQL command. What this command does is not important at this moment.

SQL> select ccode,name

  2 from courses

  3   where fee > 5000;

In the above command, we entered the command in three lines. When you enter semicolon and press enter key then SQL*PLUS will take it as the end of the command. Also note that you have to press enter key at the end of each line.

Note: Both SQL and SQL*PLUS commands are NOT case sensitive.

How to enter SQL*PLUS statements?

SQL*Plus statements are available only in SQL*PLUS. They are not part of standard SQL. SQL*Plus commands are mainly used for two purposes – editing SQL commands and formatting result of query.

The following rules are to be followed while entering these commands.

♦ The entire command must be entered on a single line.

♦ No need to terminate command with semicolon (;).

♦ Commands can be abbreviated. However, the amount of abbreviation is not fixed. Some commands are abbreviated to one letter some are abbreviated to 2 and so on.

The following example show how to use CLEAR SCREEN command of SQL*PLUS.

SQL>clear screen

Or it can be abbreviated to

SQL>cl scr

Common Errors

The following are the common errors that you get while you are trying to log on to Oracle.

Ora-01017: invalid username/password; login denied

The reason for this error is that you have entered a username or password that is not valid. Check whether username you are entering is really existing and password is correctly typed. Sql*plus gives you three chances to type username and password correctly. If you cannot log on successfully in three chances then Sql*plus will exit. However, you can restart Sql*plus again.

ORA-01034: ORACLE not available

The reason for this message is that Oracle Instance is not up and running. You have to first make sure you have started Oracle Instance. Actually there are a few other problems that occurs when Oracle Instance has not started successfully. If this is case in Oracle Server, notify administrator. If this is the case with Personal Oracle, make sure you start database as mentioned in "starting up database" section.

Summary

In this chapter, we have seen what is Oracle and what is the difference between Oracle Server and Personal Oracle. We have seen how to connect to Oracle through SQL*Plus. In the next chapter, we start creating tables and understanding elementary statements in SQL.

Exercises

♦ 1. Oracle instance is a collection of _____ and _____.

♦ What is the use of HOST STRING_____

- ◆ SQL*PLUS commands must be terminated with semicolon (;) [TRUE/FALSE]_____.

- ◆ What is the password of user DEM?

- ◆ What is difference between user SYS and SCOTT?

- ◆ What error message will you get when you try to connect to Oracle but Oracle Instance has not started?

3. GETTING STARTED WITH ORACLE8*I*

- ❏ Creating a table

- ❏ Datatypes

- ❏ Displaying table definition using DESCRIBE

- ❏ Inserting rows into a table

- ❏ Selecting rows from a table

- ❏ Editing SQL buffer

- ❏ Summary

Creating a Table

A Table is a collection of rows and columns. Data in relational model is stored in tables. Let us create a table first. Then we will understand how to store data into table and retrieve data from the table.

Before a table is created the following factors of a table are to be finalized.

❏ What data table is supposed to store.

❏ The name of the table. It should depict the content of the table.

❏ What are the columns that table should contains

❏ The name, data type and maximum length of each column of the table.

❏ What are the rules to be implemented to main data integrity of the table.

The following is an example of creation of COURSES table. We actually have six tables in the application that we use throughout the book. We will discuss more about all the tables in the next chapter. But for now, let us create COURSES table and understand how to use basic SQL commands.

The following CREATE TABLE command is used to create COURSES table.

```
SQL> create table COURSES
  2 ( ccode      varchar2(5)
  3   name       varchar2(30)
  4   duration   number(3)
  5   fee        number(5)
  6   prerequisite varchar2(100)
  7 );
```

Table Created

The above command creates a table called COURSES. This table contains 5 columns. We will discuss about rules to be implemented in this table in the next chapter, where we will recreate this table with all the required rules. For the time being I want to keep things simple. That is the reason why I am not taking you into constraint and remaining.

Well, we have created our first table. If command is successful, Oracle responds by displaying the message *Table Created*.

Rules to be followed for names

The following are the rules to be followed while naming an Oracle Object. These rules are applicable for name of the table and column.

- ❑ The name must begin with a letter - **A-Z** or **a-z**.

- ❑ Letters, digits and special characters – underscore (_), **$** and **#** are allowed.

- ❑ Maximum length of the name is **30** characters.

- ❑ It must not be an SQL reserved word.

- ❑ There should not be any other object with the same name in your account.

Note: A table can contain up to 1000 columns in Oracle8 or above, whereas in Oracle7 a table can contain only 254 columns.

Datatypes

Each column of the table contains the datatype and maximum length, if it is length is applicable. Datatype of the column specifies what type of data can be stored in the column. The datatype VARCHAR2 is to store strings that may have different number of characters, NUMBER is used to store numbers. The maximum length, which is given in parentheses after the datatype, specifies how many characters (or digits) the column can store at the most. For example, column VARCHAR2 (20) would mean it can store up to 20 characters.

Table-1 lists out datatypes available in Oracle8i along with what type of data can be stored and maximum length allowed.

Datatype	Description
VARCHAR2(len)	Can store up to **len** number of characters. Each character would occupy one byte. Maximum width is 4000 characters.
VARCHAR(len)	Same as VARCHAR2. But use VARCHAR2 as Oracle might change the usage of VARCHAR in future releases.
CHAR(len)	Fixed length character data. If **len** is given then it can store up to **len** number of characters. Default width is 1. String is padded on the right with spaces until string is of **len** size. Maximum width is 2000.
NUMBER	Can store numbers up to 40 digits plus decimal point and sign.
NUMBER (p ,s)	**P** represents the maximum significant digits allowed. **S** is the number of digits on the right of the decimal point.
DATE	Can store dates in the range 1-1-4712 B.C to 31-12-4712 AD.
LONG	Variable length character values up to 2 gigabytes. Only one LONG column is allowed per table. You cannot use LONG datatype in functions, WHERE clause of SELECT, in indexing and subqueries.
RAW and **LONG RAW**	Equivalent to VARCHAR2 and LONG respectively, but used for storing byte-oriented or binary data such as

		digital sound or graphics images.
CLOB,	**BLOB,**	Used to store large character and binary objects. Each can
NCLOB		accommodate up to 4 gigabytes. We will discuss more about it later in this book.
BFILE		Stores a pointer to an external file. The content of the file resides in the file system of the operation system. Only the name of the file is stored in the column.
ROWID		Stores a unique number that is used by Oracle to uniquely identify each row of the table.
NCHAR (size)		Same as CHAR, but supports national language.
NVARCHAR2 (size)		Same as VARCHAR2, but supports national language.

Table 1: Oracle Datatypes.

Displaying table definition using DESCRIBE

You can display the structure of a table using SQL*PLUS command DESCRIBE. It displays then name, datatype and whether the column can store null value for each column of the table.

The following is the syntax of DESCRIBE command.

DESC[RIBE] object name

Displays the column definitions for the specified object. The object may be a table, view, synonym, function or procedure.

To display the structure of COURSES table, enter:

```
SQL> DESC COURSES
```

Name	Null?	Type
CCODE	NOT NULL	VARCHAR2(5)
NAME		VARCHAR2(30)
DURATION		NUMBER(3)
FEE		NUMBER(5)
PREREQUISITE		VARCHAR2(100)

DESCRIBE is an SQL*Plus command and can be abbreviated to DESC.

Inserting rows into a table

Now, let us see how to insert rows into COURSES table. SQL command INSERT is used to insert new row into the table. While inserting rows, you may enter value for each column of the table or selected columns.

The following command inserts a row into COURSES table.

insert into courses

   values('ora','Oracle database',25,4500,'Knowledge of Windows');

Note: After inserting the required row, issues COMMIT command to make sure the changes are made permanent. We will discuss more about COMMIT command later in this book but for the time being it is sufficient to know that COMMIT command will make changes permanent. Without COMMIT, rows that are inserted might be lost if there is any power failure.

During insertion, character values are enclosed in single quotes. Unless otherwise specified we have to supply a value for each column of the table. If the value of any column is not known or available then you can give NULL as the value of the column.

For example, the following insert will insert a new row with null value for PREREQUISITE column.

insert into courses

values('c','C Programming',25,3000,null);

Note: INSERT command can insert only one row at a time. For multiple row, INSERT command must be issued for multiple times.

DATE type values must be in the format DD-MON-YY or DD-MON-YYYY, where MON is the first three letters of the month (Jan, Feb). If only two digits are given for year then current century is used. For example, if you give 99 for year, Oracle will take it as 2099 as the current century is 2000. So it is important to remember this and give four digits if required.

The following is the complete syntax for INSERT command.

INSERT INTO tablename [(columns list)]

    {VALUES (value-1,...) | subquery }

We will see how to insert row into a table using a subquery later in this book.

Inserting a row with selected columns

It is possible to insert a new row by giving values only for a few columns instead of giving values for all the available columns.

The following INSERT command will insert a new row only two values.

insert into courses(ccode,name)

    values ('odba','Oracle Database Administration');

The above command will create a new row in COURSES table with values for only two columns – CCODE and NAME. The remaining columns will take NULL value or the default value, if the column is associated with default value. We will discuss more about default value in the next chapter.

NULL value

Null value means a value that is not available or not known. When a column's value is not known then we store NULL value into the column. NULL value is neither 0 nor blank nor any other known value. We have already seen how to store null value into a column and when Oracle automatically stores null value into a column. We will discuss more about how to process null value later in this chapter.

Selecting rows from a table

Let us see how to retrieve data of a table. SELECT command of SQL is used to retrieve data from one or more tables. It implements operators of relational algebra such as projection, and selection. The following is the syntax of SELECT command. The syntax given here is incomplete. For complete syntax, please refer to online documentation.

SELECT [DISTINCT | ALL]

   {* | table.* | expr } [alias]

   [{table}.*| expr } [alias]] ...

   FROM [schema.]object

    [, [schema.]object] ...

   [WHERE condition]

   [ORDER BY {expr|position} [ASC | DESC]

    [, {expr|position} [ASC | DESC]] ...]

schema is the name of the user whose table is being accessed. Schema prefix is not required if the table is in the current account. Schema prefix is required while we are accessing a table of some other account and not ours.

The following is an example of a basic SELECT command.

select * from courses;

CCODE	NAME	DURATION	FEE	PREREQUISITE
ora	Oracle database	25	4500	Windows
vbnet	VB.NET	30	5500	Windows and programming
c	C programming	20	3500	Computer Awareness
asp	ASP.NET	25	5000	Internet and programming
java	Java Language	25	4500	C language
xml	XML Programming	15	4000	HTML,Scripting, ASP/JSP

The simplest SELECT command contains the following:

- ❏ Columns to be displayed. If * is given, all columns are selected.
- ❏ The name of the table from where rows are to be retrieved.

Projection

Projection is the operation where we select only a few columns out of the available columns. The following is an example of projection.

select name,fee from courses;

```
NAME                  FEE

-------------------- ---------

Oracle database       4500

VB.NET                5500

C programming          3500

ASP.NET               5000

Java Language          4500

XML Programming         4000
```

Using expressions in SELECT command

It is also possible to include expressions in the list of columns. For example, the following SELECT will display discount to be given for each course.

select name,fee, fee * 0.15 from courses;

```
NAME                  FEE  FEE*0.15

-------------------- --------- ---------

Oracle database       4500      675

VB.NET                5500     825

C programming          3500       525

ASP.NET               5000      750

Java Language          4500      675

XML Programming         4000       600
```

Column Alias

The column heading of an expression will be the expression itself. However, as it may not be meaningful to have expression as the result of column heading, we can give an alias to the column so that alias is displayed as the column heading.

The following example will use alias DISCOUNT for the expression FEE * 0.15.

select name, fee, fee * 0.15 DISCOUNT from courses

```
NAME                FEE  DISCOUNT
------------------- -------- --------

Oracle database      4500      675

VB.NET               5500    825

C programming        3500     525

ASP.NET              5000    750

Java Language        4500     675

XML Programming       4000     600
```

The following are the arithmetic operators that can be used in expressions.

Operator	Description
+	Add
-	Subtract

*	Multiply
/	Divide

ORDER BY clause

It is possible to display the rows of a table in the required order using ORDER BY clause. It is used to sort rows on the given column(s) and in the given order at the time of retrieving rows. Remember, sorting takes place on the row that are retrieved and in no way affects the rows in the table. That means the order of the rows will remain unchanged.

Note: ORDER BY must always be the last of all clauses used in the SELECT command.

The following SELECT command displays the rows after sorting rows on course fee.

select name, fee from courses order by fee;

```
NAME                 FEE
-------------------- ---------
C programming        3500
XML Programming       4000
Oracle database      4500
Java Language        4500
ASP.NET              5000
VB.NET               5500
```

Note: Null values are placed at the end in ascending order and at the beginning in descending order.

The default order for sorting is ascending. Use option DESC to sort in the descending order. It is also possible to sort on more than one column.

To sort rows of COURSES table in the ascending order of DURATION and descending order of FEE, enter:

select name, duration, fee from courses

order by duration , fee desc;

NAME	DURATION	FEE
XML Programming	15	4000
C programming	20	3500
ASP.NET	25	5000
Oracle database	25	4500
Java Language	25	4500
VB.NET	30	5500

First, all rows are sorted in the ascending order of DURATION column. Then the rows that have same value in DURATION column will be further sorted in the descending order of FEE column.

Using column position

Instead of giving the name of the column, you can also give the position of the column on which you want to sort rows.

For example, the following SELECT sorts rows based on discount to be given to each course.

select name, fee, fee * 0.15

from courses

order by 3;

NAME	FEE	FEE*0.15
C programming	3500	525
XML Programming	4000	600
Oracle database	4500	675
Java Language	4500	675
ASP.NET	5000	750
VB.NET	5500	825

Note: Column position refers to position of the column in the selected columns and not the position of the column in the table.

The above command uses column position in ORDER BY clause. Alternatively you can use column alias in ORDER BY clause as follows:

select name, fee, fee * 0.15 discount

from courses

order by discount;

NAME	FEE	DISCOUNT
C programming	3500	525
XML Programming	4000	600
Oracle database	4500	675

Java Language	4500	675
ASP.NET	5000	750
VB.NET	5500	825

Selection

It is possible to select only the required rows using WHERE clause of SELECT command. It implements *selection* operator of relational algebra.

WHERE clause specifies the condition that rows must satisfy in order to be selected. The following example select rows where FEE is more than or equal to 5000.

select name, fee from courses

where fee >= 5000

NAME	FEE
VB.NET	5500
ASP.NET	5000

The following relational and logical operators are used to form condition of WHERE clause. Logical operators – AND, OR – are used to combine conditions. NOT operator reverses the result of the condition. If condition returns true, NOT will make the overall condition false.

Operator	Meaning
=	Equal to
!= or <>	Not equal to
>=	Greater than or equal to
<=	Less than or equal to
>	Greater than
<	Less than
AND	Logical ANDing
OR	Logical Oring
NOT	Negates result of condition.

The following SELECT command displays the courses where duration is more than 15 days and course fee is less than 4000.

select * from courses

where duration > 15 and fee < 4000;

```
CCODE NAME              DURATION    FEE PREREQUISITE
----- ------------------ --------- --------- -------------------
c    C programming        20       3500 Computer Awareness
```

The following SELECT command retrieves the details of course with code ORA.

select * from courses

where ccode = 'ora';

```
CCODE NAME              DURATION    FEE PREREQUISITE
```

```
----- -------------------- --------- --------- ----------------
```

ora   Oracle database   25   4500 Windows

Note: When comparing   strings, the case of the string must match. Lowercase letters are not equivalent to uppercase letters.

SQL Operators

Apart from standard relational operators (= and   >), SQL has some other operators that can be used in conditions.

Operator	What it does?
BETWEEN value-1 AND value-2	Checks whether the value is in the given range. The range is inclusive of the given values.
IN(list)	Checks whether the value is matching with any one of the values given in the list. List contains values separated by comma(,).
LIKE pattern	Checks whether the given string is matching with the given pattern. More on this later.
IS NULL and IS NOT NULL	Checks whether the value is null or not null.

Table 2: SQL Operators.

Now, let us see how to use these special operators of SQL.

BETWEEN ... AND Operator

Checks whether value is in the given range. The range includes all the values in the range including the min and max values. This supports DATE type data also. To display the list of course where DURATION is in the range 20 to 25 days, enter:

select name

from courses

where duration between 20 and 25;

NAME

Oracle database

C programming

ASP.NET

Java Language

Note: BETWEEN.. AND is alternative to using >= and <= operators.

IN Operator

Compares a single value with a list of values. If the value is matching with any
of the values given in the list then condition is taken as true.

The following command will retrieve all courses where duration is either 20 or
30 days.

select name

from courses

where duration in (20,30);

NAME

VB.NET

C programming

The same condition can be formed even without IN operator using logical operator OR as follows:

Select name from courses where duration = 20 or duration = 30;

However, it will be more convenient to user IN operator compared with multiple conditions compared with OR operator.

LIKE operator

This operator is used to search for values when the exact value is not known. It selects rows that match the given pattern. The pattern can contain the following special characters.

Symbol	**Meaning**
%	Zero or more characters can take the place of %.
_ **(underscore)**	Any single character can take the place of underscore. But there must be one letter.

To select the courses where the course name contains pattern *.NET*, enter:

select name, duration, fee from courses
where name like '%.NET%'

NAME   DURATION   FEE
-------------------- --------- ---------
VB.NET   30   5500

ASP.NET   25   5000

The following example selects courses where second letter in the course code is
"b" and column PREREQUISITE contains word "programming".

select * from courses

where ccode like '_b%' and prerequisite like '%programming%';

CCODE NAME   DURATION   FEE PREREQUISITE

----- -------------------- --------- --------- ------------------------

vbnet VB.NET   30   5500 Windows and programming

Remember LIKE operator is case sensitive. In the above example, if CCODE
contains value in uppercase (VB), then it won't be a match to the pattern.

IS NULL and IS NOT NULL operators

These two operators test for null value. If we have to select rows where a
column is containing null value or not null value then we have to use these
operators.

For example the following SELECT command will select all the courses where
the column FEE is null.

select * from courses

where fee is null;

Though Oracle provides NULL keyword, it cannot be used to check whether the value of a column is null. For example, the following condition will always be false as Oracle treats two null values as two different values.

select * from courses

where fee = null;

The above command does NOT work as fee though contains null value will not be equal to NULL. SO, we must use IS NULL operator.

Selecting distinct values

DISTINCT clause of SELECT command specifies only distinct values of the specified column must be selected.

The following SELECT command will display only distinct course fee values from COURSES table.

select distinct fee from courses;

```
    FEE
---------
   3500
   4000
   4500
   5000
   5500
```

Whereas the same query without DISTINCT clause will select the following.

select fee from courses;

```
    FEE
---------
   4500

   5500

   3500

   5000

   4500

   4000
```

Editing   SQL Buffer

Whenever you enter an SQL command in SQL*Plus, it is stored in an area in the memory called as *SQL Buffer*. It is possible to edit the command that is stored in SQL Buffer using a set of commands provided by SQL*Plus. All these commands are SQL*Plus commands.

Note: SQL*PLUS commands like DESCRIBE are not stored in the buffer. Only SQL commands are stored in the buffer.

The following list of SQL*PLUS commands are used for editing and other operations related to SQL buffer.

Command	Purpose
A[PPEND] text	Adds text to the end of the current line in the buffer.
DEL	Deletes current line in the buffer.

I[NPUT] [text]	If text is given, then text is placed after the current line, otherwise it allows you to enter a series of lines and places them after the current line.
L[IST]	Displays the contents of buffer.
R[UN]	Runs the current command in the buffer.
/	Same as *RUN*, but doesn't display command being executed.
SAVE filename	Saves the contents of buffer into *filename*, which is a file in the host system.
GET filename	Places the contents of *filename* into buffer.
START filename	Executes commands that are in the given file. The file is also called as *start file* and *command file*.
EDIT [filename]	Invokes an editor in the host and places the contents of either given filename or SQL buffer if filename is not given.
HOST command	Executes the command, which is a valid command in the host system.
EXIT	Quits SQL*PLUS.

Table 3: Editing Commands.

Summary

In this chapter we have seen some fundamental SQL commands such as CREATE TABLE, INSERT and SELECT. SELECT command is the most frequently used command. It is very important to understand how to retrieve required data using SELECT command. We have seen some special operators that are available in SQL. We have seen WHERE and ORDER BY clauses of SELECT command.

Exercises

- _____ is the operator used to compare a column with null value.

- _____ operator is used to compare one value with a set of values.

- The maximum number of characters that can be stored in CHAR type is _____.

- How many LONG columns can a table contain? _____

- In LIKE operator, % stands for _____.

- _____ is used to change the heading of a column.

- SQL commands are to be terminated with _____.

- _____ command is used to display definition of a table.

- Display list of courses where course code starts with letter 'c'.

- Display rows of COURSES table in the ascending order of course fee and descending order of course code.

- Select rows from COURSES where course fee is in the range 3000 to 5000.

- Add a new row to COURSES table with the following data.

  Course code - cpp, name – C++ Programming, duration – 20, fee – 3500, prerequisite – C programming.

- Display all the rows where course fee is not known but duration is known.

4. Creating sample tables

- ❑ What is a constraint?
- ❑ Types of constraints?
- ❑ Sample tables
- ❑ Creating integrity constraints
- ❑ Creating example table
- ❑ Inserting sample data
- ❑ Summary
- ❑ Exercises

What is a constraint?

In the previous chapter we have seen how to create a table using CREATE TABLE command. Now we will understand how to define constraints. Constraints are used to implement standard and business rules. Data integrity of the database must be maintained. In order to ensure data has integrity we have to implement certain rules or constraints. As these constraints are used to maintain integrity they are called as integrity constraints.

Standard rules

Standard constraints are the rules related to primary key and foreign key. Every table must have a primary key. Primary key must be unique and not null. Foreign key must derive its values from corresponding parent key. These rules are universal and are called as standard rules.

Business rules

These rules are related to a single application. For example, in a payroll application we may have to implement a rule that prevents any row of an employee if salary of the employee is less than 2000. Another example is current balance of a bank account

Must be greater than or equal to 500.

Once the constraints are created, Oracle server makes sure that the constraints are not violated whenever a row is inserted, deleted or updated. If constraint is not satisfied then the operation will fail.

Constraints are normally defined at the time of creating table. But it is also possible to add constraints after the table is created using ALTER TABLE command. Constraints are stored in the Data Dictionary (a set of tables which stores information regarding database).

Each constraint has a name; it is either given by user using CONSTRAINT option or assigned by system. In the later case, the name is **SYS_Cn**; where **n** is a number.

Note: It is recommended that you use constraint name so that referring to constraint will be easier later on.

Types of constraints

Constraints can be given at two different levels. If the constraint is related to a single column the constraint is given at the column level otherwise constraint is to be given at the table level. Base on the where a constraint is given, constraint are of two types:

- ❑ Column Constraints
- ❑ Table Constraints

Column Constraint

A constraint given at the column level is called as Column Constraint. It defines a rule for a single column. It cannot refer to column other than the column at which it is defined. A typical example is PRIMARY KEY constraint when a single column is the primary key of the table.

Table Constraint

A constraint given at the table level is called as Table Constraint. It may refer to more than one column of the table. A typical example is PRIMARY KEY constraint that is used to define composite primary key. A column level constraint can be given even at the table level, but a constraint that deals with more than one column must be given only at the table level.

The following is the syntax of CONSTRAINT clause used with CREATE TABLE and ALTER TABLE commands.

[CONSTRAINT constraint]

{ [NOT] NULL

| {UNIQUE | PRIMARY KEY}

| REFERENCES [schema.] table [(column)]

    [ON DELETE CASCADE]

| CHECK (condition) }

The following is the syntax of table constraint.

[CONSTRAINT constraint]

{ {UNIQUE | PRIMARY KEY} (column [,column] ...)

| FOREIGN KEY (column [,column] ...)

   REFERENCES [schema.] table [(column [,column] ...)]

    [ON DELETE CASCADE]

| CHECK (condition) }

The main difference between column constraint and table constraint is that in table constraint we have to specify the name of the column for which the constraint is defined whereas in column constraint it is not required as constraint is given on immediately after the column. Now let us understand sample table to be throughout this book. It is very important to understand these tables to get the best out of this book. I have made these tables to be easy to understand.

Sample tables

The following are the sample tables used throughout the book. These tables store information about course, batches and subject. There are six tables to store the required information by typical training center.

Let us first understand the meaning of each table.

The following are the required tables of our application.

Table Name	Description
Courses	Contains the details of all the courses offered by the institute.
Faculty	Contains the details of the faculty members of the institute.
Course_facult y	This table contains information regarding which faculty can handle which course. It also contains rating regarding how good a faculty member is in handling a particular course. The rating is based on previous experience of the faulty member with that course.
Batches	Contains the information about all the batches. It contains information about all the batches that started and completed, on going and scheduled but not yet started.
Students	Contains information about all the students. Each student is assigned a new roll number whenever he/she joins a new course.
Payments	Information about all the payments made by students. A single student may pay course fee in multiple installments for a single course.

Table 1: Sample tables.

The following few tables will give the list of columns of each of the table given in table 1.

COURSES Table

Contains information related to each course. Each course is given a unique code called course code.

Column Name	Data Type	Description
CCODE	VARCHAR2(5)	Course Code. This is the primary key of the table.
NAME	VARCHAR(30)	Name of the course.
DURATION	NUMBER(3)	Duration of the course in no. of working days.
FEE	NUMBER(5)	Course fee of the course.
PREREQUISIT E	VARCHAR2(100)	Prerequisite knowledge to do the course.

The following are the required constraints of COURSES table.

- ❑ CCODE is primary key.
- ❑ FEE must be greater than or equal to 0.
- ❑ DURATION must be greater than or equal to 0.

FACULTY Table

Contains information about all the faculty members. Each faculty member is given a code called as FACCODE.

Column Name	Data Type	Description
FACCODE	VARCHAR2(5)	Faculty code. This is the primary key of the table.
NAME	VARCHAR2(30)	Name of the faculty.
QUAL	VARCHAR2(30)	Qualification of the faculty member.
EXP	VARCHAR2(100)	Experience of the faculty member.

The following are the constraints of FACULTY table.

❑ FACCODE is primary key.

COURSE_FACULTY table

Contains information regarding which faculty member can take which course. A single faculty member may be capable of handling multiple courses. However, each member is given a grade depending on his expertise in handling the subject. The grade will be wither A, B or C.

Column Name	Data Type	Description
FACCODE	VARCHAR2(5)	Faculty code.
CCODE	VARCHAR2(5)	Course the faculty can handle.
GRADE	CHAR(1)	Rating of faculty's ability to handle this particular code. A – Very good, B- Good,

		C- Average.

The following are the constraints of the table.

- FACCODE is a foreign key referencing FACCODE column of FACULTY table.
- CCODE is a foreign key referencing CCODE column of COURSES table.
- Primary key is consisting of FACCODE and CCODE.
- GRADE column must contain either A, B or C.

Batches table

Contains information about all the batches. These batches include batches that were completed, that are currently running and that are scheduled but yet to start.

Column Name	Data Type	Description
BCODE	VARCHAR2(5)	Code that is assigned to each batch. This is the primary key of the table.
CCODE	VARCHAR2(5)	Course code of the course of this batch. This is a foreign key referencing CCODE of COURSES table.
FACCODE	VARCHAR2(5)	Code of the faculty member taking this batch.
STDATE	DATE	Date on which the batch has started or scheduled to start if batch has not yet started.
ENDDATE	DATE	Date on which the batch has completed. If batch is not completed

		this will be null.
TIMING	NUMBER(1)	Number indicating the timing of the batch. 1- morning, 2 – after noon, and 3-evening.

The following are the required constraints of this table.

- ❑ BCODE is the primary key.
- ❑ CCODE is a foreign key referencing CCODE of COURSES table.
- ❑ FACCODE is a foreign key referencing FACCODE of FACULTY table.
- ❑ STDATA must be <= ENDDATE
- ❑ TIMING column must be 1, 2 or 3.

STUDENTS table

Contains information about all the students of the institute. Each student is given a roll number. Roll number will be allotted to each student of each batch.

Column Name	Data Type	Description
ROLLNO	NUMBER(5)	Roll number that is assigned to each student. This is the primary key of the table.
BCODE	VARCHAR2(5)	Code of the batch to which student belongs. This is the foreign key referencing BCODE of BATCHES table.
NAME	VARCHAR2(30)	Name of the student.
GENDER	CHAR(1)	Gender of the student. M for male and

		F for female.
DJ	DATE	Date on which the student has joined.
PHONE	VARCHAR2(10)	Contact number of the student.
EMAIL	VARCHAR2(30)	Email address of the student.

The following are the constraints of the table.

- ROLLNO is the primary key.
- BCODE is a foreign key referencing BCODE of BATCHES table.
- GENDER may be either M or F.

PAYMENTS table

Contains information about all the payment made by students of all bathes.

Column Name	Data Type	Description
ROLLNO	NUMBER(5)	Roll number of the student paying the fee.
DP	DATE	Date on which the amount is paid.
AMOUNT	NUMBER(5)	The amount paid by student.

The following are the constraints.

- Primary key is consisting of ROLLNO and DP.
- AMOUNT must be >= 25

Creating Integrity Constraints

In the following few sections we will see how to integrity constraints.

NOT NULL Constraint

Used to prevent any null value from entering into column. This is automatically defined for column with PRIMARY KEY constraint.

The following example shows how you can define course name as not null column using NOT NULL constraint.

CREATE TABLE COURSES

(...,

  name varchar2(20)

        CONSTRAINT courses_name_nn NOT NULL,

  ...

);

CONSTRAINT option is used to given a name to constraint. The convention followed here is TABLENAME_COLUMN_TYPE.

PRIMARY KEY Constraint

This constraint is used to define the primary key of the table. A primary key is used to uniquely identify rows in a table. There can be only one primary key in a table. It may consist of more than one column. If primary key is consisting of only one column, it can be given as column constraints otherwise it is to be given as table constraint.

Note: You have to use table constraint to define composite primary key.

Oracle does the following for the column that has PRIMARY KEY constraint.

- Creates a unique index to enforce uniqueness. We will discuss about indexes later in this book.
- Defines NOT NULL constraint to prevent null values.

The following example shows how to use PRIMARY KEY constraint at column level.

CREATE TABLE COURSES

(ccode varchar2(5) CONSTRAINT courses_pk PRIMARY KEY,

  ...);

The following example shows how to define composite primary key using PRIMARY KEY constraint at the table level.

CREATE TABLE COURSE_FACULTY

(...,

  CONSTRAINT COURSE_FACULTY_PK PRIMARY KEY (ccode,faccode)

);

UNIQUE Constraint

Enforces uniqueness in the given column(s). Oracle automatically creates a unique index for this column.

The following example creates unique constraint on NAME column of COURSES table.

CREATE TABLE courses

(... ,

  name varchar2(20)

      CONSTRAINT courses_name_u UNIQUE,

  ...);

If two or more columns collective should be unique then UNIQUE constraint must be given at the table level.

FOREIGN KEY Constraint

A foreign key is used to join the child table with parent table. FOREIGN KEY constraint is used to provide *referential integrity,* which makes sure that the values of a foreign key are derived from parent key. It can be defined either at the table level or at the column level. If a foreign key is defined on the column in child table then Oracle does not allow the parent row to be deleted, if it contains any child rows. However, if ON DELETE CASCADE option is given at the time of defining foreign key, Oracle deletes all child rows while parent row is being deleted.

The following example defines foreign key constraint for CCODE of COURSE_FACULTY table.

CREATE TABLE course_faculty

(ccode varchar2(5)

    CONSTRAINT course_faculty_ccode_fk REFERENCES courses(ccode),

  ...

);

Note: When the name of the column in the referenced table is same as the foreign key then column need not be given after the table name. It means **REFERENCES courses** in the above example will suffice.

Table level constraint is used when foreign key is a composite foreign key.

ON DELETE CASCADE option

As mentioned earlier, after a foreign key is defined, Oracle will NOT allow any parent row to be deleted if it has dependent rows in the child table.

For example, if CCODE in COURSE_FACULTY table is defined as foreign key referencing CCODE column of COURSES table then it is NOT possible to delete rows from COURSES table if dependent rows exists in COURSE_FACULTY table.

However, by using ON DELETE CASCADE it is possible to delete all child rows while parent row is being deleted.

The following code shows how to use ON DELETE CASCADE option.

CREATE TABLE course_faculty

(ccode varchar2(5)

    CONSTRAINT course_faculty_ccode_fk REFERENCES courses(ccode)

        ON DELETE CASCADE,

  ...

);

CHECK Constraint

Defines the condition that should be satisfied before insertion or updation is done.

The condition used in CHECK constraint may NOT contain:

- ❏ A reference to pseudo column SYSDATE
- ❏ Subquery

If it is given as column constraint, it can refer only to current column. But if it is given as table constraint, it can refer to more than one column of the table. In neither case it can refer to a column of other tables.

The following example shows how to create CHECK constraint to make sure GRADE column of COURSE_FACULTY contains letters A, B and C only.

```
CREATE TABLE course_faculty
( ...,
   grade char(1) CONSTRAINT course_faculty_grade_chk
      CHECK ( grade in ('A','B','C') ),
   ...
);
```

The above CHECK constraint does not allow any other characters other than A, B and C. It must be noted that character comparison is always case sensitive.

So to ignore case differences you can convert GRADE to uppercase before comparison made as follows:

CREATE TABLE course_faculty

(...,

  grade char(1) CONSTRAINT course_faculty_grade_chk

    CHECK (**upper(grade)** in ('A','B','C')),

  ...

);

The following is an example of CHECK constraint at table level. The constraint makes sure the starting date (STDATE) of a batch is less than or equal to ending date (ENDDATE) of the batch.

CREATE TABLE batches

(...,

  CONSTRAINT batches_dates_chk

    CHECK (stdate <= enddate),

);

Creating sample tables

Here is the script to create all six tables required in this application. Just run this script from SQL> prompt of SQL*PLUS using START command.

```
rem ******* script to create tables for oracle book  ****************

rem

rem             Author : P.Srikanth

rem             Date   : 4-aug-2001

rem             place  : Vizag.

rem

rem *******************************************************************


rem --------- first drop all existing tables -----------------

drop table payments cascade constraints;

drop table students cascade constraints;

drop table batches cascade constraints;

drop table course_faculty cascade constraints;

drop table faculty cascade constraints;

drop table courses cascade constraints;

create table  courses
(
    ccode       varchar2(5)  constraint courses_pk  primary key,
    Name        varchar2(30) constraint courses_name_u unique,
    Duration    number(3)    constraint courses_duration_chk
                         check( duration >= 1),
    fee         number(5)   constraint courses_fee_chk
```

```sql
                      check( fee >= 0 ),
   Prerequisite varchar2(100)
);


create table  faculty
(
   fCODE    Varchar2(5) constraint faculty_pk  primary key,
   Name     varchar2(30),
   qual     varchar2(30),
   exp      Varchar2(100)
);


create table  course_faculty
(
   fcode   varchar2(5) constraint course_faculty_fcode_fk
                        references faculty(fcode),
   CCODE   Varchar2(5) constraint course_faculty_ccode_fk
                        references courses(ccode),
   grade   char(1)  constraint course_faculty_grade_chk
                check ( upper(grade) in ('A','B','C') ),
   constraint course_faculty_pk  primary key(ccode,fcode)
);


create table batches
(
```

77

```
    bCODE   Varchar2(5) constraint batches_pk primary key,
    ccode   varchar2(5) constraint batches_ccode_fk
                    references courses(ccode),
    fcode   varchar2(5) constraint baches_fcode_fk
                    references faculty(fcode),
    stdate  date            constraint batches_stdate_nn not null,
    enddate date,
    timing  number(1)   constraint batches_timing_chk
                    check( timing in (1,2,3) ),
    constraint batches_dates_chk  check ( stdate <= enddate)
);


create table students
(
    rollno  number(5)   constraint students_pk primary key,
    bcode   varchar2(5) constraint students_bcode_fk
                        references batches(bcode),
    name    varchar2(30),
    gender  char(1)     constraint students_gender_chk
                    check( upper(gender)  in ('M','F')),
    dj      date,
    phone   varchar2(10),
    email   varchar2(30)
);
create table payments
```

```
(
    rollno    number(5) constraint payments_rollno_fk
                    references students(rollno),
    dp    date    constraint payments_dp_nn  not null,
    amount    number(5) constraint payments_amount_chk
                    check ( amount > 0 ),
    constraint payments_pk primary key (rollno,dp)
);
```

Getting information about tables

Data dictionary keeps track of the entire information about the database. It stores information about tables, constraints, procedures etc. Oracle provides a set of data dictionary views, which can be used to get information about these objects. Data dictionary views are not actually tables instead they are relational views. However, at this stage you can treat data dictionary views tables for the time being. We get list of tables from our schema using the followings:

```
select  * from tab;
```

It is also possible to get information about all constraints of all tables in your account by using:

```
select * from user_constraints;
```

If you want to get information about constraints of a single table, you can give the following to get names of constraints of BATCHES table.

CONSTRAINT_TYPE column of USER_CONSTRAINTS may contain any of the following characters.

Character	Meaning
C	Check
U	Unique
R	Reference
P	Primary key
V	Check on view

Note: The table name must be given in uppercase while searching based on table name as all object names (table is an object) are stored in uppercase in data dictionary.

select constraint_name from user_constraints

where table_name = 'BATCHES';

CONSTRAINT_NAME

BATCHES_STDATE_NN

BATCHES_TIMING_CHK

BATCHES_DATES_CHK

BATCHES_PK

BATCHES_CCODE_FK

BACHES_FCODE_FK

Inserting data into sample tables

The following is the script to insert a set of sample rows into all six tables.

```
rem ****script to insert sample data into table of oracle book*****
rem
rem   Author : P.Srikanth
rem   Date   : 4-aug-2001
rem   Place  : Vizag.
rem
rem ********************************************************************

rem --------- delete existing data from all tables -----------------

delete from payments;
delete from students;
delete from batches;
delete from course_faculty;
delete from faculty;
delete from courses;

rem ---------------------- COURSES --------------------------

insert into courses values('ora','Oracle database',25,4500,'Windows');

insert into courses values('vbnet','VB.NET',30,5500,'Windows and
```

programming');

insert into courses values('c','C programming',20,3500,'Computer Awareness');

insert into courses values('asp','ASP.NET',25,5000,'Internet and programming');

insert into courses values('java','Java Language',25,4500,'C language');

insert into courses values('xml','XML Programming', 15, 4000, 'HTML,Scripting, ASP/JSP');

rem ------------------------- FACULTY ---------------------------

insert into faculty values('gk','George Koch','MS Computer Science','15 years with databases');

insert into faculty values('da','Dan Appleman','CS and EE graduate', 'Extensively worked with COM');

insert into faculty values('hs','Herbert Schildt','MS Computer Science', 'Author of several books');

insert into faculty values('dh','David Hunter','MS Electronics', 'Extensively worked with Internet Tehnologees');

insert into faculty values('sw','Stephen Walther','Ph.D. in Philosophy', 'Extensively worked with Internet Tehnologees');

insert into faculty values('kl','Kevin Loney', 'MS Eletronics', 'Specialized in Oracle DBA');

insert into faculty values('jj','Jamie Jaworski','Bachlors of Electrical' ,'Developed programs for US defense department');

insert into faculty values('jc','Jason Couchman','OCP DBA','Published articles on Oracle');

rem ---------------------- COURSE_FACULTY ----------------------

insert into course_faculty values('gk','ora','A');

insert into course_faculty values('kl','ora','A');

insert into course_faculty values('jc','ora','A');

insert into course_faculty values('da','vbnet','A');

insert into course_faculty values('sw','asp','A');

insert into course_faculty values('da','asp','B');

insert into course_faculty values('hs','c','A');

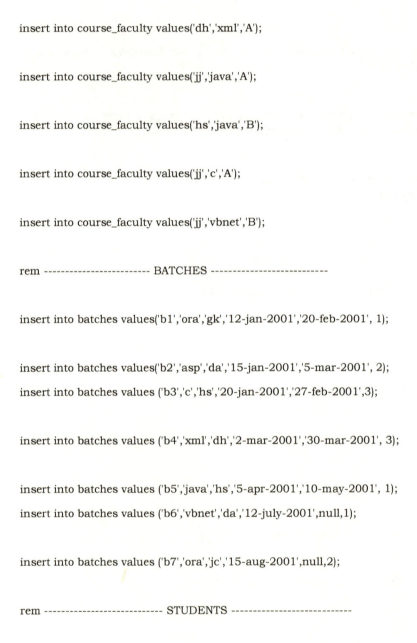

```
insert into course_faculty values('dh','xml','A');

insert into course_faculty values('jj','java','A');

insert into course_faculty values('hs','java','B');

insert into course_faculty values('jj','c','A');

insert into course_faculty values('jj','vbnet','B');

rem ----------------------- BATCHES --------------------------

insert into batches values('b1','ora','gk','12-jan-2001','20-feb-2001', 1);

insert into batches values('b2','asp','da','15-jan-2001','5-mar-2001', 2);
insert into batches values ('b3','c','hs','20-jan-2001','27-feb-2001',3);

insert into batches values ('b4','xml','dh','2-mar-2001','30-mar-2001', 3);

insert into batches values ('b5','java','hs','5-apr-2001','10-may-2001', 1);
insert into batches values ('b6','vbnet','da','12-july-2001',null,1);

insert into batches values ('b7','ora','jc','15-aug-2001',null,2);

rem ------------------------- STUDENTS -------------------------
```

insert into students values (1,'b1','George Micheal','m','10-jan-2001', '488333','gm@yahoo.com');

insert into students values (2,'b1','Micheal Douglas','m','11-jan-2001', '334333','md@hotmail.com');

insert into students values (3,'b2','Andy Roberts','m','11-jan-2001', '433554','ar@yahoo.com');

insert into students values (4,'b2','Malcom Marshall','m','16-jan-2001', '653345','mm@usa.net');

insert into students values (5,'b2','Vivan Richards','m','16-jan-2001', '641238','vr@yahoo.com');

insert into students values (6,'b3','Chirs Evert','f','14-jan-2001', null,'ce@yahoo.com');

insert into students values (7,'b3','Ivan Lendal','m','15-jan-2001', '431212','il@hotmail.com');

insert into students values (8,'b4','George Micheal','m','1-mar-2001', '488333','gm@hotmail.com');

insert into students values (9,'b5','Richard Marx','m','6-apr-2001', '876567','rm@hotmail.com');

insert into students values (10,'b5','Tina Turner','f','6-apr-2001', '565678','tinat@hotmail.com');

insert into students values (11,'b5','Jody Foster','f','7-apr-2001', '234344','jody@hotmail.com');

rem ------------------------- PAYMENTS -------------------------

insert into payments values (1,'10-jan-2001',4500);

insert into payments values (2,'11-jan-2001',3500);

insert into payments values (2,'17-jan-2001',1000);

insert into payments values (3,'13-jan-2001',2000);

insert into payments values (3,'20-jan-2001',3000);

insert into payments values (4,'16-jan-2001',3000);

insert into payments values (4,'30-jan-2001',2000);

insert into payments values (5,'16-jan-2001',5000);

insert into payments values (6,'14-jan-2001',3500);

insert into payments values (7,'15-jan-2001',3500);

insert into payments values (8,'1-mar-2001',2000);

insert into payments values (8,'2-mar-2001',2000);

insert into payments values (9,'7-apr-2001',3000);

insert into payments values (10,'10-apr-2001',4500);

insert into payments values (11,'7-apr-2001',1000);
insert into payments values (11,'10-apr-2001',3500);

commit;

Summary

In this chapter we have seen how to use integrity constraints implement standard and business rules. Constraints can be related to a single column – column constraints, or related to multiple columns – table constraints.

We have understood six tables that we need to store information about courses, students and payments. It is very important to understand what is stored in each table and the relationship among six tables. One script is used to create tables and another script is used to insert sample data into it.

Exercises

- _____ constraint can be used to implements business rules.

- _____ option of REFERENCES constraint is used to delete all child rows when parent row is being deleted.

- Data dictionary view used to get information about constraints is _____.

- When a table has a composite primary key, where the PRIMARY KEY constraint is defined?_____

♦ What is the relationship between COURSES and COURSE_FACULTY table?

♦ How do you get details of all CHECK constraints of all tables?

♦ Is it possible to create a constraint to prevent a data that is less than the system date?

5. Changing Structure and Data

❑ Altering the structure of a table

❑ Dropping a table

❑ Manipulating data

❑ Transaction

❑ Locking

❑ Read Consistency

❑ Summary

❑ Exercises

Altering the structure of a table

It is possible to modify the structure of the table even after the table is created. ALTER TABLE command is used to alter the structure of the table.

The following are the possible alterations

- Adding a new column

- Adding a new table level constraint

- Increasing and decreasing width of a column

- Changing data type of the column

- Dropping a column

- Dropping a constraint

- Disabling a constraint

- Enabling a disabled constraint

The following is the syntax of ALTER TABLE command.

ALTER TABLE Syntax

ALTER TABLE tablename

  [ADD   (column specification)]

  [MODIFY (column specification)]

  [DROP   constraint-name [CASCADE]

            | column [CASCADE CONSTRAINTS]

  [DROP UNUSED COLUMN [column]]

  [SET UNUSED column]

  [ENABLE | DISABLE constraint-name]

Let us now examine various examples using ALTER TABLE command. It is important to note that some possibilities are applicable only when certain conditions are met. These if and buts are to be remembered while modifying the structure of the table.

Adding a new column or constraint

It is always possible to add a new column to an existing table. However, if column is to be added to a table that already contains rows, then certain options are not available.

To add a new column CAT (category) to COURSES table, enter the following:

ALTER TABLE courses

    ADD (cat varchar2(5));

It is not possible to given any constraint that is not satisfied by existing data. For instance, it is not possible to add CAT as a NOT NULL column as Oracle initializes CAT column in all rows with NULL value. See the following snapshot of the screen.

SQL> alter table courses

  2 add (cat varchar2(5) not null);

alter table courses

      *

ERROR at line 1:

ORA-01758: table must be empty to add mandatory (NOT NULL) column

However, it is possible to have NOT NULL constraint in the following cases:

- ❑ If DEFAULT option is used to specify the default value for the column
- ❑ When table is empty.

The following example will work as DEFAULT option is used to specify the default value.

alter table courses add (cat varchar2(5) default 'prog' not null);

You can add a table constraint. Once table is created, it is not possible to add constraints other than NOT NULL to columns of the table. However, it is possible to add any constraint at the table level as follows:

alter table courses

   add (constraint courses_cat_chk check (length(cat) >= 2))

We will see more about functions such as **length** later in this book. The above constraint specifies that the column CAT should have at least two characters. It is added as a table constraint as it not possible to add CHECK constraint at the column level to column that already exists.

Modifying attributes of existing columns

It is also possible to modify the certain attributes of an existing column. The following are possible modifications.

- Increasing the length of the column
- Decrease the length of the column only when column is empty.
- Change the datatype of the column only when column is empty.
- Adding NOT NULL constraint. No other constraint can be added to column. However, it is possible to add constraints at table level. See the previous section.

To increase the size of the column CAT, enter the following:

alter table courses

  modify (cat varchar2(10));

You can decrease the width and even change the datatype of the column if the column is empty. That means if no row has any value for the column being altered.

Dropping a constraint

Used to drop the constraints defined on the table.

To drop a constraint, the name of the constraint is required. You may use USER_CONSTRAINTS data dictionary view to get the list of constraints.

alter table courses drop constraint courses_cat_chk;

CASCADE Option

You cannot drop a UNIQUE or PRIMARY KEY constraint that is part of a referential integrity constraint without also dropping the corresponding foreign key. To drop PRIMARY KEY or UNIQUE constraint along with REFERENCES constraint use CASCADE option.

To drop PRIMARY KEY constraint of STUDENTS along with related constraint, do the following.

alter table courses

drop primary key cascade;

Note: You can get information about all the constraint using USER_CONSTRAINTS data dictionary view.

Dropping a column

For the first time Oracle8i has provided a command to drop a column from the table. Till Oracle8, dropping a column is very lengthy task as there was no direct way to drop a column. Oracle8i has provided a new option with ALTER TABLE command to drop a column – DROP COLUMN.

Actual you have two options when you want to drop a column.

- ❑ Either you can drop unwanted column straight away. All the data related to the column being dropped will be removed immediately.
- ❑ Or you can mark the column for deletion and delete the column at a later stage. Since the column is marked for dropping, it is considered to be dropped. But the data of the column will remain until the column is physically removed.

The second options is especially useful considering the fact that dropping of a column does take a lot of time and if it is done when the load on the system is high then it will severely effect performance of the system. So you can mark a column for dropping and then drop the column when load on the system is low.

To drop column CAT of COURSES table, enter the following:

```
alter table courses drop column cat;
```

If column being dropped is either a PRIMARY KEY or UNIQUE key that is referenced by a foreign key, then it is not possible to drop the column. But it is possible if CASCADE CONSTRAINTS option is used. CASCADE CONSTRAINTS option drops all constraints that depend on the column being dropped.

To drop column FCODE column of FACULTY table along with all depending constraints, enter:

```
alter table faculty drop column fcode cascade constraints;
```

Note: When you drop a UNIQUE or PRIMARY KEY column then Oracle automatically drops the index that it creates to enforce uniqueness.

SET UNUSED option of ALTER TABLE command is used to mark a column for dropping. But the column is not physically removed. However, the column is treated as deleted. Once a column is marked as UNUSED then it cannot be accessed.

The following example marks column CAT or COURSES table as unused.

```
alter table courses set unused column cat;
```

Columns that are marked for deletion can be physically deleted using DROP UNUSED COLUMNS option of ALTER TABLE command as follows:

```
alter table courses drop unused columns;
```

Note: We can view the number of columns that are marked for deletion using USER_UNUSED_COL_TABS data dictionary view. USER_TAB_COLUMNS gives information about existing columns of a table.

Note: Until a column is physically dropped from the table it is counted as a column of the table and counted towards the absolute limit of 1000 columns per table.

Enabling and Disabling Constraints

ALTER TABLE can be used to enable and disable constraints without dropping constraints. When a constraint is disabled, Oracle does not enforce the rule defined by constraint. This may be useful when you need to insert a large number of rows and does not want Oracle to apply constraints as it takes a lot of time.

To disable PRIMARY KEY on SUBJECTS table:

ALTER TABLE courses DISABLE PRIMARY KEY;

Or you can drop any constraint by giving its name as follows:

alter table courses disable constraint courses_cat_chk;

If the constraint has depending constraints then you must use CASCADE clause to disable dependent constraints.

You can enable a disabled constraints using ENABLE clause as follows:

alter table courses disable constraint courses_cat_chk;

Note: You can find out status of a constraint by using STATUS column of USER_CONSTRAINTS data dictionary view.

Dropping a table

To drop a table, use DDL command DROP TABLE. It removes the data as well as structure of the table The following is the syntax of DROP TABLE command.

DROP TABLE tablename [CASCADE CONSTRAINTS];

CASCADE CONSTRAINTS clause is used to drop constraints that refer to primary and unique keys in the dropped table. If you do not give this clause and if referential integrity (references constraint) constraints exists then Oracle displays then Oracle displays error and doesn't drop the table.

The following command will drop FACULTY table.

DROP TABLE faculty;

Note: When table is dropped, Views, and Synonyms based on the table will be made invalid, though they remain in the system. Also note, dropping a table cannot be undone.

Manipulating data

As we have seen in the first chapter, SQL commands are divided into DML commands and DDL commands. DDL commands such as CREATE TABLE, ALTER TABLE, and DROP TABLE are dealing with definition of the table or structure of the table.

DML commands such as INSERT, DELETE and UPDATE are used to manipulate the data of the table. We have already seen how to use INSERT command to insert rows into table. Now let us see two other DML commands.

Updating rows using UPDATE command

UPDATE command is used to modify existing data in the rows. The following is the syntax of UPDATE command.

UPDATE table SET column = {expression | subquery}

      [, column = {expression | subquery}] ...

[WHERE condition];

If WHERE clause is not given then all the rows of the table will be effected by the change. In fact, it is more often the result of an error than intentional.

The following command will change course fee of ASP to 6000.

Update courses set fee = 6000

Where ccode = 'asp';

It is also possible to change more than one column at a time as follows:

update courses set fee = 6000, duration=30

where ccdoe = 'asp';

Note: We will discuss how to use **subquery** in UPDATE command later in this book.

Deleting rows using DELETE command

DELETE command is used to delete rows from a table. The following is the syntax of DELETE command.

DELETE   FROM   table

   [WHERE   condition;]

If WHERE clause is not given then all rows of the table will be deleted.

The following command will delete row where CCODE is "c".

Delete from courses

Where ccode = 'c';

It is not possible to delete a parent row while it has child rows. For example, it is not possible to delete a row from COURSES table if the row has dependent rows in BATCHES table or in COURSE_FACULTY table. However, it is possible to delete parent row along with its child rows provided ON DELETE CASCADE option is given at the time of create foreign key constraint in child table. Please see chapter 4 for more information. Changes made using INSERT, UPDATE and DELETE are not made permanent until explicitly or implicitly they are committed. See next section for more information.

Transaction

A transaction is a collection of statements used to perform a single task. These statements are logically related as they perform a single task. All these statements must be executed to successfully complete the task. If any of the statements fails then the all the statements that were executed prior to the statement that failed should be undone otherwise data in the database becomes invalid and inconsistent.

The following example will illustrate the process.

Assume that faculty with code **kl** (Kevin Loney) is leaving the institute. So all his batches are to be assigned to **jc** (Jason Couchman). For this the following steps are to be taken.

- Change FCODE of all the batches that are currently being handled by **kl** to **jc**.
- Delete rows from COURSE_FACULTY where FCODE is **kl**.
- Delete row from FACULTY where FCODE is **kl**.

That means the following are the commands to be executed to perform the above-mentioned task.

update batches set fcode = 'jc' where fcode = 'kl';

delete from course_faculty where fcode = 'kl';

delete from faculty where fcode = 'kl';

It is important to make sure that all three statements are either successfully completed or all of them are rolled back. To ensure this Oracle provides transaction mechanism.

If UPDATE command in the above set of commands begins the transaction then only COMMIT command is given after the second DELETE is executed, the changes are committed. If ROLLBACK command is given then all the changes up to UPDATE will be rolled back.

So COMMIT and ROLLBACK command are used to ensure either everything is committed or everything is rolled back.

A transaction is a collection of statements   which is to be either completely done or not done at all. In other words the process should not be *half-done.* That means ALL or NOTHING.

A transaction begins when previous transaction ends or when the session begins. A transaction ends when COMMIT or ROLLBACK is issued. See figure 1.

A new session starts when you connect to Oracle. For example, when you log on using SQL*PLUS you start a new session. When you exit SQL*PLUS the session is terminated.

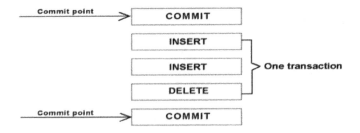

Figure 1: A transaction is a collection of commands given between two commit points.

COMMIT Command

Used to commit all changes made since the beginning of the transaction. It does the following.

- Makes all the changes made to database during transaction permanent
- Unlocks the rows that are locked during the transaction.
- Ends the transaction.
- Erases all savepoints in the current transaction(covered later).

Changes made to database such as inserting rows, deleting rows, and updating rows are not made permanent until they are committed.

Implicit Commit

Oracle Implicitly issues commit in the following cases.

- Before a DDL command.
- After a DDL command.
- At normal disconnect from the database. For example, when you exit SQL*PLUS using EXIT command.

Note: It is very important to remember not to mix DML commands with DDL command as the later commands are going to issue COMMIT, which might commit incomplete changes also.

ROLLBACK Command

Used in transaction processing to undo changes made since the beginning of the transaction.

- Undoes the changes made to database in the current transaction
- Releases locks held on rows duration transaction.
- Ends the transaction.
- Erases all savepoints in the current transaction (covered later).

ROLLBACK SEGMENT

In order to rollback changes that were made, Oracle has to store the data that was existing prior to the change so that previous data can be restored when user rolls back the changes. ROLLBACK SEGMENT is the area where Oracle stores data that will be used to roll back the changes. Every transaction is associated with a ROLLBACK SEGMENT.

Generally a few ROLLBACK SEGMENTS are created at the time of creating database. Database Administrator can create some more rollback segments depending upon the requirement using CREATE ROLLBACK SEGMENT command. Oracle assigns one rollback segment to each transaction. It is also possible to associate a transaction with a particular rollback segment using SET ROLLBACK SEGMENT command. It is not relevant to discuss more about the way ROLLBACK SEGMENT functions in a book like this. Please see Oracle Concepts for more information about ROLLBACK SEGEMENT.

SAVEPOINT Command

Savepoint is used to mark a location in the transaction so that we can rollback up to that mark and not to the very beginning of the transaction.

The following is the syntax of SAVEPOINT.

SAVEPOINT   savepoint_name;

A single transaction may also have multiple savepoints. The following example illustrates how to use savepoints.

SQL> update . . .

SQL> savepoint s1;

Savepoint created.

SQL> insert .... ;

SQL> insert .... ;

SQL> savepoint s2;

Savepoint created.

SQL> delete ...;

SQL> rollback to s1;

Rollback complete.

SQL> update...

SQL> commit;

In the above example, ROLLBACK   TO S1; will undo changes made from savepoint S1 to the point of rollback. That means it will undo INSERT, INSERT, and even DELETE given after second savepoint. It doesn't undo UPDATE given before first savepoint. The COMMIT given after last UPDATE is going to commit first UDPATE and last UPDATE. Because all the remaining are already rolled back by ROLLBACK TO S1 command.

If we have given ROLLBACK TO S2; then it would have undone only DELETE given after the second savepoint and remaining statements (update, insert, insert, and update) would have been committed.

Locking

It is important from database management system's point of view to ensure that two user are not modifying the same data at the time in a destructive manner.

Let us consider the following example to understand what will happen if two users are trying to update the same data at the same time.

Assume we have PRODUCTS table with details of products. Each product is having quantity on hand (QOH). Transactions such as sales and purchases are going to modify QOH column of the table.

The following are the steps that might take place when two transactions – one sale and one purchase – are taking place.

- Assume QOH of product 10 is 20 units.
- At 10:00 USER1 has sold 5 units and updated QOH as follows but has not committed the change. After UPDATE command QOH will be 15.

  update products set qoh = qoh – 5 where prodid = 10;

- At 10:11 USER2 has purchased 10 units and updated QOH as follows and committed. After UPDATE command QOH will be 25 as 10 it added to 15.

  update products set qoh = qoh + 10 where prodid = 10;

- If at 10:12 USER1 has rolled back the UPDATE then data that was there before the UPDATE should be restored i.e.20. But the actual data should be 30 as we added 10 units to it at 10:11 and committed.

As you can see in the above example, if two users are trying to update the same row at the same time the data may be corrupted. As shown in the above example at the end of the process QOH should be actually 30 but it is not only 20.

It is possible to ensure that two transactions are interfering with each other by locking the rows that are being modified so that only one transaction at a time can make the change. Oracle ensures that only one transaction can modify a row at a time by locking the row once the row is updated. The lock will remain until the transaction is completed. Oracle also ensures that other users will not see the changes that are not committed. That means if transaction T1 has updated a row then until the transaction is committed no other transaction in the system will see the changes made by T1. Instead other transactions will see only the data that was existing before the change was made.

The following scenario will illustrate the process in detail.

- Assume QOH of product 10 is 20.
- Transaction T1 has issued UPDATE command to update QOH of product 10. Oracle locks the row that is updated and does not allow other transactions to update the row. However, it is possible to read the data from the row.

  update products set qoh = qoh + 5 where prodid = 10;

- If T1 has issued SELECT to retrieve data then it will get 25 in QOH of product 10.
- If T2 has issued SELECT command, it will see only 20 in QOH of product

10. This is because no uncommitted changes will be available to other transactions.

♦ If T2 is trying to update product 10 then Oracle will cause transaction T2 to wait until transaction T1 (that holds lock on this row) is completed. Oracle will wail for lock to be released *indefinitely*.

♦ If transaction T1 is committed then change is made permanent and lock will be released. Now it is possible for other transactions to see the updated data and even update the row if required.

The following are the important points to be remembered about Oracle's locking mechanism.

❑ Locking in Oracle is automatic and transparent. That means we never need to ask Oracle to lock row that is being modified. Locking is transparent means user is not aware of the locking process. It happens automatically and in the background.

❑ Oracle locks the row that is being updated. That means locking is row-level. Other levels that are in user are - page-level and table-level.

❑ Oracle releases locks held by a transaction when transaction is completed either successfully – using COMMIT – or unsuccessfully – using ROLLBACK.

❑ If a transaction is trying to update a row and if row is already locked then Oracle will wait for the row that is locked to be unlocked indefinitely. It is because of the fact that rows are locked for a small duration in a typical production system. So Oracle prefers to wait to cause any error.

❑ It is possible to lock table manually using LOCK TABLE command.

Locking the rows that are being updated is an important part of Oracle. It ensures that no two transactions can update the same row at the same time. Locking mechanism is followed by all database management systems. But some smaller database management systems follow page-level locking where not the exact row that is being modified is locked instead the entire page in which the row exists is locked.

Read Consistency

When one user is trying to read data while other user is updating it, we might encounter a scenario where the data to be read by reader has already been modified by writer. In such cases Oracle provides read consistency to reader.

Read consistency ensures that whatever a user is reading is consistent to the point of starting the query. The following example will illustrate this mechanism.

- USER1 has issues a query to read data from SALES table at 10:00. The table contains 20000 rows and it may take 4 minutes to retrieve data completely. As user is only reading the data no lock is obtained on the table.

- USER2 has updated a row that is at 15000th row in the table at 10:01 and committed the change.

- USER1 has reached 15000th row at 10:03. Now USER1 get the data that was before the change as by the time query started the change didn't take place. That means Oracle has to provide the data to USER1 that existed at the time of starting the query – 10:00.

- Any changes whether committed or not made after 10:00 should not be retrieved by USER1.

Oracle uses ROLLBACK SEGMENT to store the data that was before the change to provide read consistency.

Summary

ALTER TABLE command is used to alter the structure of the table. It is possible to add column or constraint, modify attributes such as datatype and length of existing columns, and drop column or constraint. UPDATE and DELETE commands are used to update and delete rows of the table respectively. Changes made using DML commands are not committed until they are explicitly (using COMMIT command) or implicitly committed.

ROLLBACK command is used to roll back the changes since the beginning of the transaction, which is a collection of statements to perform a single task. SAVEPOINT command is used to mark a point in the transaction so that changes made after the savepoint can be rolled back. Oracle locks the rows that are being update to ensure only one transaction can update a row at a time. Oracle also ensures that the data retrieved by query is consistent to the point of starting the query – read consistency.

Exercises

♦ How do you add a check constraint to an existing column?

♦ How do you drop a constraint?

♦ Is it possible to know the name of the constraint? If yes, how?

♦ How do you give primary key constraint if two or more columns are part of the primary key?

♦ _____ command is used to mark a location in a transaction.

♦ What is ROLLBACK SEGMENT?

♦ When does a transaction begin?

♦ If a row that to be updated is already locked then what happens?

♦ What happens if a row is update and not committed or rolled back?

♦ What is read consistency?

6. Arithmetic and Date functions

- What is a function?
- Types of functions
- Arithmetic functions
- Dual table
- Date arithmetic
- Date functions
- Summary
- Exercises

What is a function?

A function is similar to an operator in operation. A function is a name that performs a specific task. A function may or may not take values (arguments) but it always returns a value as the result. If function takes values then these values are to be given within parentheses after the function name. The following is the general format of a function.

function [(argument-1, argument-2,...)]

If the function doesn't take any value then function name can be used alone and even parentheses are not required.

Types of functions

Functions are classified based on the type of data on which they perform the operation. The following are the different types of functions available in Oracle.

❑ Arithmetic Functions.

❑ Date & Time functions.

❑ String functions.

❑ Conversion functions.

❑ Miscellaneous functions.

❑ Group functions.

Arithmetic functions perform take numeric data; date functions take date type data and string functions take strings. Conversion functions are used to convert the given value from one type to another. Miscellaneous functions perform operations on any type of data. Group functions are used to perform operations on the groups created by GROUP BY clause.

Note: Group functions or aggregate functions perform their operation on a group (a collection of rows). All the remaining functions are called as *single-row* functions as they return a result for each row.

Arithmetic Functions

Arithmetic functions take numbers and perform arithmetic operations. Table 1 lists the   arithmetic functions available in Oracle.

Function	Description
ABS(value)	Absolute value of the given value.
CEIL(value)	Smallest integer larger than or equal to value
FLOOR(value)	Largest integer smaller than or equal to value
MOD(value,divisor)	Remainder of the division between the value and divisor.
POWER(value,exponent)	Value is raised to exponent.
ROUND(value[,precision])	Rounds value to precision. Precision can be negative if rounding is to be done on the left of the decimal point.
TRUNC(value[,precision])	Truncates instead of rounding. Otherwise same as ROUND.
SQRT(value)	Square root of value.
SIGN(value)	Returns 1 if value > 0, -1 if value <0, 0 if value = 0

Table 1: Arithmetic Functions.

The following are a few examples of arithmetic functions.

select mod(10,4) from dual;

The above command displays 2 as the result as the remainder of the division between 10 and 4 is 2.

ROUND and TRUNC functions

ROUND and TRUNC functions are used to round and truncate the given number to the given number of digits (either on the right or left of the decimal point). ROUND takes the leftmost digit that is being lost and accordingly adds one to the rightmost digit. TRUNC doesn't take the leftmost digit into account. It just truncates the given number to the given precision.

select round(1047.785,2), trunc(1047.785,2) from dual;

The above command will display 1047.79 and 1047.78. This is because TRUNC doesn't take the digits being lost into account.

The following examples illustrate the result of ROUND and TRUNC functions with positive and negative precision.

Function	Result
ROUND(1295.35 6,2)	1295.3 6
TRUNC(1295.356 ,2)	1295.3 5
ROUND(1295.35 6,0)	1295
ROUND(1285.35	1290

6, -1)	
TRUNC(1285.356, -1)	1280
ROUND(1295,-2)	1300

When precision in ROUND is positive then rounding takes place to the specified number of digits on the right of decimal point. For example, if precision is 2 it means round number to 2 digits on the right of the decimal point. When precision is negative; it means number is to be rounded to the left of the decimal point. In both the cases if the leftmost digit of the digits being lost is >= 5 then one is added to the rightmost digit of the digits that are retained.

In the example given above, ROUND (1285.356, -1) will result in 1290. Because one digit on the left of decimal point is to be set to zero, means 5 is replaced with 0. As the digit that is replaced with zero (5 in this case) is >= 5 one is added to digit on the left of it (8) to make it 9. So the result is 1290.

ROUND (1295,-2) results in 1300. This is because in 1295 two digits on the left of decimal point are set to zeroes(1200) and as leftmost digit out of digits that are set to zero is 9 one is added to 2, which is the rightmost digit in the remaining portion. This makes it 1300.

Note: ROUND and TRUNC functions can also be used with **date** data type. More on this later in this chapter.

CEIL & FLOOR functions

CEIL produces the smallest integer that is greater than or equal to the given value. Whereas FLOOR is opposite of CEIL. The following table illustrates the usage of these two related functions.

Function	Result
CEIL(1.3)	2
CEIL(2)	2
CEIL(-2.3)	-2
FLOOR(1.3)	1
FLOOR(2)	2
FLOOR(-2.3)	-3

DUAL Table

This is a table that is made available to every account in Oracle database. This table contains one row and one column. This table can be used with SELECT when result of the expression is to be displayed only for once.

SQL> describe dual

Name	Null?	Type
------------------------	--------	----
DUMMY		VARCHAR2(1)

For example, to display the current system date the following SELECT can be used:

SQL> select sysdate from dual;

```
SYSDATE
--------
24-AUG-01
```

As DUAL table contains only one row, the result is displayed only for once.

The following example displays the course fee by rounding it to thousands.

select ccode,name, round(fee,-3) "fee"

from courses;

```
CCODE NAME                            fee
----- ------------------------------ ---------
ora   Oracle database                5000
vbnet VB.NET                         6000
c     C programming                  4000
asp   ASP.NET                        5000
java  Java Language                  5000
xml   XML Programming                4000
```

Scientific functions

The following are the other arithmetic functions that are rarely used in business applications. They are mainly used in scientific applications. However as they are available in Oracle, we will get to know them.

Function	Description
ACOS(value)	Arc cosine of the given *value*. The value is in the range -1 to 1 and return value is in radians.
ASIN(value)	Arc sine of the *value*.
ATAN(value)	Arc tangent of the *value*.
COS(value)	Cosine of the *value*.
COSH(value)	Hyperbolic cosine of the *value*.
EXP(value)	Return **e** (2.71828183) raised to *value* power.
LN(value)	Natural logarithm of *value*.
LOG(base,value)	Logarithm with *base* of *value*.
SIN(value)	Sine of the *value*.
SINH(value)	Hyperbolic sine of the *value*.
TAN(value)	Tangent of the *value*.
TANH(value)	Hyperbolic tangent of the *value*.

Table 2: Scientific Functions.

The following are few examples of these scientific functions.

select exp(2) from dual;

  EXP(2)

7.3890561

```
select log(10,10) from dual


LOG(10,10)
----------
         1
```


```
SELECT COS(180 * 3.14159265359/180)
from dual


COS(180*3.14159265359/180)
--------------------------
                        -1
```


Date Arithmetic

When arithmetic operators are used with DATE datatype it is called as Date Arithmetic.

The following are the possible arithmetic operations on DATE type data.

- Adding a number to date to get the date after the given number of days.
- Subtracting a number from a date to get the date before the given number of days.
- Subtracting two dates to get the number of days between these two dates.

The following example displays the name of the student and number of days between system date and date of joining.

select name, **sysdate - dj** from students;

NAME	No Days
George Micheal	226.29194
Micheal Douglas	225.29194
Andy Roberts	225.29194
Malcom Marshall	220.29194
Vivan Richards	220.29194
Chirs Evert	222.29194
Ivan Lendal	221.29194
George Micheal	176.29194
Richard Marx	140.29194
Tina Turner	140.29194
Jody Foster	139.29194

In Oracle DATE datatype stores date and time. At the time of storing a date If time is not given then it will be set to 0 hours, 0 minutes and 0 seconds (beginning of the day or 12:00 a.m.).

Default date format – DD-MON-YY – doesn't include time. However time is always stored along with date and if you want to at any time you can extract the time portion a date using TO_CHAR function, which will be discussed in the next chapter.

Note: All comparisons between two dates include time portion also.

Note: The fraction portion in the result between two dates indicates the difference in time.

The following example shows the due date for first installment (assuming first installment is to be paid within 10 days from the date of joining).

select name,dj, **dj + 10** "Due Date" from students

NAME	DJ	Due Date
George Micheal	10-JAN-01	20-JAN-01
Micheal Douglas	11-JAN-01	21-JAN-01
Andy Roberts	11-JAN-01	21-JAN-01
Malcom Marshall	16-JAN-01	26-JAN-01
Vivan Richards	16-JAN-01	26-JAN-01
Chirs Evert	14-JAN-01	24-JAN-01
Ivan Lendal	15-JAN-01	25-JAN-01
George Micheal	01-MAR-01	11-MAR-01
Richard Marx	06-APR-01	16-APR-01
Tina Turner	06-APR-01	16-APR-01
Jody Foster	07-APR-01	17-APR-01

The following query displays the details of the payment that were made in the last 3 days:

select * from payments

Where **sysdate – dp <= 3;**

Date Functions

Date functions operate on values of DATE datatype. Except MONTHS_BETWEEN all date functions return DATE data type. The following is the list of DATE functions.

Function	Description
ADD_MONTHS(date, count)	Adds *count* number of months to *date*.
MONTHS_BETWEEN (date1, date2)	Returns number of months between *date1* and *date2*.
LAST_DAY(date)	Returns the last day of the month in which *date* is.
NEXT_DAY(date, 'day')	Gives the date of next *day* after the date, where *day* name of the week like 'Monday'.
NEW_TIME(date, 'this', 'other')	Returns time in *other* time zone for time of *this* time zone.
ROUND(date)	Rounds the date depending upon the time. If time is at or after 12 hours then date is incremented. Time is always set to beginning of the day (0:0:0).
TRUNC(date)	Same as ROUND (date) but doesn't

increment date.

Table 3: DATE Functions.

Adding and subtracting months

You can add or subtract months from a date using ADD_MONTHS function. If the count is positive, that many months will be added. If count is negative that many months will be subtracted.

Adding months is the process where Oracle will give the date of next specified number of months.

In the following example, Oracle will add two months to system date:

SQL> Select sysdate, add_months(sysdate,2)

  2 From dual;

SYSDATE   ADD_MONTH

--------- ---------

25-AUG-01 25-OCT-01

If the target month doesn't have the required day then the last day of the month will be taken. In the following example, 30-SEP-2001 is returned, as 31-SEP is not available. Oracle automatically adjusts the date according to the requirement.

SQL> select add_months('31-aug-2001',1) from dual;

ADD_MONTH

121

30-SEP-01

The following example will show the date on which the students of completed batches will be issued certificates assuming it will take 3 months time to issue certificates.

SQL> select bcode, ccode, enddate, add_months(enddate,3) "Cert. Date"

  2 from batches

  3 where enddate is not null;

BCODE CCODE ENDDATE   Cert. Dat

----- ----- --------- ---------

b1   ora   20-FEB-01 20-MAY-01

b2   asp   05-MAR-01 05-JUN-01

b3   c   27-FEB-01 27-MAY-01

b4   xml   30-MAR-01 30-JUN-01

b5   java 10-MAY-01 10-AUG-01

When the second parameter – *count* - is negative, date is decremented by that many months.

The following example shows the date on which the admissions for running batches have started. For a batch admissions start exactly one month before the starting date.

```
select bcode, ccode, stdate, add_months(stdate,-1)

from  batches where enddate is null
```

```
BCODE CCODE STDATE    ADD_MONTH

----- ----- --------- ---------

b6    vbnet 12-JUL-01 12-JUN-01

b7    ora   15-AUG-01 15-JUL-01
```

Getting months between two dates

You can obtain the number of months between two dates using MONTHS_BETWEEN function. The following query returns the number of months between starting date and ending date of all completed batches.

```
select bcode, ccode, stdate, enddate,

      months_between(enddate, stdate) "NO. Months"

from batches where enddate is not null;
```

```
BCODE CCODE STDATE    ENDDATE   NO. Months

----- ----- --------- --------- ----------

b1    ora   12-JAN-01 20-FEB-01 1.2580645

b2    asp   15-JAN-01 05-MAR-01 1.6774194

b3    c     20-JAN-01 27-FEB-01 1.2258065

b4    xml   02-MAR-01 30-MAR-01 .90322581

b5    java  05-APR-01 10-MAY-01 1.1612903
```

The fraction in the result is the number of days beyond the number of months. For example, the difference between 12-JAN-01 and 20-FEB-01 is 1.258. It means there is one month and 26% of another month, which comes to 8 days.

Note: The fraction is calculated based on a 31-day month and also considers time portion.

Use TRUNC function to ignore fraction in the result of MONTHS_BETWEEN as follows:

select bcode, ccode, stdate, enddate,

    trunc(months_between(enddate, stdate)) "NO. Months"

from batches where enddate is not null;

```
BCODE CCODE STDATE    ENDDATE   NO. Months
----- ----- --------- --------- ----------
b1    ora   12-JAN-01 20-FEB-01       1
b2    asp   15-JAN-01 05-MAR-01       1
b3    c     20-JAN-01 27-FEB-01       1
b4    xml   02-MAR-01 30-MAR-01       0
b5    java  05-APR-01 10-MAY-01       1
```

Note: It is possible to send the return value of a function to another function.

The following query displays the batches that we completed in the last 6 months and duration is more that 1 month.

select bcode, ccode

from batches

where months_between(sysdate,enddate) <= 6

    and months_between(enddate,stdate) > 1;

BCODE CCODE

----- -----

b2   asp

b3   c

b5   java

LAST_DAY function

LAST_DAY function returns the date of the last day of the month of the given date. The following statement displays the last day of the current month:

Select sysdate, last_day(sysdate)

From dual;

SYSDATE   LAST_DAY(

--------- ---------

25-AUG-01 31-AUG-01

The following query displays the due date by which first installment of each batch is to be paid. LAST_DAY function return the last day of the month in which batch has started and if 5 is added to that then it will be 5th of the next month – due date of first installment.

select bcode,ccode, stdate, last_day(stdate) + 5 "Due Date"

from batches

BCODE CCODE STDATE   Due Date

----- ----- --------- ---------

b1   ora   12-JAN-01 05-FEB-01

b2   asp   15-JAN-01 05-FEB-01

b3   c   20-JAN-01 05-FEB-01

b4   xml   02-MAR-01 05-APR-01

b5   java 05-APR-01 05-MAY-01

b6   vbnet 12-JUL-01 05-AUG-01

b7   ora   15-AUG-01 05-SEP-01

Similarly assuming the batches are scheduled in the last week of previous month for each batch, the following query displays the date of last week:

select bcode, ccode, stdate, last_day(add_months(stdate,-1)) - 7 | |

         ' to ' | | last_day(add_months(stdate), -1)

from batches

BCODE CCODE STDATE   Schd. Week

----- ----- --------- ------------------------

b1   ora   12-JAN-01 24-DEC-00 to 31-DEC-00

b2   asp   15-JAN-01 24-DEC-00 to 31-DEC-00

b3   c   20-JAN-01 24-DEC-00 to 31-DEC-00

b4   xml   02-MAR-01 21-FEB-01 to 28-FEB-01

b5   java 05-APR-01 24-MAR-01 to 31-MAR-01

b6   vbnet 12-JUL-01 23-JUN-01 to 30-JUN-01

b7   ora   15-AUG-01 24-JUL-01 to 31-JUL-01

NEXT_DAY function

This function returns the date of given weekday that is greater than the given date. It takes weekday – Sunday, Monday etc. – and returns the date on which the coming weekday is falling. The return value is always grater than the given date. The following example shows when is the next Friday.

select sysdate, next_day(sysdate,'Fri') from dual;

SYSDATE   NEXT_DAY(

--------- ---------

25-AUG-01 31-AUG-01

If weekday of the given date and the given weekday happen to be the same then the date of coming weekday is returned. This is because the result of this function is always greater than the given date. See the following example where though the given date - 25-AUG - is Saturday NEXT_DAY returns the next Saturday and not the same date.

select sysdate, next_day(sysdate,'Sat') from dual

```
SYSDATE   NEXT_DAY(

--------- ---------

25-AUG-01 01-SEP-01
```

But what if you want to get the same date, when day of the week of the given date is same as the one asked for? The following query will return the same date if date happens to fall on the required weekday.

```
select  sysdate, next_day(sysdate - 1,'Sat') from  dual
```

```
SYSDATE   NEXT_DAY(

--------- ---------

25-AUG-01 25-AUG-01
```

When one is subtracted from the system date, though the date happens to be on Saturday it become Friday (24-AUG) because of the subtraction. Then NEXT_DAY returns the 25-AUG as it is grater than the given date – 24-AUG.

ROUND & TRUNC functions with dates

DATE data type contains both date and time. ROUND and TRUNC function can be used to round or truncate the date based on the time portion.   The following query displays the date and time portion of system date using TO_CHAR function. It is suffice to know that TO_CHAR can be used to convert given date to character type using the given format.

```
Select to_char(sysdate,'dd-mm-yyyy hh24:mi:ss') from dual
```

TO_CHAR(SYSDATE,'DD

25-08-2001 18:42:08

Note: TO_CHAR converts a DATE type data to character type. Please see next chapter for more information on TO_CHAR.

ROUND function adds one day to the date if time portion of the date is greater than or equal to 12 noon.

select sysdate, to_char(round(sysdate),'dd-mm-yyyy hh24:mi:ss') "Round Date" from dual

SYSDATE   Round Date

--------- -------------------

25-AUG-01 26-08-2001 00:00:00

In the above query first ROUND function is used to round SYSDATE. As we have seen the time in SYSDATE is 18 hours, the date is incremented by one – 26-AUG. ROUND always sets the time portion to 0:0:0 (as seen in the output of the query).

TRUNC function doesn't increment the date based on the time, but it sets time portion to 0 hours, 0 minutes and 0 seconds. The following query shows the result of TRUNC function.

select to_char(sysdate,'dd-mm-yyyy hh24:mi:ss') "Today",

    to_char(trunc(sysdate),'dd-mm-yyyy hh24:mi:ss') "Truncated Date"

from dual

```
Today           Truncated Date

------------------- -------------------

25-08-2001 18:56:53 25-08-2001 00:00:00
```

Note: Both ROUND and TRUNC set the time portion in the DATE data type to 12 A.M. (00:00:00).

The following query is used to displays the details of the payments made today.

select * from payments

where dp = sysdate;

The above query always returns *no rows selected.* This is because when Oracle compares two dates it takes date and time portions into account. In the above query, though PAYMENTS table contains rows where DP is containing the same date as SYSDATE, the time portions will not match. The remedy is to ignore time portions and compare only date portions of the dates. The following is revised query where we truncate the dates to set both the times to 0:0:0 so that only dates are compared as times are equal.

select * from payments

where trunc(dp) = trunc(sysdate);

The following is another example where TRUNC is used to ignore time portion of DP and compare date with 10-apr-2001.

select * from payments

where trunc(dp) = '10-apr-2001'


```
  ROLLNO DP        AMOUNT

--------- --------- ---------

      10 10-APR-01    4500

      11 10-APR-01    3500
```


Getting time in different time zone

NEW_TIME is used to return the time of the specified time zone for the time of the given time zone.

The following query displays what will be the time in PST for the time in GMT.

select to_char(sysdate,'dd-mm-yyyy hh24:mi:ss') GMT ,

     to_char(new_time(sysdate,'GMT','AST'),'dd-mm-yyyy hh24:mi:ss') AST

from dual


```
TO_CHAR(SYSDATE,'DD TO_CHAR(NEW_TIME(SY

------------------- --------------------

25-08-2001 19:35:36 25-08-2001 15:35:36
```


The following are a few of the available time zones. For complete lit, please see Oracle online documentation.

Time Zone	Meaning
EST , EDT	Eastern Standard or Daylight Time
GMT	Greenwich Mean Time
HST , HDT	Alaska-Hawaii Standard Time or Daylight Time.
PST , PDT	Pacific Standard or Daylight Time
AST , ADT	Atlantic Standard or Daylight Time

Summary

A function is to perform a single operation and return a value. Functions are of different types. Arithmetic functions are used to perform arithmetic operations. Date functions perform operations on date type data. Performing arithmetic operations on dates is called as *date arithmetic.* DUAL table is with SELECT command to display the result of expression that do not relate to any table.

Exercises

♦ _____ function can be used to subtract months from a date.

♦ The return value of ROUND (2323.343,2) is _____.

♦ To get the remainder of a division____ function is used.

♦ In Date Arithmetic _____, _____ and _____ operations are allowed.

♦ _____ is the result of LAST_DAY(SYSDATE) assuming SYSDATE is 24th August.

♦ Which function can be used to set time portion of the DATE data type to 00:00:00, without affecting date portion.? _____

♦ Display details of students who have joined in the last 4 months.

♦ Display ROLLNO, NAME, DJ and number of days between current date and

DJ for each student.

- Display the first Sunday since batch with code 2 started.
- Display details of batches that started three or more months back.
- Display the details of payments of last Monday.
- _____ is the function to get number of years between two dates.

7. String, Conversion, and Miscellaneous functions

- String functions
- Conversion functions
- Miscellaneous functions

In the last chapter we have seen how to use arithmetic and date functions. In this chapter let us see how to use string, conversion and miscellaneous functions.

String Functions

String functions are functions that manipulate a set of characters. A set of characters is a string. For example, the name of the company, the address of a person all these are examples of a string. CHAR and VARCHAR data types contain strings. Let us first see how to concatenate strings in Oracle.

Concatenating Strings

Two strings can be concatenated (added one after another) to form a single string using the string concatenation operator, which is || (two pipe symbols).

The following example concatenates name of the faculty with qualification. We also put two spaces between these two values to provide required space.

select name | | ' ' | | qual from faculty

NAME| |"| |QUAL

George Koch MS Computer Science

Dan Appleman CS and EE graduate

Herbert Schildt MS Computer Science

David Hunter MS Electronics

Stephen Walther Ph.D. in Philosophy

Kevin Loney MS Eletronics

Jamie Jaworski Bachlors of Electrical

Jason Couchman OCP DBA

Table 1 shows the list of string functions. These functions generally take a string as parameter and also return a string as return value.

Function	Description
LENGTH (string)	Returns the number of characters in the *string*.
LOWER (string)	Returns the string after converting the string to lowercase.
UPPER (string)	Returns the string after converting the string to uppercase.
INITCAP (string)	Converts first character of every word to uppercase and remaining to lower case.
LPAD (string, length [, fillstring])	Makes the *string* of the given *length* by padding the string on the left either with space or with *fillstring*.
RPAD (string, length [, fillstring])	Same as LPAD but pads on the right.
LTRIM (string [, charset])	Removes all left most characters of string up to the first character that is not in the *charset*. if *charset* is not given then it defaults to blank.
RTRIM (string [, charset])	Same as LTRIM, but trims on the right.
TRIM (string)	Trims space on both sides.
SUBSTR (string, pos , length)	Extracts *length* number of characters from position *pos* in the string. If *length* is not given then extracts everything from *pos*.
INSTR (s1,s2 [,pos [,occurrence]])	Finds the starting position of *s2* in *s1*. If *occurrence* is not given then it finds first occurrence. Search starts at *pos*, if given, otherwise at the first

character in *s1*.

ASCII (string)	Returns ASCII code of the first character in the given string
CHR (number)	Returns ASCII character for the given ASCII code.
TRANSLATE (string, from, to)	Replaces characters in *from* with *to* in string.
REPLACE (string, source, replace)	Replaces *source* in *string* with *replace*.

Table 1: String functions.

Converting Case

Functions LOWER and UPPER are straightforward. And they play a very important role in string comparison. As string comparison is case sensitive, LOWER or UPPER can be used to convert strings to uniform case before they are compared.

The following query tries to retrieve details of courses related to programming.

select name,duration from courses

where name like '%programming%'

NAME   DURATION

------------------------------ ---------

C programming   20

The above query retrieves only one two whereas there are two rows that contain the word programming. It is because of the difference in the case. So the following query is converting the name to lowercase before comparison.

select name,duration from courses

where LOWER(name) like '%programming%'

NAME   DURATION
------------------------------ ---------

C programming   20
XML Programming   15

As NAME is converted to lowercase during comparison and compared with programming, which is in lowercase, the difference in case is ignored. The same result can be achieved even by using UPPER function. But in that case the string must be given in uppercase – PROGRAMMING.

INITCAP converts first letter of each word to capital and remaining letters to lowercase.

select initcap('this IS to Test INITCAP') Result

from dual;

RESULT

This Is To Test Initcap

INSTR function

INSTR returns the position in the first string where the second string starts in the first string. If second string is not found in first string, it returns **0**.

The default is to return the position of first occurrence by starting the search at the very first character in first string. However, INSTR has options using which we can specify from where the search should start and which occurrence is to be considered.

The following examples illustrate the usage of two optional parameters; *start* and *occurrence.*

select instr('How do you do','do') Postion

from dual;

POSTION

5

Though string "do" occurs for twice, the position of first occurrence is be returned. It is possible to specify to INSTR that it should start looking for *do* starting from the given position as follows.

select instr('How do you do','do',8) Postion

from dual

POSTION

    12

It is possible to specify that the position of the specified occurrence is to be returned as follows:

select instr('How do you do','do',1,2) Postion

from dual

POSTION

    12

Note: When occurrence is specified then starting position must also be specified, as third parameter cannot be omitted while fourth parameter is given.

The following example displays the details of courses where the letter p exists in the name of the course after 6th position.

select ccode,name

from courses

where instr(name,'n') > 6

```
CCODE NAME

----- -------------------------

c    C programming

java  Java Language

xml   XML Programming
```

The same query can also be written as follows using LIKE operator and six underscores to indicate that first six letters may be anything but *n* must exists after that. But INSTR version will be more flexible.

```
select ccode,name

from courses

where  name like '_____%n%'
```

```
CCODE NAME

----- ------------------------------

c    C programming

java  Java Language

xml   XML Programming
```

We will se some more applications of INSTR at a later stage.

SUBSTR function

SUBSTR is used to extract a sub string from the given string. It takes the position from where extraction starts and the number of characters to be extracted.

The following example displays the first 2 character from the code of the course.

select ccode, substr(ccode,1,2) sn from courses

CCODE SN

----- --

ora   or

vbnet vb

c   c

asp   as

java ja

xml   xm

It is possible to omit third parameter – length of the sub string. The following example illustrates it.

select substr('Srikanth Technologies',10) Result from dual

RESULT

Technologies

141

The result of one function can be passed to another function as input. We have already seen nesting functions in the previous chapter. Now let us see how we can combine SUBSTR and INSTR to get the first name of each faculty. First name is the name before space.

select name, substr(name, 1, instr(name,' ') - 1) Firstname from faculty;

NAME	FIRSTNAME
George Koch	George
Dan Appleman	Dan
Herbert Schildt	Herbert
David Hunter	David
Stephen Walther	Stephen
Kevin Loney	Kevin
Jamie Jaworski	Jamie
Jason Couchman	Jason

INSTR function is used to find out the position of first space. Then that position is used to specify the number of character to be taken from name. We subtracted one from position because position indicates the position of space but we have to take up to the character before the space.

The following is another example of these two functions. It take last name of the faculty.

select name, substr(name,instr(name,' ') + 1) Lastname from faculty

NAME	LASTNAME
George Koch	Koch
Dan Appleman	Appleman
Herbert Schildt	Schildt
David Hunter	Hunter
Stephen Walther	Walther
Kevin Loney	Loney
Jamie Jaworski	Jaworski
Jason Couchman	Couchman

The following is the sequence of steps in the above query.

- ❑ INSTR returns the position of first space in NAME
- ❑ The return value of the INSTR, after 1 is added, is passed to SUBSTR as the starting position.
- ❑ Everything on the right of the given position is taken by SUBSTR

Since Oracle converts the given values to required data type automatically, INSTR and SUBSTR can also be used with numbers and dates. The following query displays payments made in the month of April.

select * from payments

where instr(dp,'APR') <> 0

```
ROLLNO DP        AMOUNT

--------- --------- ---------

      9 07-APR-01      3000

     10 10-APR-01      4500

     11 07-APR-01      1000

     11 10-APR-01      3500
```

Trimming Strings

LTRIM and RTRIM are used to trim off unwanted characters from the left and right ends of the string respectively. Leftmost spaces are called as **leading spaces** and rightmost spaces are called as **trailing spaces.**

They trim spaces by default. Optionally, you can specify which set of characters you want to trim.

The following example is used to trim spaces on the left using LEFT. The length of the string will show the result.

```
select length(' abc  xyz  ') Before,

     length( ltrim(' abc  xyz  ')) After

from dual
```

```
BEFORE    AFTER

--------- ---------

    13        11
```

You can also trim a specified set of characters as shown below.

select ltrim('aabcbadxyabc','abc') Result from dual

RESULT

------

dxyabc

In the above example, trimming stopped at 'd' because 'd ' is the first character that doesn't fall in the character set of 'abc'.

While trimming, each character from left or right is taken and checked against the characters in the set. If character is same as any character in the character set, then character is trimmed otherwise trimming ends at that character. The same is true with RTRIM function, but it trims on the right.

TRIM function, which was introduced in Oracle8i, is used to trim both leading and trailing spaces.

select length(' abc xyz ') Before,
    length(trim(' abc xyz ')) After
from dual

    BEFORE   AFTER

```
--------- ---------
    12       8
```

Padding Strings

A string can be made of a given length by padding either on the left using LPAD or on the right using RPAD. By default Oracle uses space to pad strings. However, it is possible to specify which character(s) should be used for padding.

The following example course to 12 characters it specifies that dot is to be used for padding.

select rpad(name,12,'.') Name from courses

```
NAME
------------
Oracle datab

VB.NET......

C programmin

ASP.NET.....

Java Languag

XML Programm
```

The above example is padding strings that are shorter than 12 characters and truncating strings that are larger than 12 characters. Names like *VB.NET* and *ASP.NET* are padded on the right using dots. Whereas names like *Oracle database* and *C programming* are truncated to 12 characters.

Note: RPAD and LAPD truncate the given string if string has more number of characters than the given length.

TRANSLATE and REPLACE functions

These two functions return the string after modifying the given string. TRANSLATE works on individual characters, whereas REPLACE replaces a string with another string.

The following two examples will make the difference clear.

select replace('ABC ABAC XYZ DABC','ABC','PQR') Result from dual

RESULT

PQR ABAC XYZ DPQR

REPLACE replaces every occurrence of string 'ABC' with string 'PRQ'.

select translate('ABC ABAC XYZ DABC','ABC','PQR') Result

from dual

RESULT

PQR PQPR XYZ DPQR

TRANSLATE changes every occurrence of letter A with P, B with Q and C with R.

Conversion Functions

Conversion functions are used to convert a value from one data type into another. These functions are not required if Oracle can automatically convert the value. But there are cases where these conversion functions are required to convert the value to the required data type. The following table lists conversion functions.

FUNCTION	DESCRIPTION
TO_CHAR (value [, format])	Converts *value,* which is of DATE or NUMBER type, to CHAR type.
TO_DATE (char [, format])	Converts the given CHAR type value to DATE type.
TO_NUMBER (char)	Converts given CHAR type value to NUMBER type.

Table 2: Conversion Functions.

Before we understand how and where we use conversion functions, let us see how Oracle tries to convert the given data to the required data type.

Automatic Type Conversion

Oracle automatically converts the value to the required data type if it is possible. For example, if a number is used with string function, number is converted to string and then the function is executed. In the same way, if a DATE type value is required but if a CHAR type value is given in the format DD-MON-YY or DD-MON-YYYY then Oracle converts it to DATE type. But this automatic data type conversion is not always possible. To convert the value to the required data type, the given value must already

148

look like the data type it is being converted to. The following are guidelines that describe automatic type conversion.

GUIDELINES FOR AUTOMATIC CONVERSION OF DATA TYPE

- ❑ Any NUMBER or DATE will be converted to a CHAR.
- ❑ If DATE is a literal enclose it in quotes.
- ❑ CHAR type will be converted to NUMBER if it contains only digits, decimal point, or   minus sign on the left.
- ❑ CHAR will be converted to DATE type if it is in DD-MON-YY or DD-MON-YYYY format.
- ❑ A DATE will NOT be converted to NUMBER.
- ❑ A NUMBER will NOT be converted to DATE.

The following few examples will give you better idea about automatic conversion of data type:

In the following example NUMBER is automatically converted to CHAR before LENGTH function is used.

select length(1133) from dual;

LENGTH(1133)

    4

In the example below, a DATE given in CHAR format is converted to DATE before LAST_DAY function is applied.

select last_day('20-aug-2001') from dual;

LAST_DAY(

31-AUG-01

Similarly it is possible to use a CHAR value where a NUMBER is required, as shown below.

select 5 * '20' from dual;

  5*'20'

   100

Here are a few examples where Oracle cannot automatically convert the value.

SQL> select next_day('12-1-2001', 'Fri') from dual;
select next_day('12-1-2001', 'Fri') from dual

            *

ERROR at line 1:

ORA-01843: not a valid month

Oracle returns an error saying the date is not having valid month because Oracle expects months to be of first three letters of the month name. As we have given only month number, it is not acceptable to Oracle. In this case we need to explicitly convert the value to DATE type using TO_DATE function.

The following sections will show how to use conversion functions.

TO_CHAR Function

This function is used to convert the given DATE or NUMBER to CHAR type. TO_CHAR function may also be used to format the given date or number while converting the value to CHAR type. For example, to display date in DD-MM-YYYY format instead of standard format - DD-MON-YY, enter the following:

select to_char(sysdate,'dd-mm-yyyy') Result from dual

RESULT

15-08-2000

In fact, TO_CHAR is one of the most frequently used functions. Here in the example, below it is used to display both date and time of SYSDATE. Remember this operation needs explicit usage of TO_CHAR as by default Oracle displays only date.

select to_char(sysdate,'dd Month yyyy hh24:mi:ss')

from dual

TO_CHAR(SYSDATE,'DDMONTHYY

----

15 August   2000 02:18:56

In the above example **Month** is standing for complete month name, **yyyy** stands for four digits year, **hh24** for 24 hours based hour, **mi** minutes and **ss** for seconds.

Format in TO_CHAR function is a collection of more than 40 formatting options. Please see Table 3 for more options. For complete list, please see on-line help for *Date Format Elements*.

All options in the format are replaced with the corresponding values and remaining characters are returned as they are. In the above example, ':' between HH24 and MI is returned as it is but HH24 and MI are replaced with the corresponding values.

Format Option	Description
MM	Number of the month: 10
MON	First three letters of month name: OCT
MONTH	Complete month name: OCTOBER
DDD	Day of the year since January 1st: 340
DD	Day of the month: 16
D	Day of the week: 5
Day	Day fully spelled: Wednesday
YYYY	Four digits year: 1996

YY	Two digits year: 96
YEAR	Year spelled out: NINTEEN-NINTY-SIX
HH or HH12	Hour of the day: 5
HH24	Hour of the day: 20
MI	Minute of hour: 30
SS	Second of minute: 30
A.M. or P.M.	Displays A.M. or P.M. depending on the time.
Fm	Removes trailing spaces. 'May ' becomes 'May'
TH	Suffix to number: DDTH will produce 16th
SP	Number Spelled out: DDSP will produce THIRD for day 3.

Table 3: TO_CHAR and TO_DATE formats.

The following query retrieves details of the students who have joined in the month of April in year 2001.

```
select bcode, name from students
where  to_char(dj,'mmyyyy') = '042001';
```

BCODE NAME

----- ------------------------------

b5   Richard Marx

b5   Tina Turner

b5   Jody Foster

In the following example TO_CHAR is used to display month name of the year. However, as you can see in the output, there are trailing spaces after month name. This is because Oracle pads the name to 9 characters. Months that have smaller name than that will have trailing spaces.

select bcode, name, to_char(dj,'dd-Month-yyyy') dj from students

```
BCODE NAME                        DJ
----- ----------------------------- -----------------

b1    George Micheal               10-January -2001

b1    Micheal Douglas              11-January -2001

b2    Andy Roberts                 11-January -2001

b2    Malcom Marshall                16-January -2001

b2    Vivan Richards                16-January -2001

b3    Chirs Evert                  14-January -2001

b3    Ivan Lendal                  15-January -2001

b4    George Micheal                01-March   -2001

b5    Richard Marx                 06-April   -2001

b5    Tina Turner                  06-April   -2001

b5    Jody Foster                  07-April   -2001
```

Format fm can be used to remove these trailing spaces in months name. Here is revised version of the above query.

select bcode, name, to_char(dj,'dd-fmMonth-yyyy') dj from students

BCODE	NAME	DJ
b1	George Micheal	10-January-2001
b1	Micheal Douglas	11-January-2001
b2	Andy Roberts	11-January-2001
b2	Malcom Marshall	16-January-2001
b2	Vivan Richards	16-January-2001
b3	Chirs Evert	14-January-2001
b3	Ivan Lendal	15-January-2001
b4	George Micheal	01-March-2001
b5	Richard Marx	06-April-2001
b5	Tina Turner	06-April-2001
b5	Jody Foster	07-April-2001

Note: The output of TO_CHAR will be in the same case as the format. For example, if *Month* is given then output will be *April*; if *MONTH* is given then output will be *APRIL*.

TO_DATE function

TO_DATE is used to convert a CHAR type value to DATE type. If the value is in DD-MON-YY or DD-MM-YYYY format then TO_DATE is not needed because Oracle implicitly converts the value to DATE type.

When you insert a record with only date in DD-MON-YY format, time portion of the date is set to 00:00:00. The following INSERT inserts a new row into PAYMETS table with date as well as time.

insert into payments

    values (10,to_date('14-04-2001 10:20:00',

          'dd-mm-yyyy hh24:mi:ss'), 2000);

It is important to make sure the values given are matching with the format. That means, in the above example, as we gave *dd-mm-yyyy hh24:mi:ss* as the formation even the data is to given in the same format. The format informs to Oracle how to interpret the given values. If there is any mismatch, the values may be misinterpreted.

The *format options* are same as TO_CHAR function format options. See **Table 3** for available format options.

TO_NUMBER function

This function is required in only two occasions. The following are the two cases.

- ❑ To convert formatted number to number.
- ❑ To sort CHAR data in numeric order.

The first application of TO_NUMBER is to convert formatted number to number. The following example is trying to multiply $333 by 20. But as the number with currency symbol is not taken as a number by Oracle, it results in error.

SQL> select $333 * 20 from dual;

select $333 * 20 from dual

     *

ERROR at line 1:

ORA-00911: invalid character

TO_NUMBER function can be used to convert $333 to a number so that it is treated as a number by Oracle. The format in TO_NUMBER specified that the first character is to be taken as currency symbol and remaining as digits.

SQL> select to_number('$333','$999') * 20 from dual

TO_NUMBER('$333','$999')*20

         6660

Sorting strings in numeric order

Another usage of TO_NUMBER is to sort a column that contains numbers but stored in the form of CHAR type.

Assume the following data is existing in VNO column of VEHICLES table. Column VNO is defined as VARCHAR2(10).

SQL> select vno from vehicles;

```
VNO

----------

1133

1583

2502

5657

9

234

45
```

The following SELECT sorts the data but sorts the column VNO as a collection of strings. That means the numeric values are not taken into account and numbers are taken as a collection of characters (each digits is a character).

select vno from vehicles order by vno;

```
VNO

----------

1133

1583

234

2502

45

5657

9
```

The output show that number 9 is at the bottom. It is because of the way strings are compared in sorting – first character first and then second character and so on.

To sort the data using numeric value, issue the following command where VNO column is converted to a number before it is sorted using TO_NUMBER function.

select vno from vehicles order by to_number(vno);

VNO

9

45

234

1133

1583

2502

5657

We will see a lot of usage of conversion function TO_CHAR throughout the rest of the book.

Miscellaneous Functions

Miscellaneous functions are the functions that can be used with any data type. See table 4 for the list of miscellaneous functions.

Function	Description
DECODE(expression,cond,value, cond,value,...,elsevalue)	If *expression* is equivalent to first *cond* then first *value* is returned otherwise Oracle checks whether the *expression* is equivalent to second *cond* then second value is returned. If *expression* doesn't match with any of the values then *elsevalue* is returned.
GREATEST(value1,value2,...)	Returns the greatest of the given values.
LEAST(value1, value2, ...)	Returns the least value of the given values.
NVL(value1,value2)	Return *value2* if *value1* is null otherwise returns *value1*.

Table 4: Miscellaneous Functions.

The following examples will show you how to use miscellaneous functions.

DECODE function

This function works like a multiple IF statement or a CASE/SWITCH statement in a typical programming language.

It takes a value and compares it with the given values one by one. Wherever the value is equivalent to the given value it returns the corresponding value.

The following example shows how to decode the GRADE of COURSE_FACULTY table.

```
select fcode, ccode, decode(grade,'A','Very Good',

                'B','Good',

                'C', 'Average',

                'Unknown') Grade

from course_faculty
```

FCODE CCODE GRADE

----- ----- -------------

gk   ora   Very Good

kl   ora   Very Good

jc   ora   Very Good

da   vbnet Very Good

sw   asp   Very Good

da   asp   Good

hs   c   Very Good

dh   xml   Very Good

jj   java Very Good

hs   java Good

jj   c   Very Good

jj   vbnet Good

The function is used to display meaningful text for column GRADE, which contains only A,B or C.

The following example shows another usage of DECODE where we display the total remuneration paid to faculty. Assuming the payment is based on the time of the batch and no. of days of the batch.

select bcode,ccode,fcode, stdate, enddate,

decode(timing,1,200,2,150,175) * (enddate-stdate) Amount from batches

where enddate is not null

BCODE CCODE FCODE STDATE   ENDDATE   AMOUNT

----- ----- ----- --------- --------- ---------

b1   ora gk   12-JAN-01 20-FEB-01   7800

b2   asp da   15-JAN-01 05-MAR-01   7350

b3   c   hs   20-JAN-01 27-FEB-01   6650

b4   xml dh   02-MAR-01 30-MAR-01   4900

b5   java hs   05-APR-01 10-MAY-01   7000

GREATEST and LEAST functions

These functions take a collection of values and return a single value which is either the least or greatest of the given values as the case may be.

GREATEST is used to return the largest of the given values and LEAST the smallest of the given values.

The following example shows the discount to be given to each course. The scheme is to given discount of 10% on the course fee or 500 whichever is higher. The following query with GREATEST function will achieve the result.

select ccode, name, greatest(fee * 0.10,500) Discount from courses;

CCODE	NAME	DISCOUNT
ora	Oracle database	500
vbnet	VB.NET	550
c	C programming	500
asp	ASP.NET	500
java	Java Language	500
xml	XML Programming	500

LEAST Function can be used in the same manner but it sets the upper limit. In the following query the discount is either 10% of the course fee or 500 whichever is lower.

select ccode,name, least(fee * 0.10,500) Discount from courses

CCODE	NAME	DISCOUNT
ora	Oracle database	450
vbnet	VB.NET	500
c	C programming	350
asp	ASP.NET	500
java	Java Language	450

163

Note: GREATEST and LEAST will not treat string literal that is in date format as date. Instead these dates are taken as strings.

The following example shows how these two functions treat dates that are given in date format but as strings.

select greatest ('12-jun-2001','17-mar-2001')

from dual

GREATEST('1

17-mar-2001

The above command returns '17-mar-2001' instead of '12-jun-2001' because when these two are treated as strings, value in second position in first string (7) is greater than it corresponding value in first string (2), so 17-mar-2001 is returned as the greatest value.

NVL function

It is used to return the second value if first value is null. This function has a lot of significance since Oracle returns a null value from any expression containing a null value.

Note: Any expression involving a null value will result in a null value.

The following query is to display the details of all batches. But we get nothing – actually null value - for NODAYS of batches b6 and b7 as they are have null value in ENDDATE. Since Oracle results in null value for any expression having a null value the result of ENDDATE-STDATE is a null value.

select bcode, stdate, enddate - stdate nodays from batches;

BCODE	STDATE	NODAYS
b1	12-JAN-01	39
b2	15-JAN-01	49
b3	20-JAN-01	38
b4	02-MAR-01	28
b5	05-APR-01	35
b6	12-JUL-01	
b7	15-AUG-01	

However, now we want to take ending date if batch is completed otherwise we want to take system date as ending date.

select bcode, stdate, nvl(enddate,sysdate) - stdate nodays from batches;

BCODE	STDATE	NODAYS
b1	12-JAN-01	39
b2	15-JAN-01	49
b3	20-JAN-01	38
b4	02-MAR-01	28

165

b5   05-APR-01   35

b6   12-JUL-01 50.17985

b7   15-AUG-01 16.17985

Now we want to include even the status of the batch, which will be COMPLETED if ENDDATE is not null otherwise RUNNING.

select bcode, stdate, nvl(enddate,sysdate) - stdate nodays,

     decode(enddate,null,'Running','Completed') Status from batches;

BCODE STDATE   NODAYS STATUS

----- --------- --------- ---------

b1   12-JAN-01   39 Completed

b2   15-JAN-01   49 Completed

b3   20-JAN-01   38 Completed

b4   02-MAR-01   28 Completed

b5   05-APR-01   35 Completed

b6   12-JUL-01 50.1811 Running

b7   15-AUG-01 16.1811 Running

Summary

String functions manipulate strings. Conversion functions are used to convert the data type of a value from one to another. In fact, Oracle always tries to convert the given value to the required data type. But in some cases as Oracle cannot convert implicitly, conversion functions are to be used to convert the value to the required data type. Miscellaneous functions like DECODE and

NVL can be used with any data type. DECODE is an if-elseif-else structure. NVL returns either the first value if it is not null or second value if first value is null.

Exercises

Exercises

- _____ function performs one to one character substitution.

- _____ format option is used to get complete year spelled out in TO_CHAR function.

- _____ symbol is used to concatenate strings.

- What happens if 'replace string' is not given for REPLACE functions.

- Can a NUMBER be converted to DATE? [Yes/No] _____.

- How do you change the name of each student to uppercase in STUDENTS table.

- Display the names of the students who have more than 15 characters in the name.

- Display students 'first name' second and 'second name' first.

  For example, Louis Figo should be displayed as Figo Louis.

- Display the details of the students who have more than 10 characters in the first name.

- What is the result of AMOUNT – DISCOUNT if column DISCOUNT is null.

- How do you get the position of 5th occurrence of letter 'o' in student's name.

- What will be the result of select '10' * '20' from dual;

9. JOINING TABLES

- **Joining tables**
- **Self-join**
- **Outer Join**

Joining Tables

In a relational database system, the total required data might not be available in a single table. Generally the data is scattered. Because if the total data is stored in a single table it will lead to a lot of **redundancy.** So, often we have to bring the data of two or more tables together to get the required information. The act of combining two or more tables in such a way that you retrieve values from the columns of all the tables, to get the required data is called as *joining*. In order to join two tables, there must be a common column between those two tables. For example to join COURSES and BATCHES table, we use CCODE column as that is a common column between these two tables.

The following SELECT command is used to get information about batches from both COURSES and BATCHES table.

We take a row from BATCHES table and get the name of course from COURSES table using CCODE column of BATCHES. CCODE column of BATCHES is used to get the corresponding row from COURSES table. As we used equal to operator to join these two tables, the join is also called as **equi-join**.

select bcode, batches.ccode, name, fcode, stdate

from batches, courses

where batches.ccode = courses.ccode

```
BCODE CCODE NAME                        FCODE STDATE
----- ----- --------------------------- ----- ---------
b1    ora   Oracle database             gk    12-JAN-01
```

b2	asp	ASP.NET	da	15-JAN-01
b3	c	C programming	hs	20-JAN-01
b4	xml	XML Programming	dh	02-MAR-01
b5	java	Java Language	hs	05-APR-01
b6	vbnet VB.NET		da	12-JUL-01
b7	ora	Oracle database	jc	15-AUG-01

In the above query the following are the important points.

- Two tables are used in FROM clause. Tables are separated by comma.
- WHERE clause contains the condition using which both the tables are to be joined.
- Column CCODE is to be qualified using the table name as it exits in both the table that are used in FROM clause.

Table Alias

While joining the table we have to qualify the columns that are in more than one table using the table name. If table name is lengthy this process could be very tedious. Table alias is a short name that can be used to refer to the table name in the query. For example, the above query can be rewritten using table alias as follows:

select bcode, b.ccode, name, fcode, stdate

from batches b, courses c

where b.ccode = c.ccode

B is the alias to table BATCHES and C is the alias for COURSES. Throughout the query table BATCHES can be referred using the alias B and COURSES using alias C. As the purpose of using an alias is to shorten the reference to table, alias is generally very short. Also remember alias is available only in the query in which it is created.

Product of two tables

While tables are joined, if WHERE clause is not given then it results in PRODUCT of the table that are being joined. Product is the result in which each row of first table is joined with each row of the second table. This is also called as **Cartesian product**.

The following example will join

select bcode, b.ccode, name, fcode, stdate, enddate

from batches b, courses c;

The above command will result in 42 (6* 7) rows as we have 6 rows in COURSES and 7 rows in BATCHES table.

Product is generally the result of an error than the desired result.

Join condition and normal condition

While joining two tables the condition used to join the table is called as join condition. As we have above, without join condition, the result of joining will be product of the table. Apart from the join condition, which is required for joining, normal conditions can also be given in WHERE clause. Then Oracle uses normal condition to filter rows and then joins the filtered rows based on the join condition. The following query will get the details of batches that are completed along with name of the course. To get the name of the course it uses COURSES table and to select only those batches that are completed, it uses a normal condition as follows.

select bcode, b.ccode, name, fcode, stdate

from   batches b, courses c

where b.ccode = c.ccode and enddate is not null

BCODE CCODE NAME   FCODE STDATE

----- ----- ---------------------------- ----- ---------

b1   ora   Oracle database   gk   12-JAN-01

b2   asp   ASP.NET   da   15-JAN-01

b3   c   C programming   hs   20-JAN-01

b4   xml   XML Programming   dh   02-MAR-01

b5   java Java Language   hs   05-APR-01

It is also possible to order the result of join using ORDER BY clause as follows.

select bcode, b.ccode, name, fcode, stdate

from   batches b, courses c

where b.ccode = c.ccode and enddate is not null

order by stdate;

The above query displays the result of the join in the ascending order of STDATE column.

Joining more than two tables

Just like how two tables are joined, more than two tables can also be joined to get the required information. For example, in the above query we retrieved

171

information about batches and course name. What if we want to get name of the faculty and not just the code? Then we have to use FACULTY table along with BATCHES and COURSES table.

To get the details of batches along with name of the course and name of the faculty, give the following:

select bcode,c.name course, f.name faculty, stdate

from batches b, courses c, faculty f

where b.ccode = c.ccode and

b.fcode = f.fcode

BCODE	COURSE	FACULTY	STDATE
b1	Oracle database	George Koch	12-JAN-01
b2	ASP.NET	Dan Appleman	15-JAN-01
b3	C programming	Herbert Schildt	20-JAN-01
b4	XML Programming	David Hunter	02-MAR-01
b5	Java Language	Herbert Schildt	05-APR-01
b6	VB.NET	Dan Appleman	12-JUL-01
b7	Oracle database	Jason Couchman	15-AUG-01

The query takes data from three tables – BATCHES, COURSES and FACULTY. It uses CCODE to join BATCHES table with COURSES table. It uses FCODE to join BATCHES table with FACULTY table.

When two or more tables are joined then the minimum number of conditions to be given is derived from the following formula:

Number of join conditions = Number of tables being joined - 1

If more than one column is used to join tables then the number of join conditions may be even more.

Self Join

When a table is joined with itself it is called as self-join. This is a variant of join. In this two copies of the same table are taken and joined as if they are two different types.

The following example demonstrates self-join. It displays the details of batches that started after batch B3. We take two copies of BATCHES table. In first copy we anchor at the row where batch code is B3. Then in the second copy of the table we take row where STDATE of the batch is more than STDATE of first copy. Since we already anchored at row with batch code B3 the STDATE of first copy will be the starting date of batch B3.

```
select  b2.*

from   batches b1, batches b2

where  b1.bcode = 'b3'

    and  b2.stdate > b1.stdate;
```

```
BCODE CCODE FCODE STDATE    ENDDATE     TIMING

----- ----- ----- --------- --------- ---------

b3    c     hs    20-JAN-01 27-FEB-01      3
```

173

b3	c	hs	20-JAN-01 27-FEB-01	3
b3	c	hs	20-JAN-01 27-FEB-01	3
b3	c	hs	20-JAN-01 27-FEB-01	3

In the above example b1 and b2 are two alias to the table BATCHES. Selection b2.* would mean we want to select all columns from first table.

Outer Join

When two tables are joined, only the rows that contain the common keys are selected. That means if BATCHES and COURSES tables are joined then you get the details of courses that have corresponding values in BATCHES table. If a course has no corresponding row (batch) in BATCHES table then it is not included in the output. Let us have a look at the following data we have in BATCHES and COURSES tables.

SQL> select ccode,name from courses;

CCODE NAME

----- ------------------------------

ora   Oracle database

vbnet VB.NET

c   C programming

asp   ASP.NET

java   Java Language

xml   XML Programming

cs   C Sharp

SQL> select bcode,ccode,stdate from batches;

BCODE CCODE STDATE

----- ----- ---------

b1   ora   12-JAN-01

b2   asp   15-JAN-01

b3   c   20-JAN-01

b4   xml   02-MAR-01

b5   java   05-APR-01

b6   vbnet 12-JUL-01

b7   ora   15-AUG-01

The following SELECT command will retrieve information from both the tables.

select c.ccode, name,fee, bcode, stdate, enddate

from   courses c, batches b

where   c.ccode =b.ccode

order by c.ccode

CCODE NAME   FEE BCODE STDATE   ENDDATE

----- ------------------------------- --------- ----- --------- ---------

asp ASP.NET   5000 b2   15-JAN-01 05-MAR-01

c   C programming   3500 b3   20-JAN-01 27-FEB-01

java Java Language   4500 b5   05-APR-01 10-MAY-01

175

ora	Oracle database	4500	b1	12-JAN-01	20-FEB-01
ora	Oracle database	4500	b7	15-AUG-01	
vbnet	VB.NET	5500	b6	12-JUL-01	
xml	XML Programming	4000	b4	02-MAR-01	30-MAR-01

In the above join, we got the information about all courses except "C Sharp" because there is no corresponding row in BATCHES table for course code CS.

That means if parent table contains rows that do not have corresponding rows in child table, then Oracle will not retrieve the values of those rows of parent table.

Outer join allows you to retrieve the rows from parent table even though there is no corresponding rows for the parent table in the child table. In the following example, we get details of course CS though it doesn't have any row in BATCHES table.

```
select  c.ccode, name,fee, bcode, stdate, enddate

from   courses c, batches b

where  c.ccode =b.ccode (+)

order by c.ccode;
```

CCODE	NAME	FEE	BCODE	STDATE	ENDDATE
asp	ASP.NET	5000	b2	15-JAN-01	05-MAR-01
c	C programming	3500	b3	20-JAN-01	27-FEB-01
cs	**C Sharp**	**7000**			

java	Java Language	4500	b5	05-APR-01	10-MAY-01
ora	Oracle database	4500	b1	12-JAN-01	20-FEB-01
ora	Oracle database	4500	b7	15-AUG-01	
vbnet	VB.NET	5500	b6	12-JUL-01	
xml	XML Programming	4000	b4	02-MAR-01	30-MAR-01

Compare this output with earlier output. Here as we used outer join by using (+) on the right of BATCHES table.

The plus (+) on the right of shorter table (taking into account unique value of CCODE column) is to add extra null rows with values in common column, that do exist in the left table, but not in the right table, and then join the rows.

Note: When outer join is used, the order in which tables are listed in FROM clause is important. Also remember, (+) is to be used on the right of the table that is to be extended with null rows.

As you can see in the above output, in the row CS there is no data for BCODE, STDATE and ENDDATE columns. This is understandable as there is no row in BATCHES table for course CS.

Also remember there is no possibility of having rows in BATCHES table that do not correspond to any course code in COURSES table. It is possible to have a parent row without child rows, but it is not possible to have a child row without a parent row. If we have defined foreign key constraint on the child table, this condition is implemented by Oracle whenever you insert or update rows in child table.

SET Operators

SET operators combine the results of two queries into one result. The following are the available SET operators. These operators are part of Relational Algebra operators.

Operator	What it does?
UNION	Returns unique rows of both the queries.
UNION ALL	Returns all rows selected by both the queries including duplicates.
INTERSE CT	Returns common rows selected by both the queries.
MINUS	Returns rows that exist in the first query but not in the second query.

Table 1: Set Operators.

Assume there is a table called OLDCOURSES with the following rows:

select * from oldcourses;

CCODE NAME

----- --------------------

ora   Oracle8i

c   C Language

pas   Pascal Language

1123 Lotus 123

To get the list of all the courses from COURSES and OLDCOURSES tables by eliminating duplicates, give the following:

select ccode from oldcourses

union

select ccode from courses;

CCODE

-----

asp

c

cs

java

1123

ora

pas

vbnet

xml

Though courses ORA and C exist in both the tables they are displayed only for once as UNION ignores duplicate entries.

UNION ALL is used to retrieve all rows from both the tables. It doesn't ignore duplicates.

```
select ccode from oldcourses

union all

select ccode from courses;
```

```
CCODE
-----
ora
c
pas
1123
ora
vbnet
c
asp
java
xml
cs
```

The following query retrieves all courses that exists in both COURSES table and OLDCOURSES table using INTERSECT operator:

```
select ccode from courses

intersect
```

select ccode from oldcourses;

CCODE

-----

c

ora

To get the list of courses that exist in OLDCOURSES but not in COURSES table, give the following query with MINUS operator:

select ccode from oldcourses

minus

select ccode from courses;

CCODE

1123

pas

RULES to be followed while using SET operators

1. Both queries should select the same number of columns.
2. Corresponding columns must be of the same data type. However the length and name of the columns may be different.
3. Column names of first query will be column headings.

4. Null values are treated as identical. Normally two null values are not equal. But when dealing with SET operators, if Oracle encounters two null values, one in first table and another in second table then Oracle will treat them as identical.

The following example will make the last point clear. Assume we have a row in first table with values 10 and null for columns C1 and C2 and another row in the second table with same values (10 and null) for columns C1 and C2. When you use UNION operator, Oracle will take null values in column C2 as equal and display the row with 10 and null only for once.

Summary

In relational databases, joining is a way of life. To join tables, all tables being joined must have a common column and it will be used in WHERE clause to establish join condition. When tables are joined, all non-unique columns are to be qualified using table name. A table can be joined to itself and it is called as self-join. Outer join is the operation of extending shorter table with null rows to match with values in join column of longer table. Plus sign (+) is used for outer join.

SET operators implement operators, UNION, INTERSECT and MINUS of relational algebra.

Exercises

5. What is required to join two tables?

6. What is meant by self-join?

7. How do you qualify a column that is existing in two or more tables that are being joined?

8. What is table alias? Is it stored anywhere?

9. What happens when you join two tables without any condition?

10. Display rollno, student name, pay date and amount paid.

11. Display rollno , student name, batch code , stdate of batch and faculty code.

12. Display rollno , student name, course name , stdate of batch and faculty code.

13. Display rollno , student name, course name , faculty code and enddate of all batches that were completed.

14. Display students who have got more number of characters in name than the student with roll number 10.

15. Display rollno, student name, email , pay date and amount paid.

16. In previous query include the details of student who haven't paid anything so far.

17. Display the details of students who have paid nothing so far.

10. VIEWS

- ❑ What is a view?
- ❑ Why we need a view?
- ❑ Creating and using a view
- ❑ Simplifying query using view
- ❑ Presenting data in different forms
- ❑ Isolating application from changes in definition of table
- ❑ Changing base table through view
- ❑ Updatable join views

❑ Dropping a view

In this chapter, we will understand what is a view and how to create and use it. View is certainly one of the most important schema objects of Oracle database. It is important to understand what a view can do in Oracle.

What Is A View?

A view is a window through which you access a portion of one or more tables. View itself doesn't contain any data but it refers to the data of a table on which it is based.

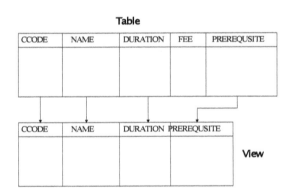

Figure 1: Example of a view.

The table on which the view is based is called as **base table**.

A view is also called as "virtual table" as it can be used when a table can be used. View retrieves the data by executing the query and presents the data in the form of a table.

Views are used to let users access only the portion of the data that they are supposed to access. Views are very commonly used objects in Oracle. In fact objects such as USER_TABLES, USER_CONSTRAINTS etc., are not actually tables and instead they are views.

Why We Need A View?

A view is required in several cases. Let us start with a simple requirement. Assume the table COURSES is owned by user "FIGO". As the owner of the table Figo will have all the privileges on that table. User Figo now wants another user – Raul to access COURSES table. To this effect Figo can grant permission to Raul. But Figo doesn't want Raul to access column FEE.

If Figo grants permission to Raul then Raul will have complete access to table and Figo cannot stop Raul from accessing FEE column. So Figo creates a view on COURSES table that includes everything from COURSES table except FEE. Then Figo grants permission on the view to Raul and not on the base table. Since Raul has access only to the view, he can access whatever data is presented by the view. See figure 1.

A view in the above requirement is quite ideal for two reasons.

♦ It fulfills the requirement without storing a separate copy of the data. A view doesn't store any data of its own and takes the data from base table.

♦ As the data is taken from base table, accurate and up-to-date information is provided to Raul. Yet the column to be hidden from Raul is hidden as it is not part of the view.

The following are the other important applications of views:

❑ Provides an extra layer on the top of table allowing only a predetermined rows or columns to be accessed.

- Allows complex queries to be stored in the database. A view stores the query that is used to create it in the database. It uses the query to retrieve the data from the base table(s). If a complex query is to be referred again and again then it can be stored in the form of a view.

- Can present the data of the table in different forms. For instance, the name of the columns can be changed and two or more columns can be presented as one column or split one column as two or more columns.

- Can isolate application from the changes in the definition of the table.

In the next section let us see how to create and use view.

Creating and using views

A view is created using CREATE VIEW command. At the time of creating the view, we have to give the name of the view and the query on which the view is based.

For example, to create a view that takes everything from COURSES table except FEE column, given the following CREATE TABLE command.

SQL> create view course_view

  2 as

  3   select ccode,name,duration, prerequisite from courses;

View created.

In the above example, COURSE_VIEW is the name of the view and COURSES is the base table. COURSE_VIEW view can access all columns of the table except FEE column.

Here is the syntax of CREATE VIEW command.

CREATE [OR REPLACE] [FORCE] VIEW viewname

    [(column-name, column-name)]

      AS Query

      [with check option];

Note: ORDER BY clause cannot be used in query used with CREATE VIEW command.

OR REPLACE Option

Allows a view to be created even if one already exists. This allows altering view without dropping, recreating and re-granting object privileges.

FORCE Option

Allows view to be created even if the base table doesn't exist. However, the base table should exist before the view is used.

I will discuss about WITH CHECK OPTION later in this chapter.

Once a view is created, a view can be used similar to a table. For example, you can use SELECT command with COURSE_VIEW as follows:

select * from course_view;

```
CCODE NAME                    DURATION PREREQUISITE

----- ------------------------------ --------- ------------------------------

ora   Oracle database           25 Windows

vbnet VB.NET                    30 Windows and programming

c     C programming             20 Computer Awareness

asp   ASP.NET                   25 Internet and programming

java  Java Language             25 C language

xml   XML Programming           15 HTML,Scripting, ASP/JSP

cs    C Sharp                   30 C Language
```

As we have seen before, a view can be used just like a table. That is the reason a view is called as **virtual table**.

It is also possible to select columns of a view, as it is illustrated below:

select name, duration from course_view;

```
NAME                    DURATION

------------------------------ ---------

Oracle database         25

VB.NET                  30

C programming           20

ASP.NET                 25

Java Language           25
```

XML Programming	15
C Sharp	30

In the same way it is possible to filter rows just like how it is done with tables.

```
select * from course_view
where  duration > 25;
```

```
CCODE NAME                    DURATION PREREQUISITE
----- ---------------------------- --------- -----------------------------
vbnet VB.NET                   30 Windows and programming
cs    C Sharp                  30 C Language
```

Note: *Though I said, a view is same as a table, it is not always right. In this chapter and in later chapters, you will come to know where, when and how a view is different from a table.*

Simplifying query using view

A view apart from providing access control can also be used to simplify query. A view is also called as "stored query". The query given at the time of creating view is stored by Oracle and used whenever the view is used. All that you get in the view is the data retrieved by the query.

Since a query is stored for view, a complex query can be stored in the form of a view. The following example creates

create view coursecount

as

select ccode, count(*) nobatches , max(stdate) lastdate

from batches

group by ccode;

Now instead of giving the lengthy query, it is possible to get the details using view COURSECOUNT as follows:

SQL> select * from coursecount;

CCODE NOBATCHES LASTDATE

----- --------- ---------

asp   1 15-JAN-01

c   1 20-JAN-01

java   1 05-APR-01

ora   2 15-AUG-01

vbnet   1 12-JUL-01

xml   1 02-MAR-01

190

If query used to create the view contains any expression then the expression must be given alias. The alias of the expression becomes the name of the column in the view.

In the above example the expression count(*) is given the alias NOBATCHES and expression max(stdate) is given the alias LASTDATE. While referring to view, we have to use these aliases to refer to the values of corresponding expressions.

The following query will display course code and most recent batches starting date using COURSECOUNT view.

select ccode, lastdate from coursecount;

CCODE LASTDATE

----- ---------

asp   15-JAN-01

c   20-JAN-01

java   05-APR-01

ora   15-AUG-01

vbnet 12-JUL-01

xml   02-MAR-01

The following query will display the courses for which we have started more than one batch so far.

select * from coursecount where nobatches > 1;

CCODE NOBATCHES LASTDATE

----- --------- ---------

ora   2 15-AUG-01

Note: Though a column is derived from group function, it can be used with WHERE clause if it is part of the view.

Presenting data in different forms using view

The following example demonstrates how views can be used to present the data of a table in different forms. FACULTY table contains the name of the faculty in NAME column. Now for some application, we have to split the name of the faculty into first name and last name. This task can be achieved using a view. No need to restructure the table.

The following view presents name of the faculty as first name and last name.

create view faculty_names

  as

  select fcode, substr(name,1, instr(name,' ') - 1) firstname,

      substr(name, instr(name,' ')+ 1) lastname

  from faculty;

Now it is possible to get the name of the faculty in two parts – firstname and lastname.

select * from faculty_names;

```
FCODE FIRSTNAME              LASTNAME

----- ------------------------------ -----------------------------

gk    George          Koch

da    Dan             Appleman

hs    Herbert           Schildt

dh    David           Hunter

sw    Stephen           Walther

kl    Kevin           Loney

jj    Jamie           Jaworski

jc    Jason           Couchman
```

Now the task of getting the details of faculty where lastname contains more than 5 characters has become easy as shown below.

SQL> select * from faculty_names where length(lastname) > 5;

```
FCODE FIRSTNAME              LASTNAME

----- ------------------------------ -----------------------------

da    Dan             Appleman

hs    Herbert           Schildt

dh    David           Hunter

sw    Stephen           Walther

jj    Jamie           Jaworski
```

Isolating application from changes in definition of table

This is another important application of a view. View can be used to isolate applications from the structure of the tables. This is achieved by creating a view on the required tables and using the view instead of the base table. The advantage with this is that if the structure of the tables is ever changed then we just need to recreate the view to continue to provide the same information as before the change to structure of the base tables.

So that though the structure of the table is ever modified, the application will not be effected by the change as application uses a view to get the required data.

Lets us see a small example to understand what I mean by isolating application from structure of the base tables.

We want to access BCODE, CCODE, STDATE and FEE of each batch. This can be done by using a query to join BATCHES and COURSES tables as follows:

select bcode, b.ccode, fee, stdate

from batches b, courses c

where b.ccode = c.ccode;

BCODE CCODE   FEE STDATE

----- ----- --------- ---------

b1	ora	4500 12-JAN-01
b2	asp	5000 15-JAN-01
b3	c	3500 20-JAN-01
b4	xml	4000 02-MAR-01
b5	java	4500 05-APR-01
b6	vbnet	5500 12-JUL-01
b7	ora	4500 15-AUG-01

This is fine but what if FEE column is moved from COURSES table to BATCHES table. Then the query needs to access only BATCHES table and COURSES table is not required. So the query is to be rewritten as follows:

select bcode, ccode, fee, stdate

from batches;

That means the application is to be modified to rewrite the query. The column FEE of COURSES table may have been used in several places and now we have to modify all those commands.

How a view can solve the problem? Instead of directly accessing tables, it is possible to create a view on the required tables. For example, we create a view to get BCODE, CCODE, FEE and STDATE from COURSES and BATCHES table as follows:

create view batchdetails

as

select bcode, b.ccode , fee, stdate

from batches b, courses c

where b.ccode = c.ccode;

Then we access the data using this view as follows:

select * from batchdetails;

If column FEE is removed from COURSES table and placed in BATCHES table, then we recreate the view to access only BATCHES table to get the required data.

create or replace view batchdetails

as

select bcode, ccode , fee, stdate

from batches;

Then accessing the view BATCHDETAILS will give the same data in spite of a change in the structure of underlying tables. That means the application will have to give as SELECT command to get the information as follows:

select * from batchdetails;

However, internally, Oracle is using only BATCHES table to get the data. All this process will be hidden from user and he is aware of only the presence of the view. As you can see, that this operation will make the programs totally independent of the structure of the database. Because even the structure of the tables changes, the view built on the tables are to be rebuild to reflect new structure of the tables. But that doesn't effect the application.

Storage of view

Oracle stores the query given at the time of creating view in data dictionary. Whenever the view is referred, Oracle executes the query and retrieves the data from the base tables. Whatever data is retrieved that is provided as the data of the view. Since all that Oracle stores regarding view is only the query, a view is also called as **stored query**.

A view may be based on tables or other views or even snapshots (a replica of remote data).

Views and dependence

A view is dependent on base tables. Base tables may be either real tables or again views. Whether a view is valid or not depends on the availability of the base tables. The following examples will illustrate the dependency.

Assume we have a table T1 created as follows:

create table t1

(c1 number(5),

  c2 number(5)

);

Let us now create a view on this table as follows:

create view v1

as

select * from t1;

Oracle stores the query in data dictionary for view. When you use * in query, Oracle expands it to include all columns of the tables. The following query shows the query stored by Oracle in data dictionary.

SQL> select text

  2 from user_views

  3 where view_name = 'V1';

TEXT

----

select "C1","C2" from t1

Note: We must use uppercase letter for object name while querying data dictionary as Oracle stores object name in uppercase.

Now let us see what happens if you drop the table T1.

drop table t1;

The view still exists and the definition of the table will remain intact. But the view cannot be used as the base table is not existing. So referring to view will displays the following error message.

SQL> select * from v1;

select * from v1

        *

ERROR at line 1:

ORA-04063: view "BOOK.V1" has errors

Oracle marks views that are dependent on the base table that is dropped as **Invalid**. You can get the status of any object using USER_OBJECTS table.

select status from user_objects where object_name = 'V1';

STATUS

INVALID

However, if you recreate the table and then try to refer to the view the view will be compiled and status of the view is changed to **valid** again.

create table t1 (c1 number(5), c2 number(5), c3 number(5));

At the time of recreating the table Oracle just checks whether columns C1 and C2 are present and doesn't mind if base table contains some new columns.

After the table is recreated, if you refer to view then Oracle will try to recompile the view and as it finds out that all the required columns are in the base table it will validate the view. You can get the status of the view using USER_OBJECTS again.

select status from user_objects where object_name = 'V1';

STATUS

VALID

In the above if table is recreated but if either column C1 or C2 is present the view cannot be made valid.

Note: The data types of the columns in the base table do not matter at the time of compiling the view. That means in the above example even columns C1 is of VARCHAR2 type in table T1 still the view will be made valid. Because Oracle precisely looks for columns C1 and C2 in table T1and not for any specific data type.

Changing Base Table Through View

Though view is generally used to retrieve the data from base table, it can also be used to manipulate base table.

However, not every view can be used to manipulate base table.   To be updatable a view must satisfy certain conditions. We will discuss when and how a view can be used to update base table.

The following manipulations can be done on base table through view:

   ❑ Delete rows from base table
   ❑ Update data of base table

❏ Insert rows into base table

If a view is to be inherently updatable, then it must not contain any of the following constructs in its query:

❏ A set operator

❏ A DISTINCT operator

❏ An aggregate function

❏ A GROUP BY, ORDER BY, CONNECT BY, or START WITH clause

❏ A collection expression in a SELECT list

❏ A subquery in a SELECT list

❏ Joins (with some exceptions)

If the view contains columns derived from pseudo columns or expression the UPDATE command must not refer to these columns.

Let us understand how to manipulate the base table through view.

Create a view called ORABATCHES as follows:

create view orabatches

as

select bcode, stdate, enddate, timing from batches where ccode = 'ora';

As this view doesn't violate any of the conditions mentioned above, it can be used to delete and update base table as follow. The following DELETE command will delete the row from base table – BATCHES – where batch code is b7.

delete from orabatches where bcode = 'b7';

It is also possible to update the ENDDATE of batch B1 as follows:

update orabatches set enddate = sysdate where bcode ='b7';

Updating join views

It is also possible to update a join view (a view that has more than one base table), provided the following conditions are true.

- The DML operations must manipulate only one of the underlying tables.
- For UPDATE all columns updated must be extracted from a key-preserved table.
- For DELETE the join must have one and only one key-preserved table.
- For INSERT all columns into which values are to be inserted must come from a key-preserved table. All NOT NULL columns of the key-preserved table must be included in the view unless we have specified DEFAULT values for NOT NULL columns.

Key-preserved table

A table is key preserved if every key of the table can also be a key of the result of the join. So, a key-preserved table has its keys preserved through a join. To understand what is a key-preserved table, take the following view.

create view month_payments

as select p.rollno, name, dp, amount from payments p, students s

where p.rollno = s.rollno;

In the above view, table PAYMENTS is key-preserved table. So it is possible to make changes to the table even though the view is based on two tables.

The following UPDATE command will update AMOUNT columns.

update month_payments set amount = 4500
where rollno = 1 and trunc(dp) ='10-jan-01';

However, it is not possible to change NAME as follows:

update month_payments set Name='Koch George'
where rollno = 1;

update month_payments set Name='Koch George'
                              *

ERROR at line 1:

ORA-01779: cannot modify a column which maps to a non key-preserved table

Column NAME doesn't belong to key-preserved table. So it is not updatable.

Getting information about updateable columns

It is possible to get the names of the columns that can be modified in a view using USER_UPDATABLE_COLUMNS data dictionary view.

select column_name, updatable, insertable, deletable from user_updatable_columns

where table_name = 'MONTH_PAYMENTS'

COLUMN_NAME	UPD	INS	DEL
ROLLNO	YES	YES	YES
NAME	NO	NO	NO
DP	YES	YES	YES
AMOUNT	YES	YES	YES

WITH CHECK OPTION

This option is used to prevent updations and insertions into base table through view that the view cannot later retrieve.

Let us create a view that retrieves information about payments where amount paid is more than 3000.

create view high_payments

as

select * from payments

where amount > 3000;

The following is the data that is retrieved by the view.

select * from high_payments;

ROLLNO DP   AMOUNT

--------- --------- ---------

      1 10-JAN-01   4500

      2 11-JAN-01   3500

      5 16-JAN-01   5000

      6 14-JAN-01   3500

      7 15-JAN-01   3500

     10 10-APR-01   4500

     11 10-APR-01   3500

As the view is updatable, Oracle allows any change to be made to the view. For example the following UPDATE statement will change the amount paid by student 11 to 2500.

update high_payments

set amount = 2500

where rollno = 11;

After the change is made if we try to retrieve the data from the view, it will NOT retrieve row that we have updated as it no longer satisfies the condition – AMOUNT > 3000.

select * from high_payments;

```
   ROLLNO DP        AMOUNT
--------- --------- ---------
       1 10-JAN-01    4500

       2 11-JAN-01    3500

       5 16-JAN-01    5000

       6 14-JAN-01    3500

       7 15-JAN-01    3500

      10 10-APR-01    4500
```

That means view allows the changes even though the changes will make the rows of the base table irretrievable after the change. However, Oracle allows you to prevent such changes by using WITH CHECK OPTION option at the time of creating view.

The following is the modified CREATE VIEW command to create HIGH_PAYMENT view. It uses WITH CHECK OPTION to make sure that all updations and insertion that are made to the base table are retrievable by the view.

create **or replace** view high_payments

as

select * from payments

where amount > 3000

with check option

constraint high_payment_wco;

The above command replaces the existing view with the new version. That is the reason why we used OR REPLACE option of CREATE VIEW command.

The command added WITH CHECK OPTION and assigned a name to that constraint. If we do not give any name then Oracle automatically assigns a name to this constraint.

Now let us see what happens if we try to insert a row into the base table – PAYMENTS through HIGH_PAYMENTS view with 2000 as the value for AMOUNT column.

SQL> insert into high_payments values (11,sysdate, 2000);

insert into high_payments values (11,sysdate, 2000)

     *

ERROR at line 1:

ORA-01402: view WITH CHECK OPTION where-clause violation

As you can see, WITH CHECK OPTION doesn't allow the insertion since the condition given in the query of the view is not satisfied by the data given in insertion.

However, it is possible to insert the same row directly to base table – PAYMENTS, but it cannot be inserted through the view HIGH_PAYMENTS if view cannot retrieve row after the insertion.

Dropping a View

DROP VIEW command is used to drop a view. Dropping a view has no effect on the base tables on which view is based. Users who were accessing the data of the base tables using view will no longer be able to access the data of the base tables.

DROP VIEW view_name;

Summary

A view is an object in Oracle database, used to provide access only to the required portion of the table by hiding the remaining part of the table. A view can simplify a query by storing complex query in the database. A view doesn't contain any data and retrieves the data from the base table whenever it is referred.

As views are used just like tables they are called as **virtual tables.** It is also possible to manipulate base table through view. Manipulations like INSERT , DELETE and UPDATE can be performed by view provided it fulfills the conditions set by Oracle.

Exercises

18. What are the major applications of a view?

19. A view can be used with ALTER TABLE command [T/F] ?_____ .

20. The table on which a view is based is called as _____.

21. When a table is dropped then all the views based on it will be dropped automatically [T/F]? _____.

22. A view can be used to manipulate base table [T/F]? _____.

23. Create a view, which contains the course code and number of students who have taken that course so far.

24. Create a view to contain the following: bcode, course name, faculty name,

208

stdate, enddate and no. of days between enddate and stdate for all completed batches.

25. Create a view to get bcode, ccode, fcode, timing , stdate and enddate for all completed batches. Also ensure the changes made to base table through view are retrievable through view.

11. SUBQUERIES

❑ What is a subquery?

❑ Multiple Subqueries

❑ Nested subquery

❑ Using subquery in DML commands

❑ Correlated subquery

❑ EXISTS, NOT EXISTS, ANY and ALL operators

What Is A Subquery

A subquery is a query within another query. The outer query is called as main query and inner query is called as subquery.

In this chapter, we will see how subqueries are used to retrieve the required data and also how to use subqueries in DML and DDL commands.

The general syntax of subquery will be as follows:

Query

(subquery)

The following is a simple example of a subquery.

```
select name, qual from faculty
where  fcode in
     ( select fcode from course_faculty
       where  ccode = 'ora')
```

NAME	QUAL
George Koch	MS Computer Science
Jason Couchman	OCP DBA
Kevin Loney	MS Electronics

In the above example we will take the details of faculty members who can handle course *ora*. COURSE_FACULTY table contains information about which faculty members can take course ora. So we first use a subquery to get the list of the codes of the faculty members who can handle Oracle course. Then we send the list of faculty codes to outer query, which will then display the details of those faculty members.

Subquery is always executed first and the result is passed to the main query. Main query is executed by taking the result from subquery.

IN operator plays a very important role in subqueries as generally subqueries generate a list of values and main query is to compare a single value against the list of values supplied by subquery.

In the above example, subquery supplies the list of faculty codes to main query. Then main query compares each faculty code of the FACULTY table with the list supplied by subquery. If the faculty code exists in the list then it will display the details of the faculty.

The following are a few other examples of subqueries.

Get the details of students who have paid today.

select * from students where rollno in

   (select rollno from payments where trunc(dp) = trunc(sysdate));

Display the details of batches handled by faculty name 'Kevin Loney'.

select * from batches

where fcode =

       (select fcode from faculty where name = 'Kevin Loney');

211

The following query displays the details of the faculty members who have not taken any batch in the last three months.

select * from faculty

where fcode NOT IN

 (select fcode from batches

 where months_between(sysdate,stdate) <= 3)

For example, the following is invalid.

SQL> select * from subjects

  2 where fulldur

  3   between 25

  4   and (select max(fulldur) from subjects);

        and (select max(fulldur) from subjects)

         *

ERROR at line 4:

ORA-00936: missing expression

Multiple Subqueries

It is possible for a main query to receive values from more than one subquery. The following example displays the details of batches that are taken by faculty with qualification MS or the course fee is more than 5000.

select from batches

where fcode in

(select fcode from faculty where qual like '%MS%')

or ccode in

(select ccode from courses where fee > 5000);

BCODE	CCODE	FCODE	STDATE	ENDDATE	TIMING
b1	ora	gk	12-JAN-01	20-FEB-01	1
b3	c	hs	20-JAN-01	27-FEB-01	3
b4	xml	dh	02-MAR-01	30-MAR-01	3
b5	java	hs	05-APR-01	10-MAY-01	1
b6	vbnet	da	12-JUL-01		1

In the above query first the subquery – select fcode from faculty where qual like '%MS%' – is executed. It then retrieves faculty codes where qualification of the faculty contains MS. Then it executes second subquery and then returns course codes of the courses where FEE is more than 5000. After both the subqueries are executed then the main query is executed with the data that is passed by subqueries to main query.

Nesting Subquery

It is also possible to nest subqueries. So far we have seen examples where a single subquery is executed and sends values to main query. It is also possible for a subquery to depend on another subquery and that subquery on another and so on.

The following example displays the details of the students who belong to batches that are taken by faculty with qualification MS.

```
select rollno,name, bcode  from students

where  bcode in

( select  bcode from batches

    where  fcode in ( select fcode from faculty where qual like '%MS%')

);
```

ROLLNO NAME   BCODE

--------- ------------------------------ -----

    1 George Micheal   b1

    2 Micheal Douglas   b1

    6 Chirs Evert   b3

    7 Ivan Lendal   b3

    8 George Micheal   b4

    9 Richard Marx   b5

  10 Tina Turner   b5

  11 Jody Foster   b5

Note: *Subqueries can be nested up to 16 levels. But that limit is seldom reached. Moreover it is not recommended to use more than 3 levels of nesting* considering the performance.

The following is another example where we will take details of payments made by students of the batch that started on 12-jul-2001.

```
select * from payments
where rollno in
  (select rollno from students
  where  bcode in
    (select bcode from batches
    where stdate = '12-jul-01'
    )
  );
```

Comparing more than one value

A subquery can return multiple columns. These multiple columns must be compared with multiple values. The following query displays the details of the batches that have taken maximum duration among the batches of the same course.

```
select * from batches
where (ccode, enddate-stdate) in
        (select  ccode, max(enddate-stdate)
        from batches
          group by ccode);
```

BCODE	CCODE	FCODE	STDATE	ENDDATE	TIMING
b2	asp	da	15-JAN-01	05-MAR-01	2
b3	c	hs	20-JAN-01	27-FEB-01	3
b5	java	hs	05-APR-01	10-MAY-01	1

215

b1   ora gk   12-JAN-01 20-FEB-01   1

b4   xml dh   02-MAR-01 30-MAR-01   3

First subquery returns the course and maximum duration for that course from BATCHES table using MAX function and GROUP BY clause. Then the values are sent to main query where they are compared with CCODE and duration of each batch. If in a row of BATCHES table the CCODE and the duration are equivalent to CCODE and maximum duration of any of rows returned by subquery then the row of BATCHES table is selected.

Now let us see few more examples of subqueries.

Get the details of course that has highest course fee.

select ccode,name,fee from courses

where fee =

   (select max(fee) from courses);

CCODE NAME   FEE

----- ------------------------------ ---------

cs   C Sharp   7000

Get the details of students who have made a payment in the last month but no in the current month.

select * from students

where rollno not in

216

```
(select rollno from payments

  where to_char(dp,'mmyyyy') = to_char(sysdate,'mmyyyy')

)

and rollno in

( select rollno from payments

  where to_char(dp,'mmyyyy')=to_char(add_months(sysdate,-1),'mmyyyy')

);
```

First we take roll numbers of students who have made payment in the current month and roll numbers of students who have made payment in the previous month. Then the outer query selects students who are not part of the first list (who made payment in current month) and part of second list (who made payment in previous month).

Subqueries in DML and DDL commands

Subqueries can also be used with DML commands. WHERE clause of UPDATE and DELETE can always contain a subquery. The following UPDATE command increases the FEE of the course if more than 5 batches have started for that course.

```
update courses set fee = fee * 1.1

where  ccode in

( select ccode from  batches

  group by ccode

  having count(*) > 5);
```

In the above example, subquery returns course codes for which more than 5 batches have started and then UPDATE will update only those courses.

The following DELETE command uses subquery in WHERE clause to find out batches for which there are no students.

delete from batches

where bcode not in (select bcode from students);

The examples above are the cases where we used subquery in WHERE clause and not precisely in DML command. The following UPDATE command updates FCODE of batch **b7** to the faculty code of the batch **b1**.

update batches set fcode =

  (select fcode from batches where bcode = 'b1')

where bcode = 'b7';

Subquery returns a single value that is to be copied to FCODE of UPDATE.

Similarly the following INSERT inserts rows into a table called COMP_BATCH. The data is taken from BATCHES table.

The following subquery creates a new table from an existing table.

create table new_batches

as select bcode, ccode,fcode, stdate ,timing from batches

where stdate > sysdate;

The subquery is used to retrieve the data using which the new table is created. The structure of the new table will be same as the structure of the query. In the above query as query selects BCODE,CCODE,FCODE, STDATE , and TIMING columns the table is also created with same columns.

The following is the structure of the new table.

SQL> desc new_batches

Name	Null?	Type
BCODE		VARCHAR2(5)
CCODE		VARCHAR2(5)
FCODE		VARCHAR2(5)
STDATE	NOT NULL	DATE
TIMING		NUMBER(1)

SQL> desc batches

Name	Null?	Type
BCODE	NOT NULL	VARCHAR2(5)
CCODE		VARCHAR2(5)
FCODE		VARCHAR2(5)
STDATE	NOT NULL	DATE

ENDDATE	DATE
TIMING	NUMBER(1)

If you observe the above two structures, you would notice that only NOT NULL constraint of STDATE of BATCHES table is taken to NEW_BATCHES table.

select * from new_batches

Will display the details of batches where STDATE of the batch is after SYSDATE.

If you want to insert details again of new batches after some time you can issue the following INSERT command.

insert into new_batches

  select bcode, ccode, fcode, stdate , timing from batches

  where stdate > sysdate;

Note: The order and type of columns in the query and NEW_BATCHES should be same. Otherwise you may have to list out columns in the query according to the requirement.

Renaming a column using subquery

The following procedure will illustrate how to use subquery with DDL to rename a column in a table. Renaming a column is not permitted in Oracle. So to rename a column, follow the given procedure. However, it is to be noted that this procedure is lengthy and not very refined. But you can consider in case of desperate need.

Assume we created a table called PRODUCTS as follows.

create table products

(id number(5) primary key ,

  name varchar2(30),

  qty number(4) check (qty >= 0),

  pric number(5)

);

But the column PRIC is misspelt. It should have been PRICE. Now let us see how to rename the column.

First create a new table called newproducts using a subquery. Give an alias to column PRIC so that the alias becomes the column name in the new table.

create table newproducts

  as select id, name, qty, pric price from products;

see the structure of the new table using DESC command.

desc newproducts

name   Null?   Type

-- -------- --------------

ID	NUMBER(5)
NAME	VARCHAR2(30)
QTY	NUMBER(4)
PRICE	NUMBER(5)

As you can see in the output of DESC command, no constraint are defined in new table - NEWPRODUCTS. So we need to define all constraints again on this table using ALTER TABLE command. But before that let us drop original table and rename NEWPRODUCTS to PRODUCTS.

SQL> drop table products;

Table dropped.

Note: If the table being dropped has any dependent tables with rows then you have to drop those rows also. For example, if you have SALES table referring to PRODUCTS table then first SALES table is to be emptied before rows in PRODUCTS table can be deleted.

SQL> rename newproducts to products;

Table renamed.

Now we have to define all constraints that we had in PRODUCTS table. This step is required as constraints of PRODUCTS table are copied to NEWPRODUCTS table.

alter table products

add (constraint products_pk primary key(id));

alter table products

add (constraint products_qty_chk check(qty >= 0));

Now see the structure of the new table using DESCRIBE command and constraints using USER_CONSTRAINTS view.

What's new in Oracle8i?

Orale8i has introduced to new possibilities related to subqueries.

Subquery in VALUES clause

Since Oracle8i it is possible to use a subquery in VALUES clause of INSERT command. Prior to Oracle8i it was possible to use subquery with INSERT command but not in VALUES clause of INSERT command.

The following INSERT command gets the next ROLLNO for a new student by using a subquery.

insert into students values ((select max(rollno) + 1 from students),

  'b7', 'Robert Lafore', 'm', sysdate, null, null);

ORDER BY is permitted in subquery – TOPn analysis

Oracle8i has allowed the ORDER BY clause to be used with subquery. The following query will use ORDER BY clause to get courses in descending order. Then main query will take the data sent by the subquery and selects only first two rows. As the result, the query will display the details of course with first two highest course fee.

223

ROWNUM pseudo column contains the row number for the retrieved rows. The query uses ROWNUM and takes only those rows that have row number less than 3.

```
select ccode,name,fee from

   (select * from courses order by  fee desc)

   where  rownum < 3;
```

```
CCODE NAME                           FEE

----- ----------------------------- ---------

cs    C Sharp                       7000

vbnet VB.NET                        5500
```

Correlated Subquery

If there is any correlation between main query and subquery then subquery is called as **correlated subquery**.

A correlated subquery is a subquery that receives some input from main query and sends result back to main query. Unlike normal subquery, a correlated subquery receives value from main query. It uses the value (generally in condition) and sends the results of the query back to main query.

Though most of the requirements can be accomplished with normal subqueries, some requirements do need correlated subquery. For example, we have to display the details of the batches where duration of the batch is more than the average duration of all the batches of that course.

Before we write the required query, let us look at the data present in BATCHES table.

select * from batches;

BCODE	CCODE	FCODE	STDATE	ENDDATE	TIMING
b1	ora	gk	12-JAN-01	20-FEB-01	1
b2	asp	da	15-JAN-01	05-MAR-01	2
b3	c	hs	20-JAN-01	27-FEB-01	3
b4	xml	dh	02-MAR-01	30-MAR-01	3
b5	java	hs	05-APR-01	10-MAY-01	1
b6	vbnet	da	12-JUL-01	31-AUG-01	1
b7	ora	gk	15-AUG-01	04-OCT-01	2
b9	ora	kl	05-MAY-01	10-JUN-01	3
b10	c	kl	15-JUN-01	20-JUL-01	2
b11	vbnet	da	15-JUN-01	30-JUL-01	2

Now let us write correlated query to get details of batches where duration (ENDDATE-STDATE) is more than the average duration of the course.

select * from batches **b1**

where enddate - stdate >=

225

(select avg(enddate - stdate)

from batches

where **ccode = b1.ccode**);

BCODE CCODE FCODE STDATE   ENDDATE   TIMING

----- ----- ----- --------- --------- ---------

BCODE	CCODE	FCODE	STDATE	ENDDATE	TIMING
b2	asp	da	15-JAN-01	05-MAR-01	2
b3	c	hs	20-JAN-01	27-FEB-01	3
b4	xml	dh	02-MAR-01	30-MAR-01	3
b5	java	hs	05-APR-01	10-MAY-01	1
b6	vbnet	da	12-JUL-01	31-AUG-01	1
b7	ora	gk	15-AUG-01	04-OCT-01	2

In correlated subquery, subquery is executed once for each row of the main query. This is required as subquery uses a value sent from main query, which may change from row to row in main query.

A correlated subquery is identified by the use of a column of main query in the subquery. In the above example, for each row of the BATCHES table the course code (CCODE) is passed to subquery and then subquery finds out the average duration of all batches of that course. The condition *ccode = b1.ccode* is used to select batches that belong to the course to which the batch in the main query belongs.

When subquery returns the average duration then main query checks whether duration of the batch is greater than or equal to the average duration sent by subquery. If the condition is satisfied then row in the main query is selected otherwise it is not selected. The process continues with the next row in the main query and so on until all rows of the main query are processed.

Differences between normal and correlated subquery

The following are the differences between a correlated subquery and ordinary subquery.

Subquery	Correlated subquery
Executed only for once before main-query	Executed once for each row of main-query.
Sends a value to main-query.	Receives value(s) from main query and sends value(s) to main-query.

Table 1: Normal subquery Vs. Correlated subquery

The following is another example of correlated subquery where we get third highest course fee.

select name, fee from courses c1

where 2= (select count(*)

from courses

where fee > c1.fee);

NAME   FEE

------------------------------- ---------

ASP.NET   5000

In the above example, subquery returns the number of courses where FEE is more than the fee of the row in the main query. If the count returned by subquery is equal to 2 then it means above that course fee there are two more. That means that course fee becomes the third highest.

The above query is pretty useful. Especially prior to Oracle8i. As Oracle8i allowed ORDER BY clause in subquery, what was achieved with this correlated subquery can to some extent be achieved with ORDER BY clause in subquery.

The following two queries, will display the details of courses with two lowest fees.

The first query uses ORDER BY clause in subquery to retrieve courses in the ascending order of FEE. Then main query retrieves only first two rows of the subquery.

select * from (select ccode, name, fee from courses order by fee)

where rownum < 3;

CCODE	NAME	FEE
c	C programming	3500
xml	XML Programming	4000

The second query uses a correlated subquery to get number of rows where FEE is less than the FEE of the row in main query. If the count returned by subquery is greater than or equal to 1 then row of the main query is retrieved.

```
select ccode,name, fee from courses c1

where  1 >= ( select count(*)

from courses

where fee < c1.fee);
```

```
CCODE NAME                      FEE

----- -------------------------------- ---------

c    C programming           3500

xml  XML Programming            4000
```

EXISTS and NOT EXISTS operators

These two operators are exclusively used in correlated subquery. EXISTS checks whether any row is returned by subquery and condition will be true if subquery returns any rows. Whereas, NOT EXISTS returns true if subquery doesn't retrieve any row.

EXISTS is different from other operators like IN,ANY etc., because it doesn't compare values of columns, instead, it checks whether any row is retrieved from subquery or not. If any row is retrieved from subquery the EXISTS returns true otherwise it returns false.

The following query displays details of courses for which at least one batch started in this month.

```
select * from courses

where  exists
```

(select * from batches

  where courses.ccode= ccode

  and to_char(stdate,'mmyy') = to_char(sysdate,'mmyy')

);

When using EXISTS operator, what you select in the inner-query does NOT matter. What does matter is whether any row is retrieved by inner query or not.

The following example displays the details of courses for which no batch has yes started.

select ccode,name,fee from courses

where **not exists**

  (select * from batches

   where ccode = courses.ccode);

CCODE NAME   FEE

----- ------------------------------ ---------

cs   C Sharp   7000

It is possible to replace the above NOT EXISTS with NOT IN operator as shown below.

select ccode,name,fee from courses

where ccode not in (select ccode from batches);


```
CCODE NAME                     FEE

----- ----------------------------- ---------

cs    C Sharp                 7000
```


Let us see two other operators ALL and ANY.

ANY and ALL Operators

Both are used for comparing one value against a set of values. ALL specifies that all the values given in the list should be taken into account, whereas ANY specifies that the condition is satisfied when any of the values satisfies the condition.

    operator ANY list

    operator ALL   list

The operator can be any one of the standard relational operators (=, >=, >, <, <=, !=) , and list is a series of values.

What if you want to display name of the courses where FEE is more than FEE of any course with DURATION 25? The following query will do just that.

select name from courses

where fee > any (select fee from courses where duration = 25);

NAME

VB.NET

ASP.NET

C Sharp

ANY operator specifies if FEE is more than any value in the list supplied by subquery then the condition is true. The same query can also be written as follows using MIN function.

select name from courses

where fee > (select min(fee) from courses where duration = 25);

NAME

VB.NET

ASP.NET

C Sharp

The following list illustrates the result of ANY and ALL operator.

Rate	ANY/ALL Operator	Result
10	Rate > ANY (15,20)	False
10	Rate > ANY (5,15)	True

10	Rate > ALL (10,20)	False
10	Rate > ALL (5,7)	True

Summary

Subquery is a query placed within another query. A subquery may return either one or multiple rows. Understanding how to use subqueries is very important. So, make sure you are comfortable with subqueries. Because subqueries, joining, and grouping the data are the areas which you must master. Subqueries can be used with DML and even DDL commands. Oracle8i has allowed ORDER BY clause in subqueries. This allows top n analysis. Oracle8i has also allowed usage of subquery in VALUES clause of INSERT command.

When a subquery takes data from main query it is called as correlated subquery. And operators EXISTS and NOT EXISTS are used exclusively with correlated subquery.

Exercises

♦ A correlated subquery is executed for _____ number of times.

♦ Subquery nesting can be up to _____ levels.

♦ What is the result of x > ANY (10,20), if x is 15? _____.

♦ Subquery always passes the result to the main-query [T/F] _____

♦ Subquery can be used in VALUES clause of INSERT command.[T/F] _____.

♦ Display details of courses taken by students who joined in the month of june, 2001.

♦ Delete the details of students who haven't paid anything so far.

♦ Display the details of course for which there are more than 3 batches.

♦ Display the details of course that has highest number of batches.

♦ Change the ENDDATE of batch B8 to the ENDDATE of most recent batch.

- Display the details of students who haven't paid total amount so far.
- Display the details of payment made by students of Oracle batch started on 5-dec-2000.

12. INDEXING, CLUSTERING, sequence and pseudo columns

- ❏ What is an index
- ❏ Why to use an index
- ❏ Creating an index
- ❏ When Oracle does not use index
- ❏ Clustering
- ❏ Sequence
- ❏ Pseudo columns

What is an Index?

I believe, the best way of understanding an index in Oracle (or any database system) is by comparing it with the index that we find at the end of a textbook. For instance, if you want to read about *indexing* in an Oracle textbook, you will use index of the book to locate the topic *indexing*. Once the topic is found in index then you take the page number of that topic from index. Then you go to the page with that page number and start reading about indexing.

The concept of indexing in Oracle is same as the concept of book index. First let us look at the features of an index of a textbook.

- ❏ It is at the end of the textbox so that you need not search for the index in the first place.
- ❏ It contains all topics of the book in the ascending (alphabetical) order of

the topics.

- After the topic the page number(s) where the topic is found in the book is listed.
- Index does increase the size of the book by a few pages.
- We use index only when we need it. In other words, we use index when we feel it is going to help locating the topic quickly.

All the characteristics of an index in a textbook will be found in an index of Oracle. The following are the characteristics of an index in Oracle.

- Index is used to search for required rows quickly.
- Index occupies extra space. Index is stored separately from table.
- Index contains the values of key – column on which index is created – in the ascending order.
- Just like the page number in book index, Oracle index stores ROWID – a unique value to internally identify each row of the table. For each entry in the index a key and corresponding ROWID are stored.
- Oracle uses index only when it feels the index is going to improve performance of the query.

Note: ROWID is a unique value assigned to each row created in a table. Once ROWID is assigned to a row it doesn't change during the lifetime of the row. Oracle access rows internally using ROWID.

An index in Oracle is internally stored as *Self-balancing binary tree*. A data structure that makes searching for a particular value faster.

Why To Use An INDEX

An index in Oracle is used for two purposes.

- ❏ To speed up searching for a particular value thereby improving performance of query.
- ❏ To enforce uniqueness

Using index to improving performance

Just like how you can quickly locate a particular topic in the book by using index at the end of the book, Oracle uses index to quickly locate the row with the given value in the indexed column. Indexed column is the one on which index is created.

For example if you want to search for a particular student by name then Oracle does the following without and with index.

- ❏ Without index, Oracle will start looking for the given name at the first row of the table and continues until it finds the name or until end of the table is reached. This could be very time consuming process especially for tables with many rows.
- ❏ With index, Oracle will use index to search for the given name. Since index is stored in the form of binary tree, locating the name in the index is going to be very fast. Then by using the ROWID obtained from index entry, Oracle will take the row from the table.

Tables with more number of rows will greatly benefit from indexes. Having an index and not having an index could make a lot of difference for large tables with thousands of rows.

Enforcing uniqueness with index

An index may also be used to enforce uniqueness in the column(s) given in the index. Once a UNIQUE index is created, Oracle makes sure values in the indexed column(s) are unique.

236

Note: A UNIQUE index is automatically created on the columns with PRIMARY KEY and UNIQUE constraints.

Creating an Index

DDL command CREATE INDEX is used to create an index. The following is the syntax of this command.

CREATE [UNIQUE] INDEX index_name

    ON table (column-1 [, column-2]...);

UNIQUE keyword is used to create a unique index. Unique index makes sure that the indexed column(s) is always unique.

To create an index on NAME column of STUDENTS table, enter:

create index students_name_idx

 on students (name);

If you want to create a unique index on NAME column of STUDENTS table, enter:

create unique index students_name_idx

    on students(name);

It is also possible to create an index on more than one column. The following command creates an index on CCODE and FCODE columns of BATCHES table.

```
create index  batches_ccode_fcode_idx

on   batches ( ccode,fcode);
```

Note: When two or more columns are used in an index then give the column in the order of frequency of usage. That means the most frequently used column should be given first.

Just like an index of the book, which is not used every time you read the book, even Oracle index is not used every time by Oracle. In the next section we will see when Oracle uses index and when not.

When Oracle does not use index?

The best part of Oracle index is; it is completely automatic. That means, you never have to explicitly refer to an index. Oracle decides whether to use an index or not depending upon the query.

Oracle can understand whether using an index will improve the performance in the given query. If Oracle thinks using an index will improve performance, it will use the index otherwise it will ignore the index.

Let us assume we have an index on NAME column of STUDETNS table. Then the following query will use the index as we are trying to get information about a student based on the name.

```
select  * from students
```

where name = 'Richard Marx';

But in the following case Oracle does NOT use index, as index's usage doesn't improve performance of the query.

SELECT doesn't contain WHERE clause

If SELECT command doesn't contain WHERE clause then Oracle doesn't use any index. Since all rows of the table are to be retrieved, Oracle will directly access the table without referring to any index.

In the following example no index of STUDENTS table will be used.

select * from students;

SELECT contains WHERE clause, but WHERE clause doesn't refer to indexed column.

In this case SELECT contains WHERE clause but the WHERE clause is not referring to any columns on which an index is created. For example, STUDETNS table contains two indexes – one on ROLLNO, as it is primary key and another on NAME (created earlier in this chapter).

The following query uses WHERE clause but condition is based on DJ column for which there is no index.

select * from students
where dj > '16-jan-2001';

However, note that if there is any index on DJ then Oracle will use that index.

WHERE clause uses indexed columns but indexed column is modified in the WHERE clause.

In this case WHERE clause refers to indexed columns but doesn't refer to indexed column as it is.

In the query below, NAME column is used but as it is used with SUBSTR function that modifies the column in the condition, index created on NAME column will not be used.

select * from students

where   substr(name,4,3) = 'Joh';

Note: Data dictionary view USER_INDEXES provides information about indexes.

Creating function-based index

Prior to Oracle8i, it is not possible to create an index with an expression as the index column. Index column must be column of the table. If any function is used with indexed column in the query then Oracle does not use index. For example, if we created an index on NAME column of STUDENTS table as follows:

create index students_name_idx

 on students (name);

Then the above index cannot be used for the following query as indexed column is used with UPPER function.

select * from students

 where upper(name) = 'RICHARD MARX';

It is also not possible to create any index based on an expression.

Oracle8i allows indexes to be created on the result of the expression. For example, the following command creates an index on the result of UPPER function.

```
create index students_name_idx
 on  students ( UPPER(name));
```

As the result if we issue the following command Oracle can use index as the expression used in the query and expression used to crate index are same.

```
select * from students
where upper(name) = 'RICHARD MARX';
```

Note: To create a function-based index, user must have QUERY REWRITE system privilege.

The following is another example of expression-based index. Here index is created on duration of the batch.

```
create index batches_duration_idx
  on batches ( enddate - stdate);
```

The following query will make use of the above index.

select * from batches

where enddate - stdate > 30;

Online indexing

Prior to Oracle8i, Oracle used to lock the table on which index is being created throughout creation process. This makes table unavailable for data manipulation during the creation of index. But Oracle8i introduced online indexing, where Oracle doesn't lock the table on which index is being built.

Online indexing is provided through the keyword ONLINE.

The following command creates index on NAME column of STUDENTS table without locking the table.

create index students_name_idx

  on students (name) online;

Note: Online indexing increases availability of the table. This is a very important facility especially for Internet databases where availability matters a lot.

Drawbacks of indexes

Though indexes increase performance of query, they can also decrease performance of data manipulation.

Many indexes on a table can slow down INSERTS and DELETES drastically. For example, if we take 5 indexes on a table then every insertion of a new row will update all 5 indexes of the table. That means, one insertion will actually result in six insertions. Similarly every change to an indexed column will need a change to index.

Having more indexes is advantageous in case of tables that are primarily used only for querying and not updated frequently.

Though the extra space occupied by indexes is also a consideration, it may not matter much since the cost of data storage has declined substantially.

Dropping an index

You can drop an index using DROP INDEX command. It removes the named index. Removing an index will effect the performance of existing applications but not the functionality in any way.

Using and not using an index is transparent to users. Oracle decides whether to use or not on its own. However, it is possible for users to control the usage of index to certain extent using **hints,** which are directive to Oracle regarding how to execute a command. But hints are too heavy in a book meant for beginners.

DROP INDEX indexname;

The following example drops the index created on NAME of STUDENTS table.

drop index student_name_idx;

243

Clustering

Clustering is a method of storing tables that are often used together (in joining) in one area of the disk. As tables that are related are stored in one area of the disk, performance of joining will improve.

In order to place tables in a cluster, tables have to have a common column. For example the following steps will create a cluster and place COURSES and BATCHES tables in the cluster.

A cluster is created with a name and a key. The key is the column, which must be present in each table that is placed in the cluster. The key is also called as *cluster key*.

Steps

The following are the required steps to create a cluster and place tables into it.

- ◆ Create a cluster with CREATE CLUSTER command.
- ◆ Create an index on the cluster using CREATE INDEX command. This must be done before you insert rows into clustered tables.
- ◆ Place the tables into cluster using CLUSTER option of CREATE TABLE command.

Creating a cluster

A cluster is created using CREATE CLUSTER command. At the time of creating a cluster the name of the cluster and data type and name of the key must be given.

The following is the syntax of CREATE CLUSTER command.

CREATE CLUSTER clustername

   (column datatype [, column datatype] ...);

The following command creates a cluster to store BATCHES and COURSES table. As CCODE is the common column of these two tables, it is to be the cluster key. We specify the data type and name of the cluster key. However, name may be anything and it is never used after cluster is created.

create cluster course_batches

   (ccode varchar2(5));

Creating cluster index

After the cluster is created and before any rows can be inserted into tables in the cluster, an index on the cluster must be created.

CREATE INDEX command is used to create an index on the cluster. Unless an index is created on the cluster no data manipulation can be done on the tables that are placed in the cluster.

create index cl_ccode_index

      on cluster course_batches;

Placing tables into a cluster

Once a cluster is created, it may be used to store tables that are related. Each table loaded into cluster, must have a column that matches with cluster key.

A table must be placed in to cluster at the time of creation. CLUSTER option of CREATE TABLE command specifies the cluster in to which the table must be placed. It also specifies the name of the column in the table that matches the cluster key of the cluster.

The following commands create COURSES and BATCHES tables and place them into cluster.

```
create table courses
(
  ccode varchar2(5),
  name  varchar2(30),
  . . .
)
cluster course_batches(ccode);
```

```
create table batches
(
  bcode   varchar2(5),
  ccode   varchar2(5),
  . . .
)
cluster course_batches(ccode);
```

Note: Placing a table into cluster is transparent to users. Users and application will use the table in the same manner whether the table is in the cluster or not.

Storage of clustered tables

When two tables are placed in a cluster, they are stored together on the disk making joining these tables faster. Apart from that storing table in a cluster will also reduce the space requirement. This is because of cluster storing common column of the clustered tables only for once. In the above example, each unique CCODE is stored only for once. That means for course ORA though there are multiple batches, the value ORA is stored only for once in the cluster.

Sequence

Sequence is an object in Oracle database, which is used by multiple users to generate unique numbers. Sequence is typically used to generate primary keys like account number, employee number etc., where uniqueness and sequence matter.

In order to use a sequence, first it is to be created using CREATE SEQUENCE command. Then pseudo columns NEXTVAL and CURRVAL are used to retrieve unique values from sequence.

The following is the syntax of CREATE SEQUENCE command .

CREATE SEQUENCE sequencename

    [INCREMENT BY integer]

    [START WITH integer]

    [MAXVALUE integer | NOMAXVALUE]

    [MINVALUE integer | NOMINVALUE]

    [CYCLE | NOCYCLE];

The following is the description of available options.

Option	Meaning
START WITH	Specifies the values at which sequence must start. Default is 1.
MAXVALUE	Maximum value the sequence can generate. Default is 10e27-1.
MINVALUE	Minimum value the sequence can generate. Default is 1.
INCREMENT BY	Specifies by how much the value of the sequence is to be incremented. If you want numbers in the descending order give negative value. Default is 1.
CYCLE	Restarts numbers from MINVALUE after reaching MAXVALUE.

Table 1: Options of CREATE SEQUENCE command.

The following command creates a sequence called ROLLNO to generate roll numbers for students.

create sequence rollno

start with 100

increment by 1;

The above sequence starts generating numbers at 100 and increments the number by 1 every time the number is taken.

Once a sequence is created, it can be used to generate unique numbers in the sequence. Once a value is taken from sequence, Oracle automatically increments the value by one (or whatever value specified using INCREMENT BY option). Oracle guarantees uniqueness. Once it gives the number then it doesn't give that number to anyone else.

The following two pseudo columns are used to access the next and current value of the sequence.

NEXTVAL

This pseudo column will yield the next value from sequence and automatically increments the value of the sequence.

CURRVAL

This returns the value that is taken by most recent NEXTVAL. This cannot be used unless NEXTVAL is first called.

The following examples will demonstrate how to use NEXTVAL and CURRVAL pseudo columns.

select rollno.nextval from dual;

    NEXTVAL

    100

As the sequence starts with 100, first NEXTVAL returned 100. And it also increments the sequence by 1. See the next example below.

select rollno.nextval from dual;

NEXTVAL

   101

CURRVAL pseudo column returns the current value of the sequence, which is the value returned by most recent NEXTVAL.   In the following example CURRVAL returns 101 since that is the most recent value returned by NEXTVAL.

select rollno.currval from dual;

CURRVAL

   101

CURRVAL is used to reuse the values returned by most recent NEXTVAL.

The real usage of sequence is in inserting rows into table. The following INSERT command will use ROLLNO sequence to get next available roll number for a new student.

insert into students

     values (rollno.nextval ,   ...);

And if you want to insert a row into PAYMENTS table immediately with the same roll number then you can use CURRVAL as follows.

insert into payments

values (rollno.currval, ...);

Though a sequence can guarantees uniqueness and sequence, its usage may not guarantee consecutiveness. See the following scenario.

insert into students values (rollno.nextval, . . .);

commit;

insert into students values (rollno.nextval, . . .);

rollback;

insert into students values (rollno.nextval, . . .);

commit;

In the above scenario, if you take the value of ROLLNO.NEXTVAL as 102 for first INSERT then the value in the second INSERT will be 103. But as second INSERT command is rolled back that number is not actually used as roll number. Third INSERT command now takes 104 but not 103 as Oracle returns next available number, which is 104.

As you can see, 103 is not used at all in the roll number. While using sequence one must be aware of this potential gaps.

Altering a sequence

Some attributes of a sequence can be altered using ALTER SEQUENCE command.

ALTER SEQUENCE sequencename

    [INCREMENT BY integer]

    [MAXVALUE integer | NOMAXVALUE]

    [MINVALUE integer | NOMINVALUE]

For instance, the following command changes MAXVALUE of ROLLNO sequence to 1000.

alter sequence rollno maxvalue 1000;

Dropping a Sequence

DROP SEQUENCE command is used to drop a sequence.

| DROP SEQUENCE sequencename;

The following command drops ROLLNO sequence.

drop sequence rollno;

Pseudo Columns

A pseudo column is used like a column in a table but it is not a column of any table. You can use pseudo columns just like table columns but you cannot modify them.

The following is the list of available pseudo columns in Oracle.

Pseudo Column	Meaning
CURRVAL	Returns the current value of a sequence.
NEXTVAL	Returns the next value of a sequence.
NULL	Return a null value.
ROWID	Returns the ROWID of a row. See ROWID section below.
ROWNUM	Returns the number indicating in which order Oracle selects rows. First row selected will be ROWNUM of 1 and second row ROWNUM of 2 and so on.
SYSDATE	Returns current date and time.
USER	Returns the name of the current user.
UID	Returns the unique number assigned to the current user.

Table 2: Pseudo Columns.

The following are a few examples on usage of pseudo columns.

253

Display the name of the current user and user's id.

SQL> select user, uid from dual;

```
USER                          UID
----------------------------- ---------
BOOK                          38
```

ROWID

Pseudo column ROWID returns the address of each row in the table. Oracle assigns a ROWID to each row. Oracle uses ROWID internally to access rows. For instance, Oracle stores ROWID in index and uses it to access the row in the table.

You can display ROWID of rows using SELECT command as follows:

select rowid, ccode from courses;

```
ROWID             CCODE
----------------- -----
AAADC5AABAAAKaSAAA ora
AAADC5AABAAAKaSAAB vbnet
AAADC5AABAAAKaSAAC c
AAADC5AABAAAKaSAAD asp
AAADC5AABAAAKaSAAE java
AAADC5AABAAAKaSAAF xml
```

AAADC5AABAAAKaSAAG cs

Oracle provides a package called DBMS_ROWID to decode ROWID. The following SELECT command displays only the row number from ROWID.

select dbms_rowid.rowid_row_number(rowid) as rownumber ,ccode

from

courses

ROWNUMBER CCODE

--------- -----

    0 ora

    1 vbnet

    2 c

    3 asp

    4 java

    5 xml

    6 cs

Note: Once a row is assigned a ROWID Oracle does not change ROWID during the lifetime of the row. As the result you may see some row numbers missing in the output of above command. It means those rows were deleted.

For more information about ROWID and DBMS_ROWID package please see online documentation.

255

ROWNUM

This pseudo column yields the order in which Oracle has selected rows.

The following command displays row number of each row.

select rownum, ccode from courses;

```
ROWNUM CCODE
--------- -----
    1 ora
    2 vbnet
    3 c
    4 asp
    5 java
    6 xml
    7 cs
```

ROWNUM can also be used in conditions but only two operators; < and <=. make sense with ROWNUM.

The following query displays first five courses.

select rownum, ccode from courses
where rownum <= 5

```
ROWNUM CCODE
--------- -----
        1 ora
        2 vbnet
        3 c
        4 asp
        5 java
```

However, the following is not meaningful usage of ROWNUM. It is because of the fact that Oracle assigns number to row after row is selected.

```
select rownum, ccode from courses
where  rownum = 5;
```

no rows selected

Also remember using Oracle assigns numbers to rows before rows are ordered using ORDER BY clause as demonstrated by the following query.

```
select rownum,ccode,duration,fee from courses
order by fee;
```

```
ROWNUM CCODE  DURATION    FEE
--------- ----- --------- ---------
        3 c         20    3500
```

6 xml	15	4000
1 ora	25	4500
5 java	25	4500
4 asp	25	5000
2 vbnet	30	5500
7 cs	30	7000

Summary

Index and cluster are used to improve performance. The concept of index in Oracle is similar to index found at the end of textbook. Oracle doesn't always use index instead Oracle uses index only when it feels, usage of index improves performance. Cluster is another method of improving performance by storing related tables together on the disk.

Sequence is an object used to generate unique number in a sequence. Pseudo column yield values and used as columns of the table though they are not columns of any table.

Exercises

1.   Which constraints automatically create index?

2.   What does ONLINE option in CREATE TABLE command do?

3.   How do you create an index on FCODE and CCODE of BATCHES table.

4.   _____ option in CREATE SEQUENCE is used to generate numbers in reverse order.

5.   _____ is the pseudo column used to get the next available number from a sequence.

6.   _____ option is used in CREATE TABLE command to place

the table in a cluster.

7.   Which option of CREATE INDEX is used to create an index on the cluster.

8.   Create a sequence called REVERSE to generate numbers in the descending order from 10000 to 1000 with a decrement of 5.

9.   Create a cluster to store STUDENTS and PAYMENTS tables and place tables into it.

10.   Change the decrement value of sequence REVERSE (created earlier) to 2.

11.   Is it possible to place an existing table into cluster? If yes how? If no, then what is the remedy you suggest?

12.   What is the purpose of ROWID?

13. SECURITY

- Users and privileges
- Object privileges
- Granting object privileges
- Using synonyms
- Revoking object privileges
- System privileges
- Using roles
- ALTER USER command
- Data dictionary views

Users and Privileges

Every user in Oracle must have a valid username and password. In order to access Oracle database, one must logon by using username and password.

At the time of creation of database, Oracle creates two users – SYSTEM and SYS. These two users have privileges to perform administrative operations such as creating users, altering and dropping users, roles, profile, tablespaces (pieces that make up the database) etc.

However, it is possible to create new users using CREATE USER command as follows:

SQL> create user srikanth identified by oraclebook;

User created.

The above command creates a new user with the name SRIKANTH and password ORACLEBOOK.

Note: In order to create a new user you must logon either as SYSTEM or as SYS.

Though the account with the name SRIKANTH is created, it cannot even logon now as shown below.

SQL> connect srikanth/oraclebook;

ERROR:

ORA-01045: user SRIKANTH lacks CREATE SESSION privilege; logon denied

CONNECT command is used to move to another user from current user. In the above example, we were moving from SYSTEM to SRIKANTH.

The error indicates that user SRIKANTH lacks CREATE SESSION privilege. CREATE SESSION is a system privilege, which allows user to create a session with Oracle (logon).

Note: A session with Oracle start from the point of login and ends when user logs out.

In order to permit user to create a session and perform other operations such as creating tables, view etc., user must be granted CONNECT and RESOURCE roles as follows.

SQL> grant connect, resource to srikanth;

Grant succeeded.

We will discuss more about roles later in this chapter. For the time being it is sufficient to know that these two roles will enable SRIKANTH to connect to Oracle database and also allow him to create and use object.

Privilege

A privilege is a right to access an object such as a table, view etc., or to execute a particular type of SQL command such as CREATE TABLE.

Privileges are classified into two categories depending upon what type of right they confer with the user.

- ❑ System privileges
- ❑ Object Privileges

System privilege

A system privilege is a right to perform certain operation in the system. For example, CREATE SESSION privilege allows user to create a session with Oracle, CREATE TABLE privilege allows user to create table and so on.

Generally system privileges are granted to users through roles. Only DBAs are concerned with system privileges.

Object privilege

An object privilege is a right to perform a particular operation on an object. An object either is a table, view, sequence, procedure, function, or package.

The next section will discuss more about object privileges.

Object Privileges

User owns the object that he/she creates. Owner has complete access to the object. For example, if the object is a table then owner can select, insert, delete, update, alter, create an index on table and even drop the table. Whereas other users do not have any access to the object, unless they are granted a privilege explicitly.

The following is the list of object privileges available in Oracle.

Privilege	What is permitted?
ALTER	Changing the definition of the object.
DELETE	Deleting rows from the object
EXECUTE	Execute the object.

INDEX	Creating an index on the object.
INSERT	Inserting rows into object
REFERENC ES	Referencing the object in foreign key constraint.
SELECT	Selecting rows from the object.
UPDATE	Updating the data of the object.

Table 1: Object Privileges.

As you see in table 1, each object privilege specifies what can be done with an object. But not all object privileges are applicable to all objects. For instance, ALTER privilege is not applicable to views, similarly EXECUTE privilege is applicable only to procedure and functions. For the list of object privileges available on different types of objects, see table 2.

Object	Privileges Available
TABLE	SELECT, INSERT, DELETE, UPDATE, ALTER, INDEX, REFERENCES.
VIEW	SELECT, INSERT, UPDATE, AND DELETE.
SEQUENCE	SELECT, ALTER.
PROCEDURE,	EXECUTE.
FUNCTION, PACKAGE and OBJECT TYPE	

Table 2: Availability of object privileges.

In the next section we will see how to grant privileges to other users so that they can access and perform required operation.

Granting Object Privileges

In order to grant object privileges use GRANT Command.

GRANT {object_priv | ALL} [(column [,column]...)]

  [,{object_priv | ALL} [(column [,column]...)]]...

  ON   object

  TO   {user | role | PUBLIC} [, {user | role | PUBLIC}] ...

  [WITH GRANT OPTION]

Object_priv is any of the object privileges listed in table 1.

ALL is used to grant all available object privileges on the object.

PUBLIC is used to grant the privilege to all the users of the system.

Now assume user SRIKANTH is the owner of COURSES table and he wants to grant SELECT privilege on COURSES table to user PRANEETH. The following command will do just that.

grant select on courses

  to praneeth;

The following command grants all available privileges on COMPBATCHES view to PRANEETH.

grant all on compbatches

to praneeth;

It is possible to restrict the privilege to a few columns in case of UPDATE, INSERT and REFERENCES privileges.

The following command will grant UPDATE privilege to PRANEETH on DURATION column of COURSES table.

grant update(duration)

on courses

to praneeth;

WITH GRANT OPTION allows the grantee to grant the privilege to other users.

Accessing other user's objects

When a user wants to access a table of other user, the table name is to be preceded by the name of the user who owns the table. Otherwise Oracle assumes that the current user owns the table and if table is not found under current user's account then Oracle displays an error.

For example, if PRANEETH is trying to access COURSES table to which he has been granted SELECT privilege, from his account, the following happens.

SQL> select * from courses;

select * from courses

      *

ERROR at line 1:

ORA-00942: table or view does not exist

Oracle assumes COURSE table belongs to user PRANEETH. To specify that COURSES table is belonging to SRIKANTH and not PRANEETH, we have to precede the table name with username.

owner.tablename

For example, to access COURSES table from user PRANEETH, give the following command.

select *

from srikanth.courses;

Using synonyms

To simplify accessing tables owned by other users, create a SYNONYM. A synonym is an alias to a table or a view. By creating a synonym you can avoid giving the owner name while accessing tables of others.

The following CREATE SYNONYM command creates a synonym, which is an alias to COURSES table of SRIKANTH.

Remember synonym is to be created in the account of PRANEETH and not in the account of SRIKANTH.

SQL>create synonym COURSES for srikanth.courses;

Synonym created.

Once a synonym is created, you can use synonym to refer to the table. So to refer to SRIKANTH.COURSES, user PRANEETH may give:

SQL>select * from courses;

PUBLIC Synonym

If synonym is to be available to all the users of the system, create a public synonym by including option PUBLIC in CREATE SYNONYM command.

The following sequence of commands will create a public synonym that is accessible to all the users in the system.

Grant select on courses to public;

The above command grants SELECT privilege on COURSES table to users of the database.

Then create a public synonym on SRIKANTH.COURSES so that any user can access the table using the synonym.

create public synonym courses

    for srikanth.courses;

Note: To create a public synonym, you must have the CREATE PUBLIC SYNONYM system privilege.

Now, it is possible for anyone in the system to access SRIKANTH.COURSES table by using the public synonym. For example, user ANURAG can access COURSES table using public synonym as follows:

```
select * from course;
```

WITH GRANT OPTION

Using option WITH GRANT OPTION with GRANT command allows grantee to grant the privilege that he/she received to other users.

In the following example, SRIKANTH grants SELECT privilege on COURSE to PRANEETH with option WITH GRANT OPTION.

```
grant select on courses

to praneeth

with grant option;
```

Now user PRANEETH can grant SELECT privilege that he has received from SRIKANTH, to ANURAG as follows:

```
grant select on srikanth.courses

to anurag;
```

Now user ANURAG can access COURSES table of SRIKANTH as follows.

```
select * from srikanth.courses;
```

Note: Though ANURAG has got privilege from PRANEETH; he has to give SRIKANTH.COURSES to access COURSES because it is owned by SRIKANTH.

Revoking Object Privilege

To revoke the privileges that were granted earlier, use REVOKE command.

The following is the syntax of REVOKE command.

Both GRANT and REVOKE commands are DCL commands.

REVOKE {object_priv | ALL}

    [,{object_priv | ALL}] ...

  ON [schema.]object

  FROM {user | role | PUBLIC} [,{user | role | PUBLIC}] ...

  [CASCADE CONSTRAINTS]

Object_priv is the privilege that is to be revoked. **ALL** revokes all privileges.

CASCADE CONSTRAINTS drops any referential constraint that was based on REFERENCES privilege granted earlier. For example, user A granted REFERENCES privilege to user B on CCODE column of COURSES table. And user B has referred to CCODE of COURSES in references constraint. If user A revokes REFERENCES privilege than references constraint will be deleted, if CASCADE CONSTARINTS options is used.

The following command will revoke SELECT privilege on COURSES from PRANEETH.

SQL> revoke select on courses

  2 from praneeth;

Revoking is cascading

When a privilege is revoked from a user, if that user has previously granted that privilege to other users then all grantees of that privilege will also lose that privilege. For example, if A grants a privilege to B and B grants that to C, then both B and C will lose the privilege when A revokes the privilege from B.

What is a Role?

Role is a collection of privileges. In cases where granting privileges user by user and table by table is lengthy, a role can come to your rescue.

The following are the important characteristics of roles:

- ❏ A role is a collection of privileges. The privileges may consist of both system and object privileges.
- ❏ A role is dynamic. Users of the role will enjoy whatever new privileges (added after the role has been granted to users) the role has been granted. In other words changes made to privileges of the role will affect all the users of the role.
- ❏ To create a role one must have CREATE ROLE system privilege.
- ❏ Oracle comes with a few predefined roles such as CONNECT, RESOURCE, and DBA.
- ❏ A single user can be granted multiple roles.
- ❏ User will use only those roles that are enabled by default. However, user can enable/disable any roles that are granted to him.

The following sections will explain how to create and use role.

Creating and using role

A role is created using CREATE ROLE command whose syntax is as follows:

CREATE ROLE rolename

[identified by password]

password is the password of the role. Users must use password of the role at the time of enabling the role. Password may be used for extra security.

The following are the three important steps related to roles. Let us see how to create and use a simple role called MANAGER.

Creating a role using CREATE ROLE command. The following command creates a role with the name MANAGER.

create role manager;

Granting required privileges to role

GRANT command can be used to grant privileges to role. The following GRANT commands are used to grant privilege to MANAGER role.

grant select on courses to manager;

grant select, update, insert, delete on batches to manager;

grant all on students to manager;

271

grant select on payments;

Granting role to users

A role can be granted to user using GRANT command as follows.

grant manager to praneeth;

grant manager to anurag;

Enabling a role

It is possible for a single user to have been granted more than one role. However, all roles granted to user may not be enabled by default. That means, the role is granted to user but user cannot use the privileges of the role.

At the time of creating user or even afterwards, administrator can specify which roles of the user must be enabled by default. The remaining roles are to be enabled explicitly.

If role MANAGER is granted to user but not enabled then user can enable the role as follows:

SQL > set role manager;

The privileges the user currently has, depend on the roles that are enabled. The roles that are not currently enabled are called as ***disabled roles*** and roles that are currently enabled are called as ***enabled roles.***

For more details on SET ROLE command, please see on-line help.

Dropping a role

It is possible to drop a role using DROP ROLE command. The following command drops role MANAGER that we created earlier.

drop role manager;

Using password with role

It is possible to assign a password to a role. The password is assigned at the time of creating the role or after the role is created using ALTER ROLE command.

create role manager identified by efficient;

Then grant a few privileges to MANAGER role. Though DBA can only create the role, any user can grant privileges to role.

grant select on courses to manager;

Now grant role to user anurag;

grant manager to anurag;

Now if user ANURAG wants to access COURSES table through the role, first he has to enable the role as follows.

set role manager identified by efficient;

273

As the role is assigned a password, user must supply password at the time of enabling role. If user doesn't supply password while enabling role, the following error occurs.

SQL> set role manager;

set role manager

*

ERROR at line 1:

ORA-01979: missing or invalid password for role 'MANAGER'

ALTER USER Command

ALTER USER command can be used to modify the characteristics of a user. For example it can be used to modify:

- Password
- Default roles

To change the password of the current user, user may give:

alter user praneeth identified by tunu;

It is possible to specify the default roles of a user using DEFAULT ROLE option of ALTER USER command as follows:

alter user book default role all except manager;

274

Note: Except changing password, user cannot change any other of his/her attributes.

Please see on-line help for remaining options in ALTER USER command and their usage.

Data Dictionary Views

Data dictionary views contain information regarding database in a simple form so that user can easily understand. All data dictionary views are based on tables owned by user SYS. Data dictionary tables and views are created at the time of creating database.

The following is the list of data dictionary views that are commonly used.

Data dictionary view	What it contains?
ALL_TAB_COLUMNS	Columns of all tables and views accessible to the user.
ALL_OBJECTS	Objects accessible to user.
DICTIONARY	Description of data dictionary view.
USER_CATALOG	Tables, views, synonyms and sequences owned by user.
USER_CLUSTERS	Description of user's own clusters.
USER_COL_PRIVS	Grants on columns for which the user is the owner, grantor or grantee.
USER_ERRORS	Current errors on stored objects owned by the user.
USER_INDEXES	Description of the user's own indexes.
USER_OBJECTS	Objects owned by the user.
USER_SEQUENCES	Description of the user's own sequences.
USER_SYNONYMS	The user's private synonyms.
USER_TABLES	Description of the user's own tables.
USER_TAB_PRIVS	Grants on tables for which the user is the owner, grantor, or grantee.
USER_TRIGGERS	Triggers owned by the user.
USER_TYPES	Object types created by user.
USER_USER	Information about the current user.
USER_VIEWS	Text of views owned by the user.

Table 3: Data dictionary views.

The following is the list of synonyms based on Data dictionary views.

Synonym	Data dictionary view
DICT	DICTIONARY
OBJ	USER_OBJECTS
CAT	USER_CATALOG
TABS	USER_TABLES
COLS	USER_TAB_COLUMN S
SEQ	USER_SEQUENCES.
SYN	USER_SYNONYM.
IND	USER_INDEXES.

Table 4: Synonyms for Data dictionary views.

To list all tables owned by current user, enter:

SQL> select * from tabs;

To list the all the objects and their types, enter:

select object_name, object_type from user_objects;

To get the query stored along with view, enter:

select view_name, text from user_views;

Summary

Security is an important feature of any multi-user database system. Oracle implements security using system privileges and object privileges. System privileges specify which commands a user can execute. Unless otherwise specified an object (table, view etc.) can be accessed only by the owner. But using object privileges a user can allow other users to access his objects.

Roles are used to group privileges. When a role is granted to a user, all the privileges that are granted to role are granted to grantee of the role. It greatly simplifies the job of implementing security because with one role many privileges can be granted.

Data dictionary views may be used to get useful information regarding objects, users, and system.

Exercises

- _____ command is used to change user password.
- Which object privilege allows user to create an index on the table _____.
- _____ Option is used to grant a privilege along with permission to grant the privilege to other users.
- A Role is _____.
- _____ Command is used to revoke a system privilege.
- _____ data dictionary view may be used to know the table that a user can access.
- _____ data dictionary view is used to know the list of tables owned by the current user.
- ____ is the synonym for USER_CATALOG data dictionary.
- Grant UPDATE privilege on STDATE column of BATCHES table to user PRANEETH with permission to grant the privilege to others.
- Create a role and assign a few privileges to that role. Assign the role to user ANURAG.
- Enable the role LEADER.

• Display the table name, column name of all columns that you can access.

14. REPORT GENERATION USING SQL*PLUS commands

❑ What is a report?

❑ Sample report

❑ Report script

❑ Break command

❑ Compute command

❑ Column command

❑ Ttitle and Btitle commands

❑ Spool command

❑ Clear command

❑ System variables

❑ Displaying information using SHOW command

What is a report?

A report is information provided in a neat and understandable format. Report contains details as well as summary information. We have so far seen different clauses of SELECT command. But no clause allows you to display details as well as summary information.. For instance, GROUP BY can be used to get summary information but it cannot display details. Simple SELECT can display details but cannot display summary information.

SQL*PLUS is a tool that is used to send SQL command to Oracle Instance.

It is an environment in which you enter SQL commands. It also provides some extra commands such as DESCRIBE, EDIT etc., which are called as SQL*PLUS commands. SQL*PLUS environment also provides a set of commands which can be used to generate report.

279

The following is a sample report that we are going to generate in this chapter. This report is generated with SQL*PLUS commands that are specifically meant for this purpose and SELECT command, which is used to retrieve data from database.

Sample Report

The following is the report to be generated. We will see in the remaining sections of this chapter how to generate this report.

The following are the various SQL*PLUS commands that are used to generate the following report. The report is used to display the details of payment made by students. The details are divided into groups based on batch and then course. The totals are displayed for each batch, each course and also for the entire report.

Payments Report

COURS	BATCH	R.NO	Student	PHONE	Date of Joining	Date of Payment	AMOUNT
asp	b2	3	Andy Roberts	433554	11-JAN-01	13-JAN-01	2,000
		3	Andy Roberts	433554	11-JAN-01	20-JAN-01	3,000
		4	Malcom Marshall	653345	16-JAN-01	30-JAN-01	2,000
		4	Malcom Marshall	653345	16-JAN-01	16-JAN-01	3,000
		5	Vivan Richards	641238	16-JAN-01	16-JAN-01	5,000
sum							15,000

```
*****                                    -------
sum                                      15,000


c    b3      6 Chirs Evert        14-JAN-01 14-JAN-01  3,500
            7 Ivan Lendal    431212   15-JAN-01 15-JAN-01  3,500
     *****                             -------
     sum                               7,000


*****                                    -------
sum                                      7,000


java b5     9 Richard Marx    876567   06-APR-01 07-APR-01  3,000
           11 Jody Foster     234344   07-APR-01 10-APR-01  3,500
           11 Jody Foster     234344   07-APR-01 07-APR-01  1,000
           10 Tina Turner     565678   06-APR-01 10-APR-01  4,500
     *****                             -------
     sum                              12,000
```

```
*****                                    -------

sum                                       12,000
```

```
ora   b1        1 George Micheal     488333    10-JAN-01 10-JAN-01  4,500

                2 Micheal Douglas    334333    11-JAN-01 11-JAN-01  3,500

                2 Micheal Douglas    334333    11-JAN-01 17-JAN-01  1,000

        *****                                    -------
```

Payments Report

```
                                     Date of   Date of

COURS BATCH    ROLLNO Student Name        PHONE      Joining   Payment
AMOUNT

----- ----- --------- -------------------- ---------- --------- --------- -------

        sum                                           9,000
```

```
ora   b7       12 Louis Figo         535555    12-JUL-01 12-JUL-01  3,000

               13 Marshall Brain     223222    13-JUL-01 13-JUL-01  2,500

               13 Marshall Brain     223222    13-JUL-01 15-JUL-01  1,000
```

```
 *****                                        -------
   sum                                         6,500


 *****                                        -------
   sum                                        15,500



 xml   b4          8 George Micheal      488333      01-MAR-01 01-MAR-01
 2,000
                   8 George Micheal      488333   01-MAR-01 02-MAR-01  2,000
   *****                                      -------
     sum                                      4,000


 *****                                        -------
   sum                                        4,000



                                              -------
   sum                                        53,500
```

Report Script

283

The following is the report script. The script is used to generate the report shown above. The following sections will explain the commands used in the script.

Type the script in any text editor under the name like payreport.sql and then run it from SQL prompt of SQL*Plus as follows.

SQL>>start c:\orabook\payreport.sql

```
rem ***********************************************
rem Purpose : Script to generate Payments Report
rem AUthor  : P.Srikanth
rem Date    : 10-Oct-2001
rem Place   : Visakhapatanam
rem ***********************************************

rem set break and compute settings

break on report on course skip page on batch skip 2
compute sum of amount on batch course report

set pagesize 24
set linesize 90
set feedback off
```

```
column amount  format 99,999

column name    format a20 heading 'Student Name'

column dj      heading 'Date of|Joining'

column dp      heading 'Date of|Payment'


ttitle  skip 1  right  'Page:' format 99 sql.pno  skip 1 center 'Payments Report'
skip 2


spool payreport.lst


select c.ccode course, b.bcode batch, p.rollno, s.name name, phone, dj, dp,
amount

from  batches b, students s, payments p, courses c

where  b.ccode = c.ccode and b.bcode = s.bcode and s.rollno = p.rollno

order by course, batch;


spool off


set feedback on


rem clear settings


clear compute
```

clear break

clear column

ttitle off

BREAK Command

Specifies how which column(s) the data selected by SELECT command is to be grouped (broken). This is also used to specify what should be done when break is given.

BRE[AK] [ON expression [*action*]] . . .

Expression is the column on which the data is to be grouped or ROW or REPORT keyword.

Action specifies what action should be taken when break is issued. The following are the possible actions.

SKI[P] n	Prints specified number of empty lines.
SKI[P] page	Issues a page break at break.
DUP[LICATE]	Prints the value of a break column in every selected row.
NODUP[LICATE]	Prints blanks instead of the value of a break column when the value is a duplicate of the column's value in the preceding row.

Note: BREAK command alone displays the current break settings

The following BREAK command issues break whenever it detects a change in BCODE column and starts a new page.

```
break on bcode skip  page
```

Note: It is important to give ORDER BY clause on the columns that are used in BREAK command.

When multiple columns are used in BREAK, SQL*PLUS issues break starting from rightmost column to leftmost.

```
break on country skip page on city skip 2
```

First it issues break on CITY and then issues break on COUNTRY. You need to makes sure the order is right.

BREAK command in script

The script above used the following break.

```
break on report on course skip page on batch skip 2
```

The above BREAK issues break on three different levels. First whenever there is a change in BATCH column, second whenever there is a change in COURSE column and finally at the end of the report.

It is important to know the order in which columns are to be given – most specific to most common.

For this break to work properly the ORDER BY clause of the SELECT must be given as follows:

order by course, batch

COMPUTE Command

This is used to compute and print summary information. The

COMP[UTE] [function [LABEL text] OF {column}...

     ON {column | REPORT | ROW} . . .]

FUNCTION is any of the functions listed in Table 1.

If you give more than one function, use spaces to separate the functions.

FUNCTION	COMPUTES	APPLIES TO DATATYPES
AVG	Average of non-null values	NUMBER
COU[NT]	Count of non-null values	all types
MAX[IMUM]	Maximum value	NUMBER, CHAR, VARCHAR, VARCHAR2
MIN[IMUM]	Minimum value	NUMBER, CHAR, VARCHAR, VARCHAR2

NUM[BER]	Count of rows	all types
STD	Standard deviation of non-null values	NUMBER
SUM	Sum of non-null values	NUMBER
VAR[IANC E]	Variance of non-null values	NUMBER

Table 1: List of functions used in COMPUTE.

Note: *Every COMPUTE requires a corresponding BREAK. COMPUTE displays summary information, only when there is a break on the given level.*

The following COMPUTE will display the subtotal and grand total of amount.

compute sum of amount on bcode report

For the above COMPUTE to function there must be a corresponding BREAK as follows.

break on bcode skip page on report

LABEL keyword specifies the text to be displayed as label for the computed value. The maximum length of the label is 500 characters.

compute sum label 'Grand Total' of amount on report

NOTE: The label is truncated to the size of first column in the SELECT.

COMPUTE command in Script

The following compute command is used in the script to generate the report.

compute sum of amount on batch course report

It will display the sum of AMOUNT column at the end of each batch, course and at the end of report.

COLUMN Command

Specifies the display attributes of a column. The following are the possible options:

- Text for the column heading
- Alignment of the column heading
- Format of NUMBER type columns
- Wrapping of text

COL[UMN] [{column | expr} [option ...]]

The following is the list of a few commonly used options of COLUMN command.

FOR[MAT] format

HEA[DING] text

JUS[TIFY] {L[EFT] | C[ENTER] | C[ENTRE] | R[IGHT]}

NUL[L] char

WRA[PPED] | WOR[D_WRAPPED] | TRU[NCATED]

FORMAT

Specifies the display format of the column.

The **format** is a string containing format characters. Format characters depend on the data type of the column.

For **CHAR** type the only available format is :

A*n*

Where *n* is the number of locations used on the screen to display the value. You can specify what action you want to take, when *n* is less than the length of the data. The valid options are:

WRAPPED	Wraps the remaining string to next line.
WORD_WRAPPED	Same as WRAPPED but moves the entire word to next line.
TRUNCATED	Truncates the extra portion of the string.

To format DATE type column we have to use TO_CHAR function.

The following are the available options to format numeric columns.

Element	Example	Description
9	9999	Represents a digit.
0	0999	Displays leading zeroes.
$	$9999	Prefixes a dollar sign to a value.
B	B9999	Displays a zero value as blank.
MI	9999MI	Displays "-" after a negative value.
PR	9999PR	Displays a negative value in angle brackets.
comma	9,999	Displays a comma in the position indicated.
period	99.99	Aligns the decimal point in the position indicated.
V	999V99	Multiplies value by 10n, where n is the number of "9s" after the "V"
EEEE	9.999EEEE	Displays in scientific notation. There should be exactly EEEE.

Table 2: List of Formats for Numeric Data.

The following format will display FEE column in the given format.

column fee format 99,999.00

HEADING
Specifies the heading to be displayed. If no heading is given, the name of the column is displayed as heading.

If heading separator (|) is used then heading is split into multiple lines.

JUSTIFY is used to align heading either to LEFT, CENTER or RIGHT.

column ccode heading 'Course | Code' justify center

NULL

Substitutes null values with the given value in the display. If not given then null is displayed as blank.

COLUMN command may also be used to show display attributes of a particular column as follows:

SQL> column name

COLUMN   name ON

HEADING 'Student | Name ' headsep ' | '

JUSTIFY center

COLUMN command in script

The following COLUMN commands in the script are used to format columns.

column amount format 99,999

column name   format a20 heading 'Student Name'

column dj   heading 'Date of | Joining'

column dp   heading 'Date of | Payment'

AMOUNT column is formatted as 99,999.

NAME column is displayed with a width of 20 columns and heading is set to "Student Name".

DJ's heading is set to two lines heading where first line is "Date of" and second line is "Joining". The same is the case with DP column.

TTITLE and BTITLE Commands

TTITLE specifies the text to be displayed   at the top of each   printed page. BTITILE displays text at the bottom of the printed page.

TTI[TLE] [options [text]] [ON | OFF]

BTI[TLE] [options [text]] [ON | OFF]

The following is the list of options:

Option	Meaning
BOLD	Prints text in bold print.
COL n	Prints title after n columns in the current line.
ENTER	Aligns title to center.
LEFT	Aligns title to left.
RIGHT	Aligns title to right.
SKIP n	Skips n number of lines before printing

TTITLE center 'First line ' skip 1 center 'Second line'

Prints the text First Line in the first line and after skipping one line then displays text Second Line.

TTITLE left 'Payments Report' right sql.pno

Prints the text Payments Report on the left and current page number on the right. SQL.PNO returns the current page number. The other variables that you can use are: SQL.USER – current username, SQL.RELEASE – current Oracle release number.

TTITLE off

Will turn off display of top title.

TTITLE command in script

The following TTITLE command is used to display the top title for payments report.

ttitle skip 1 right 'Page:' format 99 sql.pno skip 1 center 'Payments Report' skip 2

First string "Page:" is displayed followed by the page number of the current page. These two are right justified to the page. Then one line is skipped and then at the center of the line title "Payments Report" is displayed. Then two lines are skipped before the data of the page is displayed.

SPOOL Command

Stores the result of query into an operating system file. It can be used to send the content of the file to printer.

Once spooling is turned on whatever that is displayed on the screen, a copy of that is copied into spool file.

SPO[OL]   [filename | OUT | OFF]

Filena me	Specifies the name of the file into which output is to be stored. It begins spooling.
OFF	Stops spooling.
OUT	Stops spooling and sends the contents of the spool file to default printer.

The following SPOOL command sends subsequent output to file REPORT.LST.

SPOOL report.lst

SPOOL command in the script

SPOOL command is used in the script to capture the output into file PAYREPORT.LST as follows.

296

spool payreport.lst

Then after the SELECT command SPOOL command is used again to stop capturing the output using:

spool off

CLEAR Command

Resets the current value of the specified option.

CLEAR option

Where **option** may be any of the following.

Option	What it clears?
BRE[AKS]	Break settings set by BREAK.
COMP[UTE S]	Compute setting set by COMPUTE.
SCR[EEN]	Content of SQL*PLUS window.
COL[UMNS]	Column setting set by COLUMN.
BUFF[ER]	Text in the current buffer.

The following CLEAR command will rest all summary information specified by COMPUTE.

CLEAR COMPUTES

SET Variables

Set variables/system variables are used to configure SQL*PLUS environment. For instance, system variables can be used to set page pause, the length of page, size of line and so on.

SET command is used to change the value of system variables.

SET system_variable value

The following is a list of a few system variables. For the complete list of system variables and all the possible options, please see on-line help.

Some of the system variables can store more than one value. For instance, FEEDBACK stores a number and ON/OFF state.

System variable	Meaning
AUTOCOMMIT	If set to ON, automatically commits changes made by SQL command.
FEEDBACK	If set to ON, displays the number of rows selected by SELECT, if number of rows is >= the number specified by FEEDBACK variable.
LINESIZE	Specifies the number of characters that can be displayed in a single line.
PAGESIZE	Specifies the number of lines to be displayed in a single page.
NUMFORMAT	Specifies the default numeric format for numbers.

PAUSE	If set to ON, gives pause at the end of each page. Also contains the text to be displayed when pause is issued.
SERVEROUTPUT	If set to ON, enables the display of output by DBMS_OUTPUT package.
TERMOUT	If set to OFF, suppresses the display of output of start file.

Table 3: SET Variables.

The following SET commands will configure SQL*Plus for report.

set pagesize 50

set linesize 132

set feedback off

set pause off

Displaying Information Using SHOW Command

You can display the current values of system variables and other options using SHOW command.

SHO[W] option

Where **option** may be any of the following.

Option	Meaning
System_variable	Any system variable.
ERR[ORS]	Compilation error of procedures, functions.
REL[EASE]	The current release of Oracle.

TTI[TLE] BTI[TLE]	and	Current setting of title.
USER		The name of the current user.
ALL		Displays the values of all show options.

For the complete list of options, please see on-line help.

To get the name of the current user, enter:

SQL> show user

user is "SRIKANTH"

To display the current value of PAGESIZE variable, enter:

SQL> show pagesize

pagesize 24

Summary

SQL*PLUS environment, apart from providing SQL commands, has its own set of commands called as SQL*PLUS commands. These commands are basically to generate report and to change the working environment.

Exercises

♦ _____ system variable is used to automatically commit changes made to database.

- Which command is used to change the heading of a column? _____.

- _____ is the numeric format to display number 12345 as 12,345.00.

- _____ command is used to display the values of system variables.

- Display the title 'Sales Report' at the top of each printed page by aligning it to center.

- Define the following attributes for column DESC. Heading should be ' Product Description'. Allow only first 20 characters to be displayed. Display 'NONE' if the value is null.

- _____ variable is used to display the name of the user in the title.

- _____ and _____ variables are used to set the dimension of the report page.

- What is the purpose of LABEL option of COMPUTE command?

- How do you turn off top title?

15. INTRODUCTION TO PL/SQL

301

- What is PL/SQL?

- PL/SQL engine

- Features of PL/SQL

- Advantages of PL/SQL

- PL/SQL Block

- Writing first PL/SQL block

- Nested blocks

- Scope and visibility of variables

- Labeling the block

- Assignment Operator

- Displaying output from PL/SQL

What is PL/SQL?

PL/SQL is Oracle's procedural language extension to SQL. PL/SQL allows you to mix SQL statements with procedural statements like IF statement, Looping structures etc. PL/SQL is the superset of SQL. It uses SQL for data retrieval and manipulation and uses its own statements for data processing.

PL/SQL program units are generally categorized as follows:

- Anonymous blocks

- Stored procedures

Anonymous block

This is a PL/SQL block that appears within your application. In many applications PL/SQL blocks can appear where SQL statements can appear. Such blocks are called as *Anonymous blocks*.

Stored Procedure

This is a PL/SQL block that is stored in the database with a name. Application programs can execute these procedures using the name. Oracle also allows you to create functions, which are same as procedures but return a value, and packages, which are a collection of procedures and functions.

PL/SQL Engine

Every PL/SQL block is first executed by PL/SQL engine. This is the engine that compiles and executes PL/SQL blocks. PL/SQL engine is available in Oracle Server and certain Oracle tools such as Oracle Forms and Oracle Reports.

PL/SQL engine executes all procedural statements of a PL/SQL of the block, but sends SQL command to **SQL statements executor** in the Oracle RDBMS. That means PL/SQL separates SQL commands from PL/SQL commands and executes PL/SQL commands using **Procedural statement executor**, which is a part of PL/SQL engine. See figure 1.

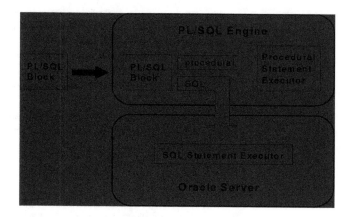

Figure 1: PL/SQL Engine.

Features of PL/SQL

The following are important features of PL/SQL.

Block structure

PL/SQL is a block-structured language. Each program written in PL/SQL is written as a block. Blocks can also be nested. Each block is meant for a particular task.

Variables and constants

PL/SQL allows you to declare variables and constants. Variables are used to store values temporarily. Variables and constants can be used in SQL and PL/SQL procedural statements just like an expression.

Control structures

PL/SQL allows control structures like IF statement, FOR loop, WHILE loop to be used in the block. Control structures are most important extension to SQL in PL/SQL. Control structures allow any data process possible in PL/SQL.

Exception handling

PL/SQL allows errors, called as exceptions, to be detected and handled. Whenever there is a predefined error PL/SQL raises an exception automatically. These exceptions can be handled to recover from errors.

Modularity

PL/SQL allows process to be divided into different modules. Subprograms called as procedures and functions can be defined and invoked using the name. These subprograms can also take parameters.

Cursors

A cursor is a private SQL area used to execute SQL statements and store processing information. PL/SQL implicitly uses cursors for all DML commands and SELECT command that returns only one row. And it also allows you to define explicit cursor to deal with multiple row queries.

Built-in functions

Most of the SQL functions that we have seen so far in SQL are available in PL/SQL. These functions can be used to manipulate variables of PL/SQL.

Advantages Of PL/SQL

The following are a few important advantages of PL/SQL. Moreover most of the features listed above are also advantages of PL/SQL.

Support for SQL

PL/SQL allows you to use SQL commands, function and operators. PL/SQL supports data types of SQL.

PL/SQL also allows SQL statements to be constructed and executed on the fly. The process of creating SQL statements on the fly is called as **Dynamic SQL**. This is different from writing SQL commands at the time of writing the program, which is called as **Static SQL**.

Starting from Oracle8i, PL/SQL support native dynamic SQL, which makes programming Dynamic SQL easier than its predecessor, where we used DBMS_SQL package.

We will see more about Dynamic SQL in later chapter.

Better performance

PL/SQL block is sent as one unit to Oracle server. Without PL/SQL each SQL command is to be passed to Oracle server, which will increase network traffic heavily. As a collection of SQL statements is passed as a block to Oracle server, it improves performance.

Portability

Applications written in PL/SQL are portable to any platform on which Oracle runs. Once you write a program in PL/SQL, it can be used in any environment without any change at all.

PL/SQL block

PL/SQL programs are written as blocks. Block allows you to group logically related statements and declarations. PL/SQL block is consisting of the following three parts:

- Declarative part
- Executable part
- Exception-handling part

The following is the syntax of PL/SQL block.

[DECLARE

    declaration of variable

    declaration of cursor

    declaration of exception]

BEGIN

executable commands

[EXCEPTION

exception handlers]

END;

Declarative Part

This is the area of the block where variables, cursors etc are declared. All variables used in the block are to be declared in declarative part.

The following is the example of declarative part. First variable is of type NUMBER(5). As we have seen before PL/SQL supports the data types of SQL. The second variable is initialized to 0.

declare

v_rollno number(5);

v_count number(2) := 0;

v_name students.name%type;

done boolean := FALSE;

Variable V_NAME is declared as of type STUDENTS.NAME column. Attribute %TYPE takes whatever is the data type of NAME column of STUDENTS table and uses the same data type to declare V_NAME variable.

Note: If the name of a variable and the name of a column are same then Oracle assumes that the column is being referenced whenever the name is used in SQL commands. That means columns names takes precedence over variable name in SQL statements.

Declarative block can also be used to declare CURSORS and EXCEPTIONS. But, I feel they are going to be heavy for now so we will defer their discussion until later chapters.

PL/SQL Datatypes

PL/SQL provides a variety of predefined datatypes, which can be divided into four categories:

Scalar   Represents a single value.

Composite Is a collection of components

Reference Is a pointer that points to another item.

LOB   Holds a lob locator.

The following are the datatypes in various categories

Scalar	NUMBER, CHAR, VARCHAR2, DATE, BOOLEAN

Composite	RECORD, TABLE and VARRAY.
Reference	REF CURSOR, REF Object_type
LOB	BFILE, BLOB, CLOB, and NCLOB.

Note: There may be minor differences between PL/SQL datatypes and SQL datatypes though they have the same name. For complete information about datatypes in PL/SQL please see PL/SQL User's guide and Reference.

Executable part

Is the area where we write SQL and PL/SQL commands that are to be executed. This is the only mandatory part of the entire block.

Exception-handling part

Is the place where we handle exceptions (errors) that are raised in executable part. Exception handlers handle exceptions. We will discuss more about this in later chapter.

Writing first PL/SQL block

The best way to get accustomed to PL/SQL is by writing a few blocks. Let us write our first PL/SQL block. PL/SQL block used here is more to highlight the syntax of a PL/SQL block rather than to show what you can do with PL/SQL block that you cannot do with SQL.

declare

    v_rollno students.rollno%type;

```
begin

    -- get roll number of the students who joined most recently

    select max(rollno) into  v_rollno
    from students;

    -- insert a new row into payments table

    insert into payments values (v_rollno,sysdate,1000);

    -- commit transaction

    commit;

end;
/
```

Follow the procedure given below to create and run the above block.

◆ Type the above program in a text editor such as Notepad and save it in a text file. Assume the file is saved under the name INSPAY.SQL. And be sure to know the directory where the file is saved.

Note: Enclose filename in double quotes at the time of giving file name in Notepad, otherwise Notepad will add the extension .TXT to the file.

- Get into SQL*PLUS. Start it and logon if you have not already logged on.
- Use START command to execute the program that is in the file INSPAY.SQL.

SQL> start c:\orabook\inspay.sql

PL/SQL procedure successfully completed.

If the block is successfully executed then PL/SQL displays the above message. If there are any errors during the execution then you have to correct the program, save the program and rerun it until you succeed.

Comments in PL/SQL

You can give comments in PL/SQL block in two ways.

First way is by preceding the comment with two hyphens (- -).

Example: -- this is single line comment

Second way is by starting the comment with /* and ending it with */.

Example: /* this comment can be of multiple lines */

SELECT... INTO

SQL*Plus displays the data retrieved by SELECT command. Whereas in PL/SQL SELECT command is used only to retrieve the data and storing and using data is to be done explicitly. So Oracle provided INTO clause with SELECT command that is used to specify the variable(s) into which the value(s) retrieved must be copied.

The following example copies the total amount paid by student with roll number 102 to variable V_SUM, which is declared as NUMBER(5) data type.

```
declare
    v_sum number(5);
    v_fee courses.fee%type;
    v_dur courses.duration%type;
begin
    select  sum(amount) into v_sum
    from payments
    where rollno = 102;


    -- take fee and duration of Ora course


    select fee, duration into v_fee, v_duration
    from    courses
    where  ccode = 'ora';


    . . .


end;
```

The number of variables and data types given after INTO clause must match the number of columns in SELECT and their data types. In the second example, SELECT selects two columns (fee, duration) so INTO clause must have two variables (v_fee, f_duration).

Declaring Constants

Constant is a PL/SQL variable whose value doesn't change. Any attempt to change the value of a constant will result in error.

variable CONSTANT datatype [precision , scale] := expression;

The following declarative statement creates a constant that takes value 500.

bonus constant number(3) := 500;

Nesting Blocks

It is possible to define a block within another block. When blocks are defined one within another they are said to be nested.

The following is an example of nested block. Main block contains a single variable X and nested block contains a single variable Y.

declare

   x number(5);

begin

   -- put executable code of main block here

```
declare      /* beginning of nested block */
   y number(3);
begin
      -- put executable code of  nested block
exception
      -- exception handing  for  nested block
end;


   -- code of main block continues.


Exception
      -- exception handling for main block
end;
```

Scope and visibility of variables

Scope of the variable refers to the region of the program in which the variable can be used. A variable is said to be *visible* when it can be referred without any qualifier.

Examine the following examples to understand scope and visibility of variables.

Example 1:

```
Declare
    num1    number(5);                              ┐
Begin                                               │
                                                    │
    Declare                                         │  Scope of
        num2  number(5);  ┐                         │  Variable NUM1
    Begin                 │  Scope of               │
        ...               │  Variable NUM2          │
    End;                  ┘                         │
                                                    ┘
End;
```

Variable NUM1 can be accessed from the point of declaration to the end of the
outer block.

Variable NUM2 can be accessed from the point of declaration to the end of
inner block.

Example2:

The following example will illustrate the difference between scope and visibility.

```
Declare
    n    number(5);        ┐
Begin                      │
                           │   n  is visible
                           │
                           ┘
    Declare
        n   number(5);     ┐   variable n  declared in main block is
    Begin                  │   not visible because the sub block has
        ...                │   declared a variable with the same name.
    End;                   ┘
                           ┐   n  is visible.
End;                       ┘
```

Variable N has scope throughout the outer block, but it is not visible in the inner block as we declared another variable (N) with the same name as the variable in outer block (N). So variable N that is declared in outer block is not visible in inner block instead N that is declared in the inner block is accessed from inner block.

It is possible to access variable N that is declared in the outer block although it is hidden by using label of the outer block.

Labeling the block

A label can be used to name a block. Label is placed within << and >> just before the beginning of the block.

The following example shows how to assign a label to a block.

<<mainblock>>

declare

   ...

Begin

   ...

end;

Label of the block can be used to access hidden objects of the block. For instance, in the previous section, we have seen two blocks declaring a variable with the same name (N), and variable N of the main block is invisible and inaccessible throughout the second block.

To access the hidden variable of main block from inner block, main block may be given a label and the label may be used to refer to hidden objects from inner block as shown below:

```
<<mainblock>>

Declare
   n number(5);
Begin

   <<nestedblock>>
   Declare
      n number(5);
   Begin
         ...


      n := 20;  -- stores  20 into N of nested block.


      /* The following stores 50 into N of main block */


      mainblock.n := 50;


   End;


End;
```

In order to access a hidden variable, we have to prefix the variable with the name of the block. In the above example to access variable N that is declared in main block but hidden in the inner block as another variable is declared with the same name, we use MAINBLOCK.N, where MAINBLOCK is the label given to the block and N is the name of the variable that we want to access.

Assignment Operator (:=)

Assignment operator allows a value to be stored in a variable.

variable := expression;

The following are examples of assignment operator:

count := 1;

name := 'Srikanth';

hra := bs * 0.05;

surname := substr('P.Srikanth',1,3);

In expression you can use the following arithmetic operators.

Operator	What it does?
+	Addition
-	Subtraction
/	Division
*	Multiplication
**	Exponentiation

Available functions

Most of the functions available in SQL are also available in PL/SQL.

The functions that are NOT available in procedural statements are:

- ◻ DECODE
- ◻ AVG, COUNT, GROUPING, MIN, MAX, SUM, STDDEV, and VARIANCE

However, these functions can be used with SQL commands and those SQL commands may be used in PL/SQL.

Another PL/SQL block

The following is a PL/SQL block to change the course fee of VBNET course with the greatest of average course fee of all courses and Oracle course fee.

```
declare
    v_avgfee courses.fee%type;
    v_orafee courses.fee%type;

begin

    -- get average fee of all courses

    select  avg(fee) into v_avgfee
    from  courses;
```

```
-- get fee of Oracle

select  fee into v_orafee
from  courses
where  ccode = 'ora';

-- update VB fee with the greatest of these two

update courses set fee = greatest( v_avgfee, v_orafee)
where  ccode = 'vbnet';

-- commit changes

commit;

end;
/
```

Displaying output from PL/SQL

In order to display output from a PL/SQL block, we have to use
DBMS_OUTPUT package.   A package is a collection of procedures and
functions. We will see more about package in later chapter.

DBMS_OUTPUT is a package that comes along with Oracle database and used to display data onto screen from a PL/SQL block. The following are the procedures available in DBMS_OUTPUT package.

PUT and PUT_LINE procedures

Both these procedures are used to display a NUMBER, VARCHAR2 or DATE type value. PUT allows you to put multiple pieces that make up a line. PUT_LINE puts the given data followed by end-of-line character.

In order to see the output sent using these procedures, the following must satisfy:

- The program unit from where they are called must be completed
- **SERVEROUPUT** variable of SQL*PLUS must be set to ON.

Note: You must set SERVEROUPUT variable on (shown below) in SQL*PLUS before you run this PL/SQL program. This is to be done in each new session of SQL*PLUS.

.

SQL> SET SERVEROUPUT ON

The following program is used to display the difference between average duration of Oracle batches and the duration of Oracle course.

321

```
declare

    v_amtcltd  number(6);

    v_totamt   number(6);

    v_orafee   courses.fee%type;

    v_studcnt  number(3);

    v_diff     number(6);

begin


    -- get total amount collected from Oracle students


    select  sum(amount) into v_amtcltd

    from payments

    where rollno in

        ( select rollno from students

          where  bcode in

          (

            select bcode

            from  batches

            where ccode = 'ora'

          )

        );
```

-- get total amount to be collected from Oracle students

-- first get course fee of Oracle

```
select  fee into v_orafee
from  courses
where ccode = 'ora';
```

-- get no. of students in Oracle batches

```
select count(*) into v_studcnt
from  students
where  bcode in
   (
      select bcode from batches
      where  ccode  = 'ora'
   );
```


```
/* calculate difference between total amount to be collection
      and the amount colleted so far */
```

```
v_diff := v_orafee * v_studcnt - v_amtcltd;
```

dbms_output.put_line('Oracle arrears : ' || v_diff);

end;

/

The following are the important steps in the above program:

❖ Getting total amount collected from Oracle students. This can be done by taking rows related to payments of Oracle students.

❖ Finding out the number of Oracle students.

❖ Finding out the course fee for Oracle.

❖ Then multiplying the number of Oracle students with Oracle course fee. This will yield the total amount to be collected from Oracle students.

❖ Subtract total amount collected from the figure obtained from previous step to get total amount yet to be paid by Oracle students. Display this value.

Summary

In this chapter, we have seen what is PL/SQL, its features, and advantages. PL/SQL Engine is the component of Oracle that executes PL/SQL blocks. PL/SQL programs are written as PL/SQL blocks where each block contains Declarative Part, Executable Part, and Exception Handler part.

PL/SQL allows programmers to retrieve the data from database using SQL and then process the data with its conditional statements and looping structures. PL/SQL is a superset of SQL.

Exercises

❖ In _____ part of PL/SQL block errors are handled.

❖ ___, ___ and ___ are the valid values for BOOLEAN data type.

❖ The part of Oracle Server that executes SQL commands is called as _____.

❖ _____ is an example of Oracle tool that contains PL/SQL engine.

❖ _____ is the operator for exponentiation.

❖ _____ is used for commenting a single line.

❖ Write PL/SQL block to change the DURATION of courses C++ to the duration of Java course.

❖ Insert a new row into COURSE_FACULTY table with the following details:

❖ Course name is Oracle8i, Faculty name is Kevin Loney, and grade is B.

16. CONTROL STRUCTURES

❏ IF statement

❏ Loop...End Loop

❏ Exit command

❏ While Loop

❏ For loop

❏ Goto statement

IF statement

IF statement is used to check the condition and execute statements depending upon the result of the condition.

The following is the syntax of IF statement.

IF condition-1 THEN

    statements_set_1;

[ELSIF condition-2 THEN

    statements_set_2;] ...
[ELSE

    statements_set_3;]

END IF;

Condition is formed using relational operators listed in table 1.

Operator	Meaning
>	Greater than
>=	Greater than or equal to
<	Less than
<=	Less than or equal to
=	Equal to

<>, !=, ~=, ^=	Not equal to
LIKE	Returns true if the character pattern matches the given value.
BETWEEN..AND	Returns true if the value is in the given range.
IN	Returns true if the value is in the list.
IS NULL	Return true if the value is NULL.

Table 1: Relational Operators.

In order to combine two conditions, logical operators – AND and OR are used. When two conditions are combined with AND then both the conditions must be true to make the entire condition true. If conditions are combined with OR then if any one condition is true then the entire condition will be true.

The following are valid conditions:

If amt > 5000 then

If rate > 500 and qty < 10 then

If rate between 100 and 200 then

Now, let us write a simple PL/SQL block that uses IF statement.

The following program will increase the course fee of Oracle by 10% if more than 100 students have joined for Oracle, otherwise it will decrease the course fee by 10%.

declare

327

```
   v_ns  number(5);
begin

   -- get no. of students of the course

   select  count(*) into v_ns
   from students
   where  bcode in ( select bcode from  batches
              where  ccode = 'ora');

   if  v_ns > 100 then
        update courses set fee = fee * 1.1
        where  ccode = 'ora';
   else
        update courses set fee = fee * 0.9
        where  ccode = 'ora';
   end if;

   commit;

end;
/
```

The above block uses IF statement to check whether the variable V_NS is greater than 100. If the condition is satisfied it will increase the course fee by 10% otherwise it will decrease the course fee by 10%.

The above program will either increase the course fee by 10% or decrease it by 10%.

That means it will take either of two possible actions. But in some cases we may have more than two actions. For instance, what if we have to change the course fee as follows based on the number of students joined in Oracle course:

No. of Students Percentage of change

No. of Students	Percentage of change
>100	Increase by 20
>50	Increase by 15
>10	Increase by 5
<=10	Decrease by 10

The following program will change course fee of Oracle according to the above table.

```
declare

  v_ns  number(5);

  v_fee courses.fee%type;


begin


  -- get no. of students of the course


  select  count(*) into v_ns
```

```
from students
where  bcode in ( select bcode from  batches
            where  ccode = 'ora');

select fee into v_fee
from   courses
where  ccode = 'ora';

if  v_ns > 100 then
      v_fee := v_fee * 1.2;  -- 20%
elsif  v_ns > 50 then
      v_fee := v_fee * 1.15;  -- 15%
elsif  v_ns > 10 then
      v_fee := v_fee * 1.15;  -- 15%
else
      v_fee := v_fee * 0.90;  -- 10% decrease

end if;

-- update fee in table

update courses set fee = v_fee
where  ccode = 'ora';
```

end;

/

The above program first checks whether the number of students is more than 100. If so, it increases course fee by 20%. If the first condition is not satisfied then it checks whether second condition is true ($v\_no > 50$) and if so it executes the statement after that ELSIF.

The IF statement will be terminated once a condition is true and the corresponding statements are executed.

If none of the conditions is true then it executes statements given after ELSE.

Every IF must have a matching END IF. However, ELSIF that is used to check for a condition need not have corresponding END IF. Also note that ELSIF can be used only after an IF is used.

Apart from checking condition and executing statements depending on the result of the condition, PL/SQL also allows you to repeatedly execute a set of statements. Repeatedly executing a set of statements is called as looping structure.

In the next few sections we will discuss about looping structures.

LOOP

This is used to repeatedly execute a set of statements. This is the simplest form of looping structures.

LOOP

    Statements;

END LOOP;

Note: Loop... End Loop has no termination point. So unless you terminate loop using EXIT command (discussed next) it becomes an infinite loop.

Statements are the statements that are to be repeatedly executed. In case of LOOP, these statements must make sure they exit the loop at one point or other. Otherwise the statements will be executed indefinitely.

EXIT

This is used to exit out of a Loop. This is mainly used with LOOP statement, as there is no other way of terminating the LOOP.

The following is the syntax of EXIT command.

EXIT [WHEN condition];

If EXIT is used alone, it will terminate the current loop as and when it is executed.

If EXIT is used with WHEN clause, then the current loop is terminated only when the *condition* given after WHEN is satisfied.

The following examples show how you can use EXIT and EXIT WHEN to exit a Loop.

Example 1:

```
LOOP
    ...

    IF count > 10 THEN
        EXIT;    -- terminates loop
    END IF;

    ...

END  LOOP;
```

Example 2:

```
LOOP
    ...

    EXIT WHEN count >10; -- terminates loop

    ...

END LOOP;
```

The following program will display numbers 1 to 10 using LOOP.

```
declare

    i number(2) := 1;

begin

    loop

        dbms_output.put_line(i);

        i := i + 1;

        exit when i > 10;

    end loop;

end;
/
```

In the above program, we first initialized variable **I** to 1. Then LOOP starts and displays the value of **I** on the screen. Then **I** is incremented by one. EXIT statement checks whether **I** is greater than 10. If the condition is true then EXIT is executed and LOOP is terminated otherwise it enters into loop again and redisplays the value of **I**.

Nested Loops

It is possible to have a loop within another loop. When a loop is placed within another loop it is called as nested loop. The inner loop is executed for each iteration of outer loop.

The following example will display table up to 10 for numbers from 1 to 5.

334

```
declare

    i number(2);
    j number(2);

begin

    i := 1;

    loop

        j:= 1;

        loop

            dbms_output.put_line(i || '*' || j || '=' || i * j);
            j := j + 1;
            exit when j > 10;

        end loop;

        i := i + 1;

        exit when i > 5;
```

end loop;

end;

/

It is possible to exit current loop using EXIT statement. It is also possible to use EXIT statement to exit any enclosing loop. This is achieved using **loop label**.

A loop label is a label that is assigned to a loop. By using this label that is assigned to a loop, EXIT can exit a specific loop instead of the current loop.

The following example uses EXIT to exit the outer loop.

```
<<outerloop>>
LOOP

   ...

   LOOP

      ...

      EXIT outerloop WHEN ...  – exits outer loop


   END LOOP;
```

...

END LOOP;

EXIT statement uses label to specify which enclosing loop is to be terminated. EXIT uses *outerloop*, which is the label given to outer loop, to terminate outer loop.

WHILE

Executes a series of statements as long as the given condition is true.

WHILE condition LOOP

    Statements;

END LOOP;

As long as the *condition* is true then statements will be repeatedly executed. Once the condition is false then loop is terminated.

The following example will display numbers from 1 to 10.

declare

   i number(2) := 1;

begin

   while i <= 10

```
loop

    dbms_output.put_line(i);

     i := i + 1;

    end loop;


end;

/
```

As long as the condition (I<=10) is true statements given within LOOP and END
LOOP are executed repeatedly.

The condition is checked at the beginning of iteration. Statements are executed
only when the condition is true otherwise loop is terminated.

FOR

This looping structure is best suited to cases where we have to repeatedly
execute a set of statements by varying a variable from one value to another.

FOR counter IN [REVERSE] lowerrange .. upperrange   LOOP

        Statements;

END LOOP;

lowerrange and   *upperrange* may also be expressions.

FOR loop sets *counter* to lower range and checks whether it is greater than
upper range. If *counter* is less than or equal to upper range then statements
given between LOOP and END LOOP will be executed. At the end of execution

of statements, counter will be incremented by one and the same process will repeat.

The following is the sequence of steps in FOR LOOP.

Steps

The following is the sequence in which FOR will take the steps.

- Counter is set to lowerrange.
- If counter is less than or equal to upperrange then statements are executed otherwise loop is terminated.
- Counter is incremented by one and only one. It is not possible to increment counter by more than one.
- Repeats step2.

The following example will display numbers from 1 to 10.

```
begin

    for i in 1..10
    loop
        dbms_output.put_line(i);
    end loop;

end;
/
```

If REVERSE option is used the following steps will take place:

❖ Counter is set to upper range.

❖ If counter is greater than or equal to lower range then statements are executed otherwise loop is terminated.

❖ Counter is decremented by one.

❖ Go to step 2.

The following FOR loop uses REVERSE option to display number from 10 to 1.

begin

```
    for i in REVERSE 1..10
    loop
        dbms_output.put_line(i);
    end loop;

end;
/
```

Note: It is not possible to change the step value for FOR loop.

Sample program using FOR loop

The following example will display the missing roll numbers. The program starts at lowest available roll number and goes up to largest roll number. It will display the roll numbers that are within in the range and not in the STUDENTS table.

```
declare

    v_minrollno  students.rollno%type;
    v_maxrollno  students.rollno%type;
    v_count      number(2);

begin

  -- get min and max roll numbers

  select  min(rollno) , max(rollno) into  v_minrollno, v_maxrollno
  from  students;

  for i  in v_minrollno .. v_maxrollno
  loop

      select count(*) into v_count
      from students
      where rollno = i;

      -- display roll number if count is 0
      if  v_count = 0 then
          dbms_output.put_line(i);
      end if;
```

```
  end loop;


end;

/
```

The above program takes minimum and maximum roll numbers using MIN and MAX functions. Then it sets a loop that starts at minimum roll number and goes up to maximum roll number. In each iteration it checks whether there is any student with the current roll number (represented by variable i). If no row is found then COUNT (*) will be 0. So it displays the roll number if count is zero.

GOTO statement

Transfers control to the named label. The label must be unique and should precede an executable PL/SQL statement or PL/SQL block.

The following example shows how to create label and how to transfer control to the label using GOTO statement.

```
BEGIN


        ...

        GOTO   change_details;

        ...


        <<change_details>>
```

update students ... ;

END;

GOTO statement transfers control to UPDATE statement that is given after the label *change_details*

Label is created by enclosing a name within two sets of angle brackets (<< >>). The label must be given either before an executable PL/SQL statement or a block.

Restrictions

The following are the restrictions on the usage of GOTO statement.

❑ Cannot branch into an IF statement

❑ Cannot branch into a LOOP

❑ Cannot branch into a Sub block.

❑ Cannot branch out of a subprogram – a procedure or function.

❑ Cannot branch from exception handler into current block.

❑

The following is an **invalid** usage of GOTO statement as it tries to enter into an IF block:

BEGIN

   ...

    /* following is invalid because GOTO can not

     branch into an IF statement */

```
    GOTO change_details;

    ...

    IF  condition  THEN

        ...

        <<change_details>>

        update  students  ... ;

        ...

    END IF;

END;
```

Summary

Any programming language has basic control structures like IF statement, looping structures etc. These control structures are an important part of PL/SQL, because they allow data processing. In this chapter, we have covered basic control structure, but the practical usage of these control constructs will be better understood as you write more programs.

Exercises

- ❖ Write a PL/SQL block to decrease the duration of the course C++ if more than 2 batches have started in the last two months.
- ❖ Write a PL/SQL block to insert a new row into PAYMENTS table with the following data:
- ❖ Roll number is the number of student with the name *George Micheal.*
- ❖ Date of payment is previous Monday.
- ❖ Amount is the balance amount to be paid by the student.

❖ Display how many students have joined in each month in the current year.

17. EXCEPTION HANDLING

- ❑ What is an exception?
- ❑ How to handle exceptions?
- ❑ Predefined exceptions
- ❑ When NO_DATA_FOUND exception is not raised?
- ❑ User-defined exception
- ❑ Reraising an exception
- ❑ Associating an exception With An Oracle Error

- Exception propagation
- When is a PL/SQL block successful or failure?

What is an Exception?

In PL/SQL, errors and warnings are called as *exceptions.* Whenever a predefined error occurs in the program, PL/SQL raises an exception. For example, if you try to divide a number by zero then PL/SQL raises an exception called ZERO_DIVIDE and if SELECT can not find a record then PL/SQL raises exception NO_DATA_FOUND.

PL/SQL has a collection of predefined exceptions. Each exception has a name. These exceptions are automatically raised by PL/SQL whenever the corresponding error occurs.

In addition to PL/SQL predefined exceptions, user can also create his own exceptions to deal with errors in the applications. Understanding how to handle exception raised by PL/SQL is as important as understanding how to write code to achieve task. Because exception handling is an important part of any application and application is not complete without exception handling.

How to handle exceptions?

When PL/SQL raises a predefined exception, the program is aborted by displaying error message. But if program is to handle exception raised by PL/SQL then we have to use *Exception Handling* part of the block.

Exception handling part is used to specify the statements to be executed when an exception occurs. Control is transferred to exception handling part whenever an exception occurs. After the exception handler is executed, control is transferred to next statement in the enclosing block. If there is no enclosing block then control returns to Host (from where you ran the PL/SQL block).

The following is the syntax of exception handling part.

WHEN exception-1 [or exception -2] ...   THEN

     statements;

[WHEN exception-3 [or exception-4] ... THEN

     statements;] ...

[WHEN OTHERS THEN

     statements;]

exception-1, exception-2 are exceptions that are to be handled. These exceptions are either pre-defined exceptions or user-defined exceptions.

The following example handles NO_DATA_FOUND exception. If SELECT statement doesn't retrieve any row then PL/SQL raises NO_DATA_FOUND exception, which is handled in exception handling part.

declare

    ...

begin

    select ...

exception

347

```
        when no_data_found then

            statements;

end;
```

When two or more exceptions are given with a single WHEN then the statements are executed whenever any of the specified exceptions occur.

The following exception handling part takes the same action when either NO_DATA_FOUND or TOO_MANY_ROWS exceptions occur.

```
declare

    ...

begin

    select ...


exception

    when no_data_found or too_many_rows then

        statements;

end;
```

The following snippet handles these two exceptions in different ways.

```
declare

    ...

begin
```

```
    select ...

exception

    when no_data_found then

        statements;

    when too_many_rows then

        statements;

end;
```

WHEN OTHERS is used to execute statements when an exception other than what are mentioned in exception handler has occurred.

Note: If an exception is raised but not handled by exception handling part then PL/SQL block is terminated by displaying an error message related to the exception.

Sample Programs

The following is an example of exception handler. This program assigns course fee of "C" to course "C++". If course "C" does not exist then it sets course fee of "C++" to average fee of all courses.

```
declare

    v_fee courses.fee%type;

begin

    select fee into v_fee
```

```
from  courses

where ccode  = 'c';


update courses

 set fee = v_fee

where  ccode='c++';


exception

 when no_data_found then

    update courses

     set fee = ( select avg(fee) from courses)

    where ccode = 'c++';

end;

/
```

If SELECT cannot find a row course code "c" then it raises NO_DATA_FOUND exception. When exception is raised, control is transferred to exception handling part and course fee of "c++" is set to average course fee of all courses. If course code "c" is found then it sets the course fee of course "c++" to the course fee of "c".

Getting information about error - SQLCODE and SQLERRM

In WHEN OTHERS section of exception handler, you can use SQLCODE and SQLERRM functions to get the error number and error message respectively. As there is no predefined exception for each of Oracle errors, you will not get a particular exception for most of the errors. However, it is possible to know the error code and error message of the most recently occurred error using these two functions. This is one way of knowing which Oracle error has exactly occurred. The other method is associating an exception with an Oracle error. Please see "Associating an exception with Oracle error" section for details.

The following example demonstrates how to use SQLCODE and SQLERRM.

```
declare
    newccode varchar2(5) := null;
begin
    update courses
       set ccode = newccode
    where  ccode = 'c';
exception
    when dup_val_on_index then
        dbms_output.put_line('Duplicate course code');
    when others then
        dbms_output.put_line( sqlerrm);
end;
```

If you run the above program, the following output will be generated.

ORA-01407: cannot update ("BOOK"."COURSES"."CCODE") to NULL

PL/SQL procedure successfully completed.

The above output is generated by WHEN OTHERS part of exception handling part. SQLERRMS returns the error message of the most recent error. As we are trying to set CCODE, which is a not null column to NULL value, PL/SQL raises an exception. But as the error (-01407) is not associated with any predefined exception, WHEN OTHERS part of exception handling part is executed.

Note: You cannot use SQLCODE or SQLERRM directly in a SQL statement. Instead, you must assign their values to variables then use the variables in the SQL statement.

Predefined exceptions

PL/SQL has defined certain common errors and given names to these errors, which are called as *predefined exceptions*.   Each exception has a corresponding Oracle error code.

The following is the list of predefined exceptions and the corresponding Oracle error code.

Exception	Oracle Error	SQLCODE Value
ACCESS_INTO_NULL	ORA-06530	-6530
COLLECTION_IS_NULL	ORA-06531	-6531
CURSOR_ALREADY_OPEN	ORA-06511	-6511
DUP_VAL_ON_INDEX	ORA-00001	-1
INVALID_CURSOR	ORA-01001	-1001
INVALID_NUMBER	ORA-01722	-1722
LOGIN_DENIED	ORA-01017	-1017
NO_DATA_FOUND	ORA-01403	+100
NOT_LOGGED_ON	ORA-01012	-1012
PROGRAM_ERROR	ORA-06501	-6501
ROWTYPE_MISMATCH	ORA-06504	-6504
SELF_IS_NULL	ORA-30625	-30625
STORAGE_ERROR	ORA-06500	-6500
SUBSCRIPT_BEYOND_COUNT	ORA-06533	-6533
SUBSCRIPT_OUTSIDE_LIMIT	ORA-06532	-6532
SYS_INVALID_ROWID	ORA-01410	-1410
TIMEOUT_ON_RESOURCE	ORA-00051	-51
TOO_MANY_ROWS	ORA-01422	-1422
VALUE_ERROR	ORA-06502	-6502
ZERO_DIVIDE	ORA-01476	-1476

Table 1: Predefined Exceptions

The following is the description of some of the pre-defined exceptions.

CURSOR_ALREADY_OPEN	Raised if you try to open an already open cursor.
DUP_VAL_ON_INDEX	Raised if you try to store duplicate values in a database column that is constrained by a unique index.
INVALID_CURSOR	Raised if you try an illegal cursor operation.
INVALID_NUMBER	Raised in an SQL statement if the conversion of a character string to a number fails because the string does not represent a valid number.
NO_DATA_FOUND	Raised if a SELECT INTO statement returns no rows or if you reference an un-initialized row in a PL/SQL table.
	See the section "When NO_DATA_FOUND is not raised?".
SUBSCRIPT_BEYOND_COUNT	Raised when the program references a nested table or varray element using an index number larger than the number of elements in the collection.
TOO_MANY_ROWS	Raised if a SELECT INTO statement returns more than one row.
VALUE_ERROR	Raised if an arithmetic, conversion, truncation, or size–constraint error occurs.
ZERO_DIVIDE	Raised when your program attempts to

divide a number by zero.

When NO_DATA_FOUND exception is not raised?

As NO_DATA_FOUND exception is most commonly used exception, let us have a close look at this exception. We have so far understood that NO_DATA_FOUND exception is raised by PL/SQL whenever SELECT command doesn't retrieve any rows.

In the following cases NO_DATA_FOUND exception is not raised by PL/SQL even though no row is retrieved or effected:

- When a group function is used in the SELECT statement.
- When UPDATE and DELETE commands are used.

When SELECT command uses any group function then NO_DATA_FOUND exception will be not be raised by PL/SQL although no row is retrieved. For example, if SUM function is used in SELECT no record is retrieved by the SELECT command then SUM function returns NULL value but doesn't raise NO_DATA_FOUND exception. Please see examples given below.

Note: When COUNT function is used in SELECT and no row is retrieved then COUNT function returns 0 and not NULL value.

The following example is used to display the average duration of C++ batches. If no C++ batch has been completed then it displays a message. Since AVG function returns NULL when no row is retrieved by SELECT, we check the return value of AVG and display error message if it is NULL.

declare

    v_avgdur number(3);

```
begin
        -- get average duration of C++ batches

        select avg( enddate - stdate) into v_avgdur

        from  batches

        where enddate is not null and ccode = 'c++';


        /* display error if AVG return null */


        if  v_avgdur is null then

          dbms_output.put_line ('No batch of C++ has been completed');

        else

          dbms_output.put_line ('Average duration of C++ :' || v_avgdur);

        end if;

end;
/
```

We will understand how to detect whether UPDATE or DELETE command has affected any row in the table, in the next chapter.

User-defined exception

PL/SQL allows you to create exceptions of your own. These exceptions are available to the block in which they are created. Unlike a predefined exception, which is predefined and automatically raised whenever the corresponding error occurs, a user-defined error has the following steps.

Declaring userdefined exception

A userdefined exception is to be declared in the declare section of the block. The following is the syntax to declare an exception.

exception-name exception;

exception-name is the name of the exception to be created.

The following example declare an exception classed OUT_OF_STOCK.

declare

out_of_stock   exception;

begin

statements;

end;

Raising userdefined exception using RAISE command

Unlike predefined exceptions, userdefined exception is to be raised explicitly using RAISE command.

RAISE exception-name;

We have to decide when the user-defined exception has to be raised. For example, if you want to raise OUT_OF_STOCK exception when value of variable QTY is less then 10, give the following:

if qty < 10 then

        raise out_of_stock;

    end if;

Once a userdefined exception is raised using RAISE command, it is to be handled just like a predefined exception. So handling exception OUT_OF_STOCK is no way different from what we have seen so far.

The following PL/SQL block will declare, raise and handle a user-defined exception.

declare

    out_of_stock   exception;   -- declare exception
begin

    if condition then

        raise out_of_stock;   -- raise userdefined exception

    end if;

exception

    when out_of_stock then -- handle userdefined exception

    . . .

end;

Reraising an exception

RAISE command can also be used to reraise an exception so that the current exception is propagated to outer block. If a sub block executes RAISE statement without giving exception name in exception handler then the current exception is raised again.

The following example will illustrate the process of re-raising an exception.

```
declare
    out_of_stock exception;
begin
    ...
    begin  ---------- sub-block (inner block) begins
        ...
        if ... then
            raise out_of_stock;  -- raise the exception
        end if;
        .
        .
    exception
        when out_of_stock then
            -- handle the error in the sub block
            raise;  -- reraise the current exception, which is out_of_stock
        ...
    end;  ------------ sub-block ends
```

exception

when out_of_stock then

-- handle the exception (that is reraised) in outer block

...

end;

Note: RAISE statement without exception name is valid only in exception handler.

Associating an exception With An Oracle Error

It is possible to connect a userdefined exception with an Oracle error number so that whenever the Oracle error occurs then the user-defined exception will be raised by PL/SQL automatically.

The following example associates exception NULL_VALUE_ERROR with error number –1407, which occurs when a not null column is set to null value, using PRAGAMA EXCEPTION_INIT statement.

declare
  null_value_error   exception;

  pragma exception_init(no_privilege, -1407);

Now, whenever Oracle error -1407 occurs, NULL_VALUE_ERROR exception is raised by PL/SQL. The following example will illustrate important points related to associating an Oracle error with a user-defined exception.

declare

```
    null_value_error   exception;
    pragma exception_init(null_value_error, -1407);

    newccode varchar2(5) := null;
begin
    update courses
       set ccode = newccode
    where  ccode = 'c';


exception


  when null_value_error then
    dbms_output.put_line('trying to set null value to a not null column');
  end;
  /
```

Exception propagation

When an exception is raised by PL/SQL and if it not handled in the current block then the exception is propagated. That means, the exception is sent to enclosing blocks one after another from inside to outside until an error handler is found in one of the enclosing blocks or there are no more blocks to search for handlers.

When an exception is not handled in any of the enclosing blocks then it is sent to host environment.

The following figures illustrate how exceptions propagate.

In figure 1, exception A is raised by inner block. As there is an exception handler for exception A, the exception is handled there itself. After the exception is handled, control resumes with statements after inner block in outer block.

As the exception is handled in the block in which exception is raised, the exception is not propagated and control resumes with the enclosing block.

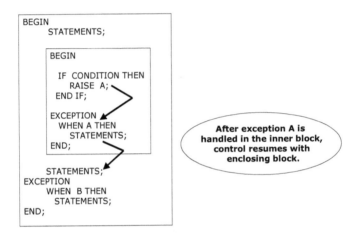

Figure 1: Exception handling.

Exception propagating to outer block

In figure 2, inner block raises exception "A" but as it is not handled in the current block (in inner block) it is propagated to first outer block. As there is an exception handler for "A" in the outer block, control is passed to it and exception is handled in the outer block.

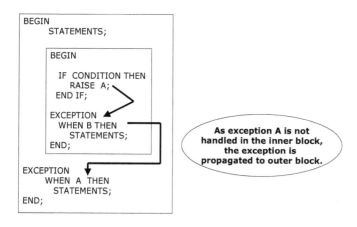

Figure 2: An exception is propagated from inner block to outer block.

Exception propagating to host

In figure 3, exception "A" is neither handled in the block in which it is raised nor handled in any of the outer blocks. As the result exception is propagated to host (the environment from where you ran the outer most block). When an exception is propagated to host the action taken by host depends on host. Examples for host are SQL* PLUS, Oracle forms, and Oracle Server.

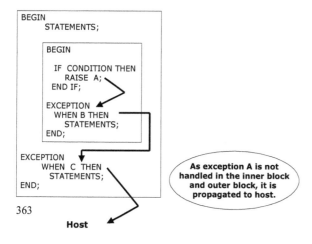

363

Figure 3: An exception propagating to Host.

In the next section we will see when a PL/SQL is considered to be successful or failure.

Exception raised in Declaration

When an exception is raised in the declaration of a block, the exception is immediately propagated to enclosing block and not handled in that block.

The following example illustrates how an exception that is raised in the declaration of inner block is propagated to outer block.

```
begin
    dbms_output.put_line('in outer block');
    declare
        ccode varchar2(5) := 'abcdef';
    begin
        -- some statements
        dbms_output.put_line('in inner block');
    exception
        when others  then
            dbms_output.put_line(sqlerrm);
    end;
    dbms_output.put_line(' back in outer block');
exception
```

when others then

dbms_output.put_line('Error in outer block: ' || sqlerrm);

end;

/

When you run the above block, the following output will be generated:

in outer block

Error in outer block: ORA-06502: PL/SQL: numeric or value error: character string buffer too small

When is a PL/SQL block successful or failure?

Each PL/SQL block exits either successfully or unsuccessfully. The exit status of PL/SQL block plays a very important role at a later stage (for example in database triggers). But for now let us just understand when a PL/SQL block is considered to be successful and when is it considered to be a failure.

A PL/SQL block is successful if it:

- ❑ Exits without raising any exceptions.

- ❑ Raises an exception but the exception is handled within the block's exception handling part.

A PL/SQL block is unsuccessful if it:

- ❑ Exits with an unhandled exception. That means the executable part raises an exception (either predefined or user-defined) and it is not handled in the block's exception handler.

❑ Executes RAISE_APPLICATION_ERROR procedure to generate an user-defined error.

Detecting where exception is raised

It is sometimes important to know which statement has actually raised the exception. Especially when two or more SELECT statements are there in the block and if one of them has raised NO_DATA_FOUND exception, it is difficult to know which statement has actually caused the problem.

The following example will use a variable to know which SELECT statement has actually raised the exception.

```
declare

    n number(1) :=0;

begin

    select ...

    n := 1;

    select ...

    n:= 2;

    select ...


exception

    when no_data_found then

        if n = 0 then

            ...

        elsif n = 1 then

            ...
```

```
       else

          ...

       end if

end;

/
```

In the above example, variable N is set to 0 at the time of declaration. If first SELECT statement raised NO_DATA_FOUND exception then control is transferred to exception handler and the value of N will be 0. If first SELECT succeeds and second SELECT has failed then the value of N will be 1 and similarly the value of N will be 2 if second SELECT also succeeds but third SELECT fails.

In the exception handler, it is possible to know which SELECT has failed by using the value of variable N.

Summary

Errors and warnings in PL/SQL are called as exceptions. PL/SQL exceptions may be either predefined or user-defined. Predefined exceptions are those that represent a general failure. User can also define exception, in addition to predefined, and use them identical to predefined exceptions. But user-defined exceptions are to be explicitly declared and raised.

Oracle allows errors to be associated with user-defined exceptions using PRAGMA EXCEPTION_INIT statement. When an exception is raised first PL/SQL tries to handle the exception in the current block. If current block doesn't have an exception handler for the exception then exception is propagated to outer block. This propagation will go either until the exception handler is found in one of the enclosing block or until Host is reached.

Exercises

♦ Look for student number 1008. If it is not found then write a suitable error message on the screen otherwise display the total amount paid by student so far.

♦ _____ statement is used to re-raise an exception.

♦ _____ function is used to get error message of the most recent error.

♦ How do you associate an Oracle error with a user-defined error.

♦ When UPDATE command could not update any rows then which of the following will happen?

    1. NO_DATA_FOUND exception occurs

    2. INVALID_UPDATE exception occurs

    3. No exception is raised

♦ When an exception is not handled in the current block

    1. It results in error and terminates the block

    2. It is propagated to outer block

    3. It is ignored.

18. CURSOR HANDLING

- What is a cursor?
- When do we need explicit cursor?
- Handling explicit cursor
- Cursor FOR loop
- Sample program
- Implicit cursor

- Cursor attributes

- Input arguments to cursor

- FOR UPDATE and CURRENT OF clauses

What is a cursor?

Oracle uses a work area to execute SQL commands and store processing information. PL/SQL allows you to access this area through a name using a cursor.

Cursors that you use in PL/SQL are of two types:

- Implicit cursor

- Explicit cursor

Implicit Cursor

PL/SQL declares an implicit cursor for every DML command, and queries that return a single row. The name of the implicit cursor is *SQL*. You can directly use this cursor without any declaration. We will see more about this later in this chapter.

Explicit Cursor

PL/SQL's implicit cursor can handle only single-row queries. If you ever need to select more than one row using SELECT in PL/SQL then you have to use explicit cursor.

When do we need an explicit cursor?

SELECT command in PL/SQL block can retrieve only one row. If SELECT command retrieves no row then NO_DATA_FOUND exception will be raised. If SELECT retrieves more than one row then TOO_MANY_ROWS exception occurs.

370

So, a SELECT command will succeed only when it retrieves a single row. The reason for this is; SELECT command copies the values of columns that it retrieved into variables. If multiple rows are retrieved then multiple values for each column are to be copied to a single variable and that creates the problem.

```
declare
    v_ccode  varchar2(5);
    v_fee    number(5);
begin

    select  ccode,fee  into  v_ccode, v_fee
    from  courses
    where  duration > 25;

end;
```

SELECT command in the above example will raise TOO_MANY_ROWS exception if more than one course is having duration more than 25.

An explicit cursor is the solution to the problem. A cursor can store a collection of records retrieved by a query. Then it allows us to fetch one record from cursor at a time and thereby enabling to process all the records in the cursor.

As you can see in figure 1, SELECT retrieves rows from database into cursor. Cursor stores the collection of record retrieved by SELECT. Then the program can fetch one row at a time from cursor and apply the required process to it.

SELECT command given at the time of declaring the cursor is used to retrieve the data from database. Records in the cursor will be fetched one at a time using FETCH statement, which fetches the data from current row of the cursor and copies the data into variables.

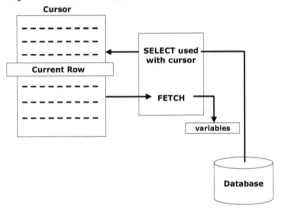

Figure 1: An explicit cursor.

Handling explicit cursor

Explicit cursor is a name used to refer to an area where you can place multiple rows retrieved by SELECT. You must use an explicit cursor whenever you have to use a multi-row query in PL/SQL.

The following are the steps required to create and use an explicit cursor:

- ❏ Declare the cursor in Declare section
- ❏ Open the cursor using OPEN statement in Executable part
- ❏ Fetch one row at a time using FETCH statement.
- ❏ Close the cursor after all the records in the cursor are fetched and processed by using CLOSE.

The following section will discuss each step in detail.

Declaring a cursor

A cursor is declared in Declare section using CURSOR statement. At the time of declaration the name of the cursor and the associated SELECT statement are mentioned.

CURSOR cursor_name [(parameter[, parameter]...)]

    IS select_statement

    [FOR UPDATE [OF column,column, . . .];

The following example shows how to declare a cursor.

```
declare
  cursor course_det is
    select ccode, name, fee
    from   courses;
begin


end;
```

COURSE_DET is the name of the cursor, which will be populated with the rows retrieved by the given SELECT at the time of opening the cursor.

We will discuss more about parameters in declaration of cursor in the section "Input Arguments".

The following example declares a cursor that takes course code and number of batches of the course in the ascending order of number of batches.

Opening a cursor using OPEN statement

OPEN statement is used to execute the SELECT command associated with the cursor and place the rows retrieved by the query into cursor.

OPEN cursor_name [(input arguments)];

Cursor_name is the name of the cursor that is to be opened.

Input_arguments are the values to be passed to the parameters of the cursor. More on this later in the section "Input Arguments".

The following statement opens the cursor COURSE_DET and places the rows retrieved by the query into the cursor.

```
declare
  cursor course_det is
    select ccode, name, fee
    from   courses;

begin
  open course_det;
```

end;

Fetching rows using FETCH statement

Once cursor is opened using OPEN statement, cursor has a set of rows, which can be fetched using FETCH statement. FETCH statement takes the data of the current row in the cursor and copies the values of the columns into variables given after INTO keyword.


```
FETCH cursor_name INTO variable-1, variable-2, . . .;
```


For each column in the cursor there should be a corresponding variable in FETCH statement. Also make sure the data types of variables and corresponding columns are matching.

The following snippet demonstrates how to fetch and copy data from current row of the cursor to variables given after INTO.


```
declare
  cursor course_det is
    select ccode, name, fee
    from   courses;


    v_ccode  courses.ccode%type;

    v_name   courses.name%type;

    v_fee    courses.fee%type;


begin
```

```
open course_det;

loop

    fetch course_det into v_ccode, v_name, v_fee;

    . . .

end loop;

end;
```

FETCH statement is to be used inside the loop to repeatedly fetch rows from the cursor. The process of fetching should stop once all rows of the cursor are fetch (reached end of cursor).

The following code will show how to exit cursor when cursor is completely processed.

```
loop

    fetch course_det into v_ccode, v_name, v_fee;

    exit  when course_det%notfound;

end loop;
```

NOTFOUND attribute of the cursor returns TRUE when previous FETCH doesn't successfully read a row from cursor.

We will discuss more about attributes of explicit and implicit cursors later in his chapter.

Closing a cursor using CLOSE command

CLOSE statement is used to close cursor after the cursor is processed. Closing a cursor would release the resources associated with cursor.

CLOSE cursor_name;

The following example closes COURSE_DET cursor:

declare

begin

  open ..

  loop

    ...

  end loop;

close course_det;

end;

Cursor For Loop

In order to process a cursor, you can use cursor FOR loop to automate the following steps.

- ❏ Opening cursor
- ❏ Fetching rows from the cursor
- ❏ Terminating loop when all rows in the cursor are fetched
- ❏ Closing cursor

The following is the syntax of cursor for loop. This for loop is specifically meant to process cursors.

FOR rowtype_variable IN cursor_name

LOOP

    Statements;

END LOOP;

rowtype_variable is automatically declared by cursor for loop. It is of ROWTYPE of the cursor. It has columns of the cursor as fields. These fields can be accessed using *rowtype_variable.fieldname.*

The following example shows the process involved without using cursor for loop and using for loop.

DECLARE

  cursor courses_cursor is

```
        select  ccode,fee

        from    courses;
BEGIN

    -- open cursor

    open courses_cursor;


    loop

        fetch  courses_cursor into v_ccode, v_fee;

        -- if previous fetch failed then exit loop

        -- NOTFOUND attribute of the cursor return true if

        -- previous fetch has failed.

        exit when  courses_cursor%notfound;


        -- process the record fetched from cursor

        . . .

    end loop;


    close  courses_cursor;
END;
```

The same program can also be written using cursor for loop as follows:

declare

```
cursor  courses_cursor  is

    select  ccode,fee

    from   courses;

begin

    -- cursor is opened and one row at a time is fetched

    -- loop is automatically terminated if all records are fetched


    for rec in  courses_cursor

    loop

        -- process the record fetched from cursor

        if  rec.fee > 5000 then

            -- do something here

        end if;


    end loop;


end;
```

The following are the important steps in the above program:

- ❑ Cursor COURSES_CURSOR is automatically opened by cursor for loop.
- ❑ REC is declared automatically by cursor for loop as:
- ❑ *REC courses_cursor%ROWTYPE;*

□ But REC is available only inside the cursor for loop. It contains the same columns as the cursor. In order to access a column of the current row of the cursor, in the cursor for loop, use the format:

□   *rowtype_variable.columnname*

□ Statements in the cursor for loop are executed once for each row of the cursor. And for each row of the cursor, row is copied into rowtype_variable.

□ Loop is terminated once end of cursor is reached. And cursor is closed.

The following section will summarize what we have seen so far by showing how to write a simple program using cursor.

Sample program

Let us now put all pieces together and write a complete program that makes use of cursor.

The sample program is to update FEE of each course based on the following table.

No. of students	Percentage of change
> 10	10% increase
> 20	15% increase
Otherwise	5% decrease

/* Author : P.Srikanth

Date   : 22-10-2001

Place : Vizag.

Purpose: Sample cursor program to illustrate how to handle a cursor*/

```
declare
    cursor courses_cursor is
        select c.ccode, count(*) count
        from   batches b, students s
        where  c.ccode = b.ccode and b.bcode = s.bcode
        group  by c.ccode;


v_per number(5,2);


begin
        -- rec is automatically declared
        for rec in courses_cursor
        loop
          if  rec.count > 20 then
              v_per:= 1.15;
          elsif  rec.count > 10 then
              v_per := 1.10;
          else
              v_per := 0.90;
          end if;


        -- update row in the table


        update courses set fee = fee * v_per
```

```
            where  ccode = rec.ccode;


        end loop;


end;

/
```

The above program is used to declare a cursor that takes course code and no. of students joined into that course using a SELECT that joins BATCHES and STUDENTS table. Depending upon the no. of students joined into each course, it updates the course fee of the course.

It uses cursor for loop to take one row at a time from COURSES_CURSOR and updates the FEE of COURSES table after the process.

Implicit cursor

Oracle implicitly opens a cursor to process each SQL statement not associated with an explicitly declared cursor. You can refer to this cursor using the name SQL.

You cannot use the OPEN, FETCH, and CLOSE statements with SQL cursor. But, you can use cursor attributes to get information about the most recently executed SQL statement.

The following example shows how to use implicit cursor to know whether the most recent UPDATE has updated any rows or not.

declare

```
begin

    update . . .

    if SQL%NOTFOUND then

        statements;

    end if;

end;
```

NOTFOUND is an attribute of implicit cursor that returns true if previous UPDATE command has not affected any row.

Cursor attributes

Cursor attributes allow you to get information regarding cursor. For example, you can get the number of rows fetched so far from a cursor using ROWCOUNT attribute and whether a row is fetched or not using FOUND attribute.

Use the following syntax to access cursor attributes:

cursor_name%Attribute

Explicit cursor attributes

The following is the list of available cursor attributes and their meaning for explicit cursor.

Attribute	What it returns?
NOTFOUN	True, if previous fetch failed.

D

FOUND	True, if previous fetch succeeded.
ROWCOU NT	Number of rows fetched from cursor so far.
ISOPEN	True, if cursor is currently open

Table 1: Explicit Cursor Attributes.

Implicit cursor attributes

Cursor attributes do not have the same meaning for both explicit and implicit cursors. The following table shows the meaning of cursor attributes with implicit cursor.

Attribute	What it returns?
NOTFOUN D	True, if previous DML operation didn't affect any row.
FOUND	True, if previous DML operation affected any row.
ROWCOU NT	Number of rows affected by the most recent DML operation.

Table 2: Implicit Cursor Attributes.

The following example shows how to use ROWCOUNT attribute with implicit cursor to know how many rows were updated with most recent UPDATE command.

begin

    update courses set   fee = fee & 1.1

    where duration > 25;

```
/*  if more than 5 rows are effected

    then rollback updation */


if  SQL%ROWCOUNT  >  5 then

    rollback;

else

    commit;

end if;

end;
```

The following is how you use cursor attributes with explicit cursors. Attribute NOTFOUND returns true if previous FETCH statement couldn't fetch any row.

```
LOOP
        fetch  courses_cursor into  v_ccode, v_fee;


        /* exit loop if previous FETCH failed */


        exit  when    students_cursor%NOTFOUND;


        /* process the record fetched */
END LOOP;
```

In the above example EXIT is executed when NOTFOUND attribute of cursor CORUSES_CURSOR returns TRUE.

Input arguments to cursor

Input arguments are the values that are passed to cursor at the time of opening the cursor. These values are passed to parameters that are declared in cursor and they are used while executing the query.

The following example will illustrate the process.

```
declare
        cursor  batch_cursor ( pccode varchar2) is
        select * from batches where ccode = pccode;

begin

        -- open the cursor and get all batches of course oracle.
        open  batch_cursor('ora');
        -- process the cursor

        close batch_cursor;

        -- open the same cursor but with a different course code
        open  batch_cursor('vb');
```

```
        -- process the cursor, which contains details of batches of vb


        close batch_cursor;
end;
```

Cursor BATCH_CURSOR is declared to take a parameter or input argument – PCCODE. The parameter is used to retrieve details of the batches of the given course.

At the time of opening the cursor, the value for parameter PCCODE is to be passed by enclosing the value within parentheses. The value is passed to PCCODE, which is then used in the query of the cursor.

The advantage of the input arguments, as you can see in the example above, is that you can use the same cursor to represent different sets of records at different points of time. In the above example, first cursor contains the batches of Oracle course then that cursor is closed and reopened with course code VB to take the details of batches of VB.

In case of cursor for loop, values to input arguments are passed at the time of using cursor in for loop as follows:for rec in batch_cursor('ora')

  loop

      ...

  end loop;

Note: The size of data type of input arguments should not be given. That means, we should give only VARCHAR2 and not VARCHAR2 (10).

FOR UPDATE and CURRENT OF

By default, Oracle locks rows while manipulating the rows. But it is possible to override default locking by using FOR UPDATE option of SELECT command.

FOR UPDATE option clause can be used with SELECT while declaring cursor to lock all records retrieved by cursor to make sure they are not locked by others before we update or delete them. As Oracle automatically locks rows for you, FOR UPDATE clause is required only when you want to lock rows ahead of update or delete - at the time of opening cursor.

CURRENT OF clause with UPDATE and DELETE commands can be used to refer to the current row in the cursor.

Note: FOR UPDATE must be given if you want to use CURRENT OF clause to refer to current row in the cursor.

The following example shows how to use FOR UPDATE OF and CURRENT OF clauses:

DECLARE

```
CURSOR course_details  IS

    SELECT ccode, name, fee from courses

    FOR UPDATE OF fee;

  ...
BEGIN

  OPEN course_details;


  LOOP

    FETCH  course_details INTO...

      ...

    /* Update the current record in the cursor

        course_details */


    UPDATE courses SET fee =  new_fee

      WHERE CURRENT OF course_details;
    END LOOP;


    CLOSE   course_details;


END;
```

Summary

A cursor is always used by PL/SQL to execute single-row queries and DML command. But, in order to use multi-row query, you have to use an explicit cursor. An explicit cursor contains a row-set, which is retrieved by multi-row query. Implicit cursor is used to get information about the most recent DML operation.

Cursor FOR loop is used to open, fetch rows until end of cursor, and close the cursor.

Input arguments of the cursor can be used to pass values to cursor at the time of opening cursor so that these values are used by SELECT command of the cursor. FOR UPDATE clause is used to override default locking and CURRENT OF is used to refer to current record in the cursor.

Exercises

- Which attribute is used to find out how many rows were fetched from cursor so far.

- Can we use ISOPEN attribute with implicit cursor.

- How can we know whether the most recent DML operation has affected any row?

- How do you declare an input arguments for the cursor and how do you pass value to it?

- What is the use of CURRENT OF clause in DELETE and UPDATE commands?

- Create table called COURSE_DETAILS with the columns:

  Course Code, No. of batches completed, Total amount collected so far

19. PROCEDURES, FUNCTIONS and packages

- ❑ What is a stored procedure?
- ❑ Advantages of stored procedures
- ❑ Creating a stored procedure
- ❑ Creating a stored function
- ❑ Recompiling
- ❑ Types of parameters
- ❑ Parameter modes
- ❑ NCOPY compiler hints
- ❑ RAISE_APPLICATION_ERROR procedure
- ❑ Packages

What is a stored procedure?

As we have seen in the introduction to PL/SQL that there are two types of PL/SQL blocks – anonymous and stored procedures.

A stored procedure is a PL/SQL block that is stored in the database with a name. It is invoked using the name. Each procedure is meant for a specific purpose.

A stored procedure is stored in the database as an object. It is also called as database procedure as it is stored in the database.

A procedure may take one or more parameters. If a procedure takes parameters then these parameters are to be supplied at the time of calling the procedure.

What is a function?

A function is similar to procedure, except that it returns a value. The calling program should use the value returned by the function.

Advantages of stored procedures

Stored procedures and functions offer the following benefits.

Reduced network traffic

Stored procedures are stored in the database on the server. In order to invoke a stored procedure a client has to use only the name of the stored procedure. This results in reduced network traffic because only the name is passed to server and not the entire PL/SQL block.

Better Performance

Stored procedures improve performance because the database accessed by stored procedures and stored procedures themselves are stored in the database. Furthermore, because a stored procedure's compiled form is available in the database, no compilation step is required to execute the code.

Apart from this, stored procedures make use of shared memory. That means if a stored procedure is called by user-1, then it is brought into server's memory. As a result there is a chance of finding the stored procedure in memory, when user-2 later wants to use the same procedure. In this case stored procedure need not be brought into memory since it is already in the memory. This saves time and increases performance.

Easy Maintenance

If there is any change in the application, only the concerned stored procedures are to be modified to incorporate the change. As all the clients access stored procedures, they automatically use the modified definition. You only have to change business login once in the stored procedure. Therefore stored procedures improve the integrity and consistency of your applications.

Security

Stored procedures help enforcement of data security. You can allow users to access only the stored procedures and not the table that are manipulated by stored procedures.

Whenever a stored procedure runs, it runs with the privileges of the owner and not the user running it. Because users only have the privilege to execute the procedure and not the privileges to access the underlying tables, it increases security.

Owner rights

When a stored procedure is run under the privileges of the owner of the stored procedure, it is called as owner rights.

Invoker rights

When a stored procedure is executed with the privileges of the invoker and not under the privileges of the owner, it is called as invoker rights.

We will discuss about the difference between these two ways of running a stored procedure in detailed later in this chapter.

Creating a stored procedures

A stored procedure is created using CREATE PROCEDURE command.

CREATE [OR REPLACE] PROCEDURE name [(parameter[,parameter, ...])] {IS |
AS}

[local declarations]

BEGIN

    executable statements

[EXCEPTION

    exception handlers]

END [name];

OR REPLACE   is used to create a procedure even a procedure with the same
name is already existing.

Oracle creates procedure even though the procedure is not valid but it displays
the message saying that the procedure is created with errors. Then you have
to rectify the errors and recreate the procedure. If OR REPLACE option is not
given Oracle doesn't allow you to replace an existing stored procedure. So, it is
better you use OR REPLACE option so that the existing invalid version of the
procedure will be replaced with the valid version.

SHOW ERRORS

During the creation of the procedure if there are any errors Oracle displays the
message saying procedure is created but with errors with the following
message:

Warning: Procedure created with compilation errors.

In order to displays errors in the most recent CREATE PROCEDURE statement, use SHOW ERRORS command.

The following stored procedure inserts a new record into PAYMENTS table with the given roll number and amount.

```
create or replace procedure  newpayment(rollno number, amt number)
is
begin
   insert into payments values(rollno, sysdate,amt);
   commit;
end;
/
```

Once a stored procedure is stored in the database, it can be invoked using EXECUTE command by using the name of the procedure.

EXECUTE command

A procedure can be executed using EXECUTE command. To execute a procedure either you must be the owner of the procedure or you must have EXECUTE privilege on the procedure.

The following example shows how to invoke NEWPAYMENT procedure.

```
SQL> execute newpayment(10,2000);
```

PL/SQL procedure successfully completed.

In the above example, NEWPAYMENT is invoked by passing 10 and 2000. It inserts a new row into PAYMENTS table with values 10, sysdate, and 2000.

Creating a stored function

A stored function is same as a procedure, except that it returns a value. CREATE FUNCTION command is used to create a stored function.

CREATE [OR REPLACE] FUNCTION name

       [(parameter[,parameter, ...])]

       RETURN datatype

{IS | AS}

[local declarations]

BEGIN

     executable statements

       RETURN value;

[EXCEPTION

     exception handlers]

END [name];

OR REPLACE is used to create a function even though a function with the same name already exists

RETURN datatype specifies the type of data to be returned by the function.

RETURN statement in the executable part returns the value. The value must be of the same type as the return type specified using RETURN option in the header.

The following stored function takes roll number of the student and return the amount yet to be paid by the student.

```
create or replace function  getdueamt(prollno number)

return number

is

v_fee     number(5);

v_amtpaid number(5);

begin

   -- get total amount paid by student

   select sum(amount) into  v_amtpaid

   from  payments

   where  rollno = prollno;

   -- get course fee of the course into which student joined

   select fee into v_fee

   from courses

   where ccode = ( select ccode from batches

          where bcode in

          ( select bcode from students

           where  rollno = prollno)

        );
```

```
-- return the difference
   return v_fee - v_amtpaid;
end;
/
```

The above function can be called from a PL/SQL block as follows:

```
begin
   dbms_output.put_line(getdueamt(10));
end;
```

User-defined PL/SQL functions can be used in SQL in the same manner as the standard functions such as ROUND and SUBSTR..

For example, the function GETDUEAMT can be invoked from SELECT command as follows:

```
SQL> select rollno, getdueamt(rollno)
  2  from students;
```

```
ROLLNO GETDUEAMT(ROLLNO)
--------- -----------------
     1           0
     2           0
     3           0
     4           0
```

5	0
6	0
7	0
8	0
9	1500
10	2000
11	0
12	1500
13	0

Getting source code

It is possible to see the source code of stored procedures and function by using USER_SOURCE data dictionary view.

The following SELECT command will display the source code of NEWPAYMENT stored procedure.

SQL> select text

  2 from user_source

  3 where name = 'NEWPAYMENT';

TEXT

----

procedure newpayment(rollno number, amt number)

is

begin

insert into payments values(rollno, sysdate,amt);

commit;

end;

Privileges required

To create a stored procedure, you must have CREATE PROCEDURE system privilege.

You must also have required object privileges on the objects that are referred in the procedure in order to successfully compile the procedure.

Note: The owner of the procedure CANNOT obtain required privileges on the stored procedure through ROLES.

Recompiling

Stored procedures and functions are compiled at the time of creation and stored in the compiled form. If a procedure becomes invalid afterwards, it is to be recompiled before it is executed. Oracle implicitly compiles the procedure when an invalid procedure is referred. However, it is possible to explicitly recompile

In order to recompile a stored procedure use ALTER PROCEDURE and ALTER FUNCTION to recompile a procedure and function respectively.

ALTER PROCEDURE procedurename   COMPILE;

ALTER FUNCTION functionname   COMPILE;

The following sequence will illustrate the importance of recompilation.

❑ Assume user SCOTT has created NEWPAYMENT procedure as follows

```
create or replace procedure  newpayment(rollno number, amt number)
is
begin
   insert into book.payments values(rollno, sysdate,amt);
   commit;
end;
/
```

❑ Since SCOTT doesn't have INSERT privilege on PAYMENTS table of BOOK, the procedure is created but marked as invalid. You can see the status of the procedure using the following command.

```
select status from user_objects where object_name = 'NEWPAYMENT';


STATUS
-------
INVALID
```

❑ Now, user BOOK has granted INSERT privilege on PAYMENTS table to SCOTT as follows:

```
GRANT INSERT ON PAYMENTS to SCOTT;
```

❑ Then any subsequent reference to NEAPAYMENT procedure in SCOTT will implicitly recompile the procedure. But in order to avoid extra time taken to recompile the procedure at runtime, it can be recompiled using ALTER PROCEDURE command as follows:

ALTER PROCEDURE newpayment COMPILE;

❑ After recompilation, the procedure will have status VALID as provide by the following query.

select status from user_objects where object_name = 'NEWPAYMENT';

STATUS

VALID

Types of Parameters

Parameters of a procedure are of two types.

❑ Formal parameters
❑ Actual Parameters

Formal Parameters

The parameters declared in the definition of procedure are called as **formal parameters**. They receive the values sent while calling the procedure.

procedure increase_fee (pccode varchar2, pamt number)

In the above procedure, PCCODE, PAMT parameters are called as formal parameters.

Actual Parameters

The values given within parentheses while calling the procedure are called as **actual parameters.**

increase_feepaid (v_ccode, 2000);

v_ccode and   2000 are actual parameters.   These values are copied to the corresponding formal parameters - pccode and p*amt.*

Parameter Modes

Parameter mode is used to specify what can be done with formal parameter. The following are the available modes.

- IN
- OUT
- IN OUT

IN mode

IN parameters lets you pass a value to the subprogram being called. The value cannot be changed inside the subprogram. It is like a constant in the subprogram. Therefore it cannot be assigned a value.

procedure increase_fee (pccode in varchar2, pamt number) is

begin

   . . .

end;

The actual parameter corresponding to IN parameter can be a variable, constant, or expression.

The default parameter mode is IN. In the above example though we didn't specify the parameter mode for PAMT is it taken as IN parameter.

OUT Mode

An OUT parameter lets the subprogram pass a value to caller. Inside the subprogram OUT parameter is an uninitialized variable.

Subprogram has to place a value in the OUT parameters, which will be used by caller program. Whatever changes are made to formal parameter, the changes will be made available to actual parameter.

The actual parameter corresponding to OUT parameter must be a variable.

IN OUT Mode

It is same as IN and OUT modes put together. It can get a value from the calling program and return value to calling program. The value of this type of parameter can be used in the subprogram and

The actual parameter corresponding to IN OUT parameter must be a variable.

The following procedure takes course code and returns the dates on which the first and last batches of that course have started.

```
create or replace procedure get_dates( pccode in  varchar2,
                        first_date  out  date,
                        last_date out  date) is
begin

        select  min(stdate)  into  first_date
        from   batches
        where  ccode = pccode;


        select  max(stdate)  into  last_date
        from   batches
        where  ccode = pccode;


end;
```

Once the procedure is created, it can be called as follows:

```
declare
    min_date date;
```

```
    max_date date;

begin

    get_dates( 'ora',  min_date, max_date);
    dbms_output.put_line( min_date  ||   ':'  ||  max_date);

end;
```

The output of the above program will be:

12-JAN-01:15-AUG-01

NOCOPY Compiler Hint

By default, OUT and IN OUT parameters are passed by value. That means, the value of an IN OUT actual parameter is copied into the corresponding formal parameter. Then, if the procedure exits normally, the values assigned to OUT and IN OUT formal parameters are copied into the corresponding actual parameters.

When the parameters hold large data structures such as records, and instances of object types (which we will in later chapters), copying slows down execution and uses up more memory. To prevent that, you can specify the NOCOPY hint, which allows the PL/SQL to pass OUT and IN OUT parameters by reference.

PROCEDURE change(pstudent IN OUT NOCOPY student_type) IS ...

407

In the above example parameter PSTUDENT is of object type – STUDENT_TYPE. It is now passed by reference as we used NOCOPY option with it.

Invoker Rights vs. definer rights

By default, when a user executes a procedure, the procedure is executed with the privileges of the owner. That means, the privileges of invoking user (invoker) are not taken into account only the privileges of definer (owner) of the procedure will be considered.

If the procedure is to be called by user other than the owner then the use must be granted EXECUTE privilege on the procedure.

When the procedure is executed using the privileges of definer then, it is called as definer rights.

Definer rights is the default option. All object references in the procedure will be referring to objects of definer and not invoker. Let us see an example to understand this point further.

Assume we have procedure ADDMESSAGE created by user SRIKANTH as follows:

create or replace procedure addmessage(msg varchar2)

is

begin

insert into messages values (msg, sysdate);

commit;

end;

Then user SRIKANTH has granted EXECUTE privilege to user PRANEETH as follows:

grant execute on addmessage to praneeth;

Now user PRANEETH can execute the procedure as follows:

execute Srikanth.addmessage('First message');

The message "First message" is inserted into MESSAGES table of SRIKANTH – the definer of the procedure.

What if user PRANEETH also has MESSAGE table with the same structure as MESSAGES table of SRIKANTH? The answer is; even now the message goes to MESSAGES table of SRIKANTH, since all references to objects in the procedure are resolved to definer of the procedure.

Invoke Rights

Oracle8i has introduced invoker rights. In case of invoker rights, procedure is executed with the privileges of invoker and not the definer of the procedure.

If you want the procedure to be executed with invoker rights and not with definer right, then the procedure is to be created with AUTHID CURRENT_USER option as follows.

create or replace procedure addmessage(msg varchar2)

authid current_user as

is

begin

    insert into messages values (msg, sysdate);

    commit;

end;

AUTHID CURRENT_USER option specifies that the procedure to be executed under the privileges of invoking user. Also remember that all object references are resolved to invoker and not the definer. However, if any object is qualified with schema (username) then it will refer to object in that schema. In other words, all unqualified object are taken from invoker's schema.

Now if you execute ADDMESSAGE procedure from user PRANEETH, it will fail, as there is no MESSAGES table in that schema.

SQL> execute srikanth.addmessage('Second message');

BEGIN srikanth.addmessage('fine'); END;

*

ERROR at line 1:

ORA-00942: table or view does not exist

ORA-06512: at "SRIKANTH.ADDMESSAGE", line 4

ORA-06512: at line 1

As you can understand, the above message is complaining about missing MESSAGES table. If you create MESSAGES table in PRANEETH schema, then the procedure will succeed and the message is inserted into MESSAGES table of PRANEETH account.

The advantage of invoker rights is that it allows you to centralized code whereas the data is stored in individual schema. That means though users use the same common code the data is stored in objects of their schema.

RAISE_APPLICATION_ERROR Procedure

This procedure is used to create your own application error numbers and messages.

When you have to terminate a PL/SQL program, you can display an error message and send error code to host environment using this procedure.

RAISE_APPLICATION_ERROR (errornumber, errormessage);

errornumber   is a number in the range -20001 and -20999.

errormessage   is the message to be displayed.

The following PL/SQL block displays the error message along with error number (-20100) when NO_DATA_FOUND exception is raised.

declare

411

```
    v_fee courses.fee%type;
begin

    select fee into v_fee
    from   courses
    where  ccode = 'ora';

    -- remaining statements

exception
    when  no_data_found then
        raise_application_error(-20100,'Invalid course code');
end;
/
```

Packages

A package is a collection of related procedures, functions, variables and data types. A package typically contains two parts – specification and body.

Specification

Package specification contains declarations for items, procedure and functions that are to be made public. All public objects of package are visible outside the package. In other words, public objects are callable from outside of the package.

Private items of the package can be used only in the package and not outside the package.

The following is the syntax to create package specification.

```
CREATE PACKAGE package_name AS

    /* declare  public objects  of package */

END;
```

Body

Body of the package defines all the objects of the package. It includes public objects that are declared in package specification and objects that are to be used only within the package – private members.

```
CREATE PACKAGE BODY package_name AS
    /* define objects of package */
END;
```

- ❑ procedures declared in the package specification
- ❑ functions declared in the package specification
- ❑ definition of cursors declared in the package specification
- ❑ local procedures and functions, not declared in the package specification
- ❑ local variables

Calling a procedure of package

413

In order to access a public object of a package use the following syntax:

package_name.object_name

package_name is the name of the package whose object you want to access.
object_name   is the name of a public object in the package.

Let us now create a package called COURSE_PKG that contains two subprograms – CHANGEFEE and GETBATCHCOURSE.

We have to first create package specification and then body a follows:

```
create or replace package  course_pkg  as

    procedure changefee (pccode varchar2, newfee number);
    function  getbatchcourse(pbcode varchar2) return varchar2;


end;
/
```

The following CREATE PACKAGE BODY statement creates the body of the package.

```
create or replace package  body course_pkg  as

    procedure changefee (pccode varchar2, newfee number)
    is
```

```
begin
    update courses set fee = newfee
    where  ccode = pccode;
    if  sql%found  then
        commit;
    else
        raise_application_error(-20010,'Invalid course code');
    end if;
end;


function  getbatchcourse(pbcode varchar2) return varchar2
is
  v_ccode courses.ccode%type;
begin
    select  ccode into v_ccode
    from batches
    where  bcode = pbcode;


    return v_ccode;


exception
    when no_data_found then
        raise_application_error( -20011,'Invalid batch code');


end;
```

end;

/

In order to call procedure CHANGEFEE of the package, use the package name followed by procedure name as follows:

Execute course_pkg.changefee('ora',5000);

Initializing package

It is possible to execute some code when a user refers the package for the first time. Any code that you feel is to be executed at the time of a user referring to the package for the first time can be put in initialization part of the package.

The following is the structure of initialization part.

create package body name as

    /* definition of package body */

begin

    /* code to be executed when package is referred for the first time */

end;

Summary

Stored procedure and functions are sub programs stored in database. Functions return a single value whereas procedure doesn't return any value. Stored procedures have important advantages such as improving performance, making maintenance and security implementation easy.

Oracle allows parameters of three types – in, out, and in out. OUT and IN OUT parameters are used to return values back to calling program. They can be passed by either value (default) or by reference using NOCOPY hint.

Procedures are executed under privileges of owner of the procedure. However, it is possible to execute procedure with the privileges of invoker using AUTHID CURRENT_USER option of CREATE PROCEDURE command.

Standard procedure RAISE_APPLICATION_ERROR is used to raise an application error with the given error number and message. Package allows a group of related procedures and function to be identified by a single name. It is used to avoid name conflicts between names of different procedures.

Exercises

♦ _____ command is used to display errors that occurred during compilation of a stored procedure.

♦ _____ view provides information about stored procedures.

♦ _____option is used to specify that a parameter is both input and output parameter.

♦ What is the command used to compile a procedure explicitly?

♦ Create a procedure to insert a new row into payments with the given roll number. DP is system date and AMOUNT is the amount to be paid by the student.

♦ Create a function to take batch code and return the number of students in the batch.

♦ Create a function to return the first missing roll number. If no roll number is missing then return the highest roll number + 1.

♦ Create a function to take faculty code and return the number of batches the faculty can handle.

♦ Create a procedure to take course code and return minimum and maximum duration of batches of that course.

- Create a package to contain the following procedures and functions.

  Function BATCHSTATUS – takes batch code and returns S - if batch is yet to start, C – if batch is completed, R – if batch is currently running.

  Function BATCHAMOUNT – return the total amount collected from the given batch code.

20. DATABASE TRIGGERS

- What is a database trigger?
- Types of Triggers
- Creating a database trigger
- Correlation names
- Instead-of triggers
- Knowing which command fired the trigger
- Enabling and disabling trigger
- Dropping a trigger

What is a Database Trigger?

Database trigger is a PL/SQL block that is executed on an event in the database. The event is related to a particular data manipulation of a table such as inserting, deleting or updating a row of a table.

Triggers may be used for any of the following:

- To implement complex business rule, which cannot be implemented using integrity constraints.
- To audit the process. For example, to keep track of changes made to a

table.

- To automatically perform an action when another concerned action takes place. For example, updating a table whenever there is an insertion or a row into another table.

Triggers are similar to stored procedures, but stored procedures are called explicitly and triggers are called implicitly by Oracle when the concerned event occurs.

Note: Triggers are automatically executed by Oracle and their execution is transparent to users.

Types of Triggers

Depending upon, when a trigger is fired, it may be classified as :

- Statement-level trigger
- Row-level trigger
- Before triggers
- After triggers

Statement-level Triggers

A statement trigger is fired only for once for a DML statement irrespective of the number of rows affected by the statement.

For example, if you execute the following UPDATE command STUDENTS table, statement trigger for UPDATE is executed only for once.

update students   set bcode='b3'

where bcode = 'b2';

However, statements triggers cannot be used to access the data that is being inserted, updated or deleted. In other words, they do not have access to keywords NEW and OLD, which are used to access data.

Statement-level triggers are typically used to enforce rules that are not related to data. For example, it is possible to implement a rule that says "no body can modify BATCHES table after 9 P.M".

Statement-level trigger is the default type of trigger.

Row-level Trigger

A row trigger is fired once for each row that is affected by DML command. For example, if an UPDATE command updates 100 rows then row-level trigger is fired 100 times whereas a statement-level trigger is fired only for once.

Row-level trigger are used to check for the validity of the data. They are typically used to implement rules that cannot be implemented by integrity constraints.

Row-level triggers are implemented by using the option FOR EACH ROW in CREATE TRIGGER statement.

Before Triggers

While defining a trigger, you can specify whether the trigger is to be fired before the command (INSERT, DELETE, and UPDATE) is executed or after the command is executed.

Before triggers are commonly used to check the validity of the data before the action is performed. For instance, you can use before trigger to prevent deletion of row if deletion should not be allowed in the given case.

AFTER Triggers

After triggers are fired after the triggering action is completed. For example, If after trigger is associated with INSERT command then it is fired after the row is inserted into the table.

Possible Combinations

The following are the various possible combinations of database triggers.

- Before Statement
- Before Row
- After Statement
- After Row

Note: Each of the above triggers can be associated with INSERT, DELETE, and UPDATE commands resulting in a total of 12 triggers.

In the next section, we will see how to create database triggers.

Creating a Database Trigger

CREATE TRIGGER command is used to create a database trigger. The following details are to be given at the time of creating a trigger.

- Name of the trigger
- Table to be associated with
- When trigger is to be fired - before or after
- Command that invokes the trigger - UPDATE, DELETE, or INSERT
- Whether row-level trigger or not

❏ Condition to filter rows.

❏ PL/SQL block that is to be executed when trigger is fired.

The following is the syntax of CREATE TRIGGER command.

```
CREATE  [OR REPLACE] TRIGGER trigername
{BEFORE | AFTER}
{DELETE | INSERT | UPDATE [OF columns]}
      [OR {DELETE | INSERT |UPDATE [OF columns]}]...
ON table
[FOR EACH ROW [WHEN condition]]
[REFERENCING  [OLD AS old] [NEW AS new]]
PL/SQL block
```

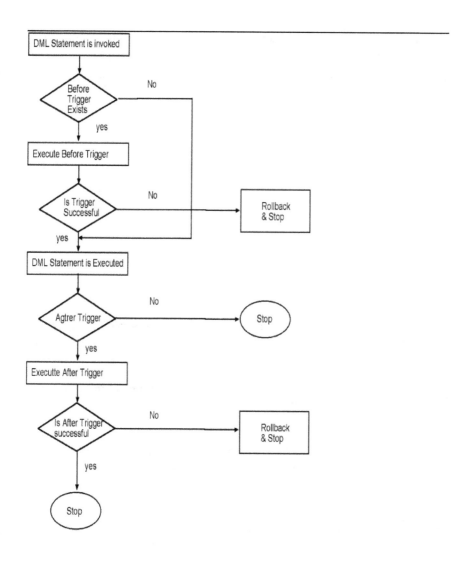

Figure 1: Execution sequence of database triggers.

If FOR EACH ROW option is used then it becomes a row-level trigger otherwise it is a statement-level trigger.

WHEN is used to fire the trigger only when the given condition is satisfied. This clause can be used only with row triggers.

For example, the following trigger is fired only when AMOUNT is more than 1000.

```
create or replace trigger ..

before insert on payments

for each row

when :new.amount > 1000
```

OF option allows you to specify updation of which columns will fire trigger. The list of columns can be given by separating column by comma.

REFERENCING is used to use new names instead of default correlation names OLD and NEW. See the section "Correlation Names "

The following is a simple database trigger that is used to check whether date of joining of the student is less than or equal to system date. Otherwise it raises an error.

```
create or replace trigger students_bi_row

before insert

on students

for each row

begin
```

```
if :new.dj > sysdate then

  raise_application_error

    (-20002,'Date of joining cannot be after system date.');

end if;

end;
```

STUDENTS_BI_ROW is the name of the trigger. It represents table name – STUDENTS, event of the trigger – BI (before insert) and type – ROW. Though trigger name can be anything, it is better you follow a convention while naming it.

FOR EACH ROW specifies that this trigger is a row-level trigger.

Condition :NEW.DJ > SYSDATE checks whether the value of DJ of the row being inserted is greater than system date. If the condition is true then it raises an error using RAISE_APPLICATION_ERROR procedure.

Note: Use data dictionary view USER_TRIGGERS to list the existing triggers.

The following command can be used to display the name and body of each trigger in the current account.

select trigger_name, trigger_body from user_trigger;

Column TRIGGER_BODY is of LONG type. How many characters of this column will be displayed is determined by variable LONG in SQL*Plus. Set variable LONG to a larger value to see the complete body of the trigger. The default value of LONG is 80.

The following is another trigger used to implement a rule that cannot be implemented by integrity constraints. The trigger checks whether payment made by the student is more than what the student is supposed to pay.

```
create or replace trigger payments_bi_row

before insert

on payments

for each row

declare

  v_dueamt number(5);

begin

  v_dueamt := getdueamt(:new.rollno);

  if :new.amount > v_dueamt then

        raise_application_error(-20112,'Amount being paid is more than what is
to be paid');

  end if;

end;
```

The above trigger makes use of GETDUEAMT function that we created in the previous chapter. It first gets the due amount of the given roll number. If the amount being paid – values of AMOUNT column – is more than the due amount then trigger fails.

Statement-level trigger example

The following is an example of statement-level trigger. As we have seen in the previous section, a statement trigger is fired only for once for the entire statement irrespective of the number of rows affected by the statement.

```
create or replace trigger payments_biud

before insert or update or delete

on payments

begin

  if to_char(sysdate,'DY') = 'SUN' then

    raise_application_error(-20111,'No changes can be made on sunday.');

  end if;

end;
```

The above trigger is fired whenever an UPDATE or DELETE or INSERT command is executed on PAYMENTS table. Trigger checks whether day of week of the system date is Sunday. If condition is true then it raises an application error. Since the trigger is not concerned with data, it uses a statement-level trigger.

Valid Statements in trigger body

The following are the only valid statements in trigger body. Trigger can make use of existing stored procedures, functions and packages (as shown in the previous example).

- DML commands
- SELECT INTO command

Correlation Names

The default correlation names are NEW for new values and OLD for old values of the row. So, in order to access the values of new row use NEW and to access the values of old (existing) row, use OLD.

It is also possible to change these correlation names using REFERENCING option of CREATE TRIGGER command. This is done mainly to avoid names conflicts between table names and correlation names.

See the table 1, to understand the availability of correlation name with triggering commands.

Command	NEW	OLD
DELETE	No	Yes
INSERT	Yes	No
UPDATE	Yes	Yes

Table 1: Availability of correlation names

NEW is not available with DELETE command because there are no new values. In the same way, OLD is not available with INSERT because a new row is being inserted and it doesn't contain old values. Triggers based on UPDATE command can access both NEW and OLD correlation names. OLD refers to values that refer to values before the change and NEW refers to values that are after the change.

The following trigger prevents any change to AMOUNT column of PAYMENTS table. This is done by comparing old value with new value and if they differ that means the value is changed and trigger fails.

```
create or replace trigger payments_bu_row

before update

on payments

for each row

begin

   if :new.amount <> :old.amount then

           raise_application_error(-20113,'Amount cannot be changed. Please
   delete and reinsert the row, if required');

   end if;

end;
```

Instead-of Trigger

These trigger are defined on relation-views and object-views. These triggers are used to modify views that cannot be directly modified by DML commands. Unlike normal trigger, which are fired during the execution of DML commands, these triggers are fired instead of execution of DML commands. That means instead of executing DML command on the view, Oracle invokes the corresponding INSTEAD-OF trigger.

The following is a view based on STUDENTS and PAYMENTS tables.

```
create view  newstudent

as

select  s.rollno, name, bcode,gender, amount

from students s, payments p

where  s.rollno = p.rollno;
```

429

If you try to insert data into NEWSTUDENT table then Oracle displays the following error.

SQL> insert into newstudent values (15,'Joe','b2','m',2000);

insert into newstudent values (15,'Joe','b2','m',2000)

*

ERROR at line 1:

ORA-01779: cannot modify a column which maps to a non key-preserved table

But, we want the data supplied to NEWSTUDENT view to be inserted into STUDENTS and PAYMENTS table. This can be done with an instead of trigger as follows:

```
create or replace trigger newstudent_it_bi_row

instead of insert

on newstudent

for each row

begin
    -- insert into STUDENTS table first

    insert into students(rollno,bcode,name,gender,dj)
        values(:new.rollno, :new.bcode, :new.name, :new.gender,sysdate);

    -- insert a row into PAYMENTS table

    insert into payments
```

```
            values(:new.rollno, sysdate, :new.amount);

end;
```

The above INSTEAD-OF trigger is used to insert one row into STUDENTS table with roll number, name, batch code and gender of the student. It then inserts a row into PAYMENTS table with roll number, date of payment - sysdate, and amount.

Since we created an INSTEAD-OF trigger for INSERT command, Oracle invokes this trigger when an INSERT command is executed on NEWSTUDENTS view.

```
SQL> insert into newstudent values (15,'Joe','b2','m',2000);
```

So the above command inserts two rows – one into STUDENTS table and another into PAYMENTS table. The following two queries will ratify that.

```
select rollno, bcode,name, gender, dj

from students where rollno = 15;


   ROLLNO BCODE NAME                    G DJ

--------- ----- ----------------------------- - ---------

      15 b2    Joe                     m 30-Oct-01



select * from payments where rollno = 15;


   ROLLNO DP         AMOUNT
```

431

---------- ---------- ----------

    15 30-OCT-01   2000

Knowing which command fired the trigger

When a trigger may be fired by more than one DML command, it may be required to know which DML command actually fired the trigger.

Use the following conditional predicates in the body of the trigger to check which command fired the trigger.

- ❏ INSERTING
- ❏ DELETING
- ❏ UPDATING

The following example is used to log information about the change made to table COURSES. The trigger makes use of a COURSES_LOG table, which is created with the following structure.

```
create table courses_log
( cmd  number(1),
  pk   varchar2(20),
  dc   date,
  un   varchar2(20)
);
```

Now a row level trigger is used to insert a row into COURSES_LOG table whenever there is a change to COURSES table.

432

```
create or replace trigger  courses_biud_row

before insert or delete or update

on courses

for each row

begin

    if  inserting then

        insert into courses_log values (1, :new.ccode,sysdate, user);

    elsif  deleting then

        insert into courses_log values(2,:old.ccode,sysdate,user);

    else

        insert into courses_log values(3,:old.ccode,sysdate,user);

    end if;

end;
```

After the trigger is created, if you execute an UPDATE command as follows:

```
update courses set fee = fee * 1.1 where ccode = 'ora';
```

it will fire COURSES_BIUD_ROW trigger, which will insert a row into COURSES_LOG table as follows:

```
SQL> select * from courses_log;


    CMD PK              DC      UN

--------- -------------------- --------- --------------------
```

Enabling and disabling triggers

A database trigger may be either in enabled state or disabled state.

Disabling trigger my improve performance when a large amount of table data is to be modified, because the trigger code is not executed.

For example,

UPDATE students set name = upper(name);

will run faster if all the triggers fired by UPDATE on STUDENTS table are disabled.

Use ALTER TRIGGER command to enable or disable triggers as follows:

alter trigger payments_bu_row disable;

A disabled trigger is not fired until it is enabled. Use the following command to enable a disabled trigger.

alter trigger payments_bu_row enable;

The following command disables all triggers of STUDENTS table.

alter table students disable all triggers;

Dropping a Trigger

When a trigger is no longer needed it can be dropped using DROP TRIGGER command as follows.

drop trigger payments_bu_row;

Summary

Database triggers are used to implement complex business rules that cannot be implemented using integrity constraints. Triggers can also be used for logging and to take actions that should be automatically performed.

Trigger may be fired before the DML operation or after DML operation. Trigger may be fired for each row affected by the DML operation or for the entire statement.

INSTEAD-OF trigger are called instead of executing the given DML command. They are defined on relational-views and object-views (will be discussed later in this book).

A trigger can be disabled to increase the performance when a lot of data manipulations are to be done on the table.

Exercises

- Which data dictionary view contains information about triggers? _____

- How many before trigger can we create?_____

- Is it possible to create two or more trigger for the same event(BEFORE INSERT)?_____.

- What is the default type of trigger?[Statement/row]___

- Create a trigger to prevent any changes to FEE column of COURSES table in such a way that increase is more than the half of the existing course fee.

- Create a trigger to prevent all deletions between 9p.m to 9 a.m.

21. LOBs

❑ Introduction

❑ LOB Data types

❑ Defining and Manipulating LOBs

❑ DBMS_LOB Package

Introduction

Oracle supports LOBs(Large Objects) which can hold large amount of raw binary data, such as graphics images, as well as large amount of character data.

Oracle extended SQL DDL and DML to provide support for LOBs. You can also manipulate LOBs using DBMS_LOB package and OCI (Oracle Call Interface).

Depending upon the way in which LOBs are stored they can be classified as follows.

Internal LOBs

These are stored in the database tablespace. They support transaction processing like any other scalar data type. CLOB, BLOB and NCLOB belong to this category.

External LOBs

These are not stored in the database. Instead they are stored in the Operating System files. Only a pointer pointing to the actual data is stored in the database. They do not support transaction processing and integrity checking. BFILE data type belongs to this category.

See figure 1, to understand how data is stored in internal lob and external lob.

LOB Datatypes

The following are the different LOB datatypes that are supported by Oracle8.

437

Data Type	Description
CLOB	The data is consisting of single-byte character data.
NCLOB	The data is consisting of multi-byte or single-byte fixed length character data that corresponds to the national character set.
BLOB	The data is consisting of RAW binary data, such as bitmap images.
BFILE	The data is stored in an operating system file. Only a reference to the file is stored in the database. This is the example for External LOB.

Table 1: LOB Datatypes.

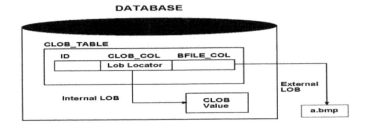

In the above example the table contains three columns – ID, CLOB_COL and BFILE_COL. CLOB_COL is of CLOB type and BFILE_COL is of BFILE type. CLOB column stores lob locator, which points to the location where the complete data is stored. BFILE column contains the name of the file (a.bmp) but the file is physically stored outside the database as a file in the operating systems file system.

LOB Locator

The data of the LOB column is NOT stored in the row along with the other columns of the row, instead only a locator is stored in the database and the actual data is stored elsewhere. The locator is similar to a pointer and points to the location where the data is actually stored. In case of Internal LOB the data is stored within the database, and in case of external LOB the data is stored outside the database as a file in the file system of the operating system.

The value that is stored in the row to point to the actual location of the Internal LOB is called as LOB Locator. It is used to locate the LOB data that is stored elsewhere in the database.

LONG vs. LOBs

LONG datatype and LOBs are similar in some respects and differ in other. LOB data types can be taken as an extension to LONG RAW data type. LONG RAW is the only data type that supported large binary data in Oracle7. The following are the differences between LONG RAW data type and LOB data types.

LONG type	LOB type
Can contain up to 2 GB of data	Can contain up to 4 GB of data
A table can contain only one	A table can contain more than

LONG column	one LOB column
A sub-query cannot select a LONG column	A subquery can select LOB column

Defining and Manipulating LOBs

A LOB column is defined just like any other column. Data of the LOB column can be accessed either directly or through DBMS_LOB package. Let us first see how to create a table with LOB columns.

The following example creates a table with a CLOB type column and a BFILE type column.

```
create table  lob_table

(    id    number(5),

     clob_col    clob,

     bfile_col    bfile

);
```

The following functions are used to manipulate LOB columns.

EMPTY_BLOB and EMPTY_CLOB Functions

These functions are part of the SQL DML. They are used to initialize LOB locator to empty locator in INSERT and UPDATE commands.

Note: Before you start writing data to a LOB using either OCI or DBMS_LOB package, the LOB column must be initialized to empty locator using these functions.

The following example stores empty locator into CLOB_COL.

insert into lob_table (id, clob_col)

    values (100, empty_clob());

BFILENAME Function

This is used to initialize a BFILE column. This is used in SQL INSERT and UPDATE commands.

BFILENAME(Directory_alias, Filename) RETURN BFILE;

Directory_alias   Is the alias of the directory in which the file is stored. This directory alias is created using CREATE DIRECTORY command.

Filename   Is the name of the file, which contains the contents that are accessed using BFILE column.

insert into lob_table

values(101, EMPTY_CLOB(), BFILENAME('IMAGES','BMP1.BMP'));

The above INSERT command inserts a row into LOB_TABLE in which BFILE_COL refers to BMP1.BMP file in directory with alias IMAGES.

Directory Alias

Directory alias is to be created using CREATE DIRECTORY command. Directory alias is used to refer to a physical directory (directory in the file system of the operating system) using an alias in Oracle.

441

The directory alias can be used to change the physical directory to which alias points, without having to change the alias itself. This makes the job of making BFILE column pointing to the right directory and right file easier, even though the files are moved from one physical directory to another.

```
create directory "IMAGES" as 'c:\bitmaps';
```

The above statement creates a directory alias called IMAGES, which is an alias to the physical directory C:\BITMAPS.

Note: The directory alias is case sensitive. When using directory alias in BFILENAME function, if proper case is not given then Oracle doesn't recognize the directory alias. But at the time of creation, Oracle converts the directory alias to uppercase if the name is not given in double quotes (" "). So if you want to preserve the case of the directory alias then enclose it in double quotes.

Now, the alias IMAGES can be used to refer to the physical directory in BFILENAME function as shown in the example below.

```
Insert into lob_table
values(101, 'Some data in CLOB cloumn',
     BFILENAME('IMAGES','BMP1.BMP'));
```

Note: it is not possible to display the value of BFILE column using SELECT command in SQL*PLUS.

Users who have to access the directory, should be granted privilege to access the directory as follows:

grant read on directory LOB_DIR to Srikanth;

The above GRANT command grants READ permission on LOB_DIR directory to user SRIKANTH.

Deleting LOBs

When a LOB value is deleted, the locator to the LOB value as well as the LOB value are deleted in case of internal LOBs (CLOB, NCLOB, and BLOB). But in case of BFILE (external LOB) only the locator is deleted and the actual data is not deleted. This is obvious considering the fact that in case of external LOBs database stores only a pointer to the actual content but not the content itself. So for BFILEs you need to delete data manually.

Note: The function discussed above deal with complete LOB column. They do not allow you to modify a part of the LOB column. For information regarding modifying a part of the LOB column, see DBMS_LOB package, later in this chapter.

DBMS_LOB Package

Functions and procedures in DBMS_LOB package can be used to perform various operations related to LOBs. These methods of DBMS_LOB are very important while dealing with LOBs as normal functions such as SUBSTR cannot be used with LOBs.

The following is the list of functions and procedures in DBMS_LOB package.

Method	Description

READ(locator,nobytes,offset, output)	Reads *nobytes* of a LOB value starting from *offset* and places the read piece in *output*.
WRITE(locator, nobytes, offset, buffer)	Writes *nobytes* from *buffer* into a LOB starting at *offset* in a LOB value.
APPEND(dest_locator, source_locator)	Appends one LOB value at the end of another LOB value.
ERASE(locator, nobytes, offset)	Erases *nobytes* from the given *offset* of a LOB value.
TRIM(locator, newlength)	Reduces the size of a LOB value by trimming characters on the right.
SUBSTR(locator, nobytes, offset)	Extracts a portion of a LOB value and returns that value. The difference between this and READ procedure is that READ procedure places the extracted value in the given variable whereas this returns the value.
COPY(dest,source,nobytes, dest_offset,source_offset)	This is a combination of READ and WRITE procedures. This modifies a LOB value by replacing a part of it with data from another LOB.
GETLENGTH(locator)	Returns the length of a LOB value.
INSTR(locator,pattern,offset,occur)	Searches for the given *pattern* and returns the position at which the pattern is found. If *offset* is given search starts at the offset. And if occur parameter is also given then it looks for occur number of *occurrence*.
COMPARE(locator1,locator2,nobytes,offset1,offset2)	Compares two LOB values and returns 0 if they are same, 1 if first one is bigger than second one, and -1 if second one is bigger than first one. offset1 and offset2 may be used to specify at which position in first and

| | second LOBs the search should begin. nobytes specifies the number of bytes to be compared. |

Table 2: DBMS_LOB Functions and Procedures

Examples using DBMS_LOB Package

The following examples use procedures and functions given in the table 2.

INSTR function
The following example looks for the pattern 'Oracle' in   CLOB_COL column
of the row where ID is 10 in LOB_TABLE.

```
declare

   c_lob     CLOB;

   pos       Number(2);

begin

   /* get the value of  CLOB_LOB column

     from the  row where ID is  10  */


   select  clob_col  into   c_lob

   from  lob_table

   where   id =  10;


   /* Use INSTR  function  to find out the

     position where the pattern  'Oracle'

     occurs  in the  LOB value.
```

Search start at first character and look for the

first occurrence of the pattern

```
*/


pos := dbms_lob.instr(c_lob,'Oracle',1,1);


-- if INSTR returns 0 if means pattern is not found
if  pos = 0 then
    dbms_output.put_line('Could not file pattern Oracle');
else
    dbms_output.put_line('Found Oracle at =' || to_char(pos));
  end if;


end;
```

COPY procedure

The following example copies 10 characters of one LOB to another lob.

```
declare
  source_clob    CLOB;
  dest _clob     CLOB;


begin
    /* get  CLOB_COLs of  ID  20   */
    select  clob_col  into    source_clob
```

from   lob_table

where   id = 20;

/* retrieve CLOB_COL of id 10 for

   updation */

select clob_col into   dest_clob

from   lob_table

where   id = 15

for update; -- required to update LOB value

/*Now copy data with the following parameters

    No. of character to be copied = 10

    Offset in the destination LOB = 50

    Offset in the source LOB   = 10 */

dbms_lob.copy(dest_clob,source_clob,10,50,10);

end;

BFILE Related Procedures and Functions

The following are the procedures and functions in DBMS_LOB that are related
to BFILE data type.

Procedure   or Description

Function	
FILEOPEN(bfile,m ode)	Opens the specified file.
FILECLOSE(bfile)	Closes the specified file
FILECLOSEALL	Closes all open files.
FILEEXISTS(bfile)	Checks whether the file referenced by BFILE locator exists.
FILEGETNAME(loc ,dir,file)	Gets the name of external file referenced by BFILE locator.
FILEISOPEN(bfile)	Checks whether external file is currently open.

Table 3: BFILE Related Procedures and Functions in DBMS_LOB Package.

The following example displays the directory and filename of a BFILE column.

```
declare
    bf      bfile;
    d varchar2(20);
    f varchar2(20);
begin
    /* get the  BFILE_COL value for the  ID  20 */
    select   bfile_col into  bf
    from     lob_table
    where    id = 20;

    /* get directory name into d and filename into f */
    dbms_lob.filegetname(bf,d,f);
```

```
    dbms_output.put_line('Directory: ' || d || ' File : '|| f);
end;
```

The following example checks whether the file referenced by a BFILE_COL is existing on the disk.

```
declare
 bf bfile;
begin
   /* get the BFILE_COL value for the ID 20 */
   select bfile_col into bf
   from   lob_table
   where  id = 20;

   /* FILEEXISTS returns non-zero if the given locator
   points to an existing file on the disk */

   if dbms_lob.fileexists(bf) <> 0 then
     dbms_output.put_line(' BFILE for ID 20 is found ');
   else
     dbms_output.put_line(' BFILE for ID 20 is not found');
   end if;

end;
```

449

The following program is used to read the content of BFILE_COL of LOB_TABLE.

```
declare
    value BFILE;
    buf char(100);
    amt BINARY_INTEGER := 100;
    pos INTEGER :=1;
BEGIN
    SELECT bfile_col INTO value FROM lob_table
    WHERE id = 1;
    dbms_lob.fileopen(value, dbms_lob.file_readonly);
    LOOP
        dbms_lob.read(value,amt,pos, buf);
        -- process contents of buf
        pos := pos + amt;
    END LOOP;
    EXCEPTION
      WHEN NO_DATA_FOUND THEN
        dbms_lob.fileclose(value);
end;
/
```

The above program first retrieves BFILE_COL column's data from LOB_TABLE. Then FILEOPEN method is used to open the file using BFILE locator. Then

LOOP is used to read contents from BFILE using READ method until READ method raises NO_DATA_FOUND exception. Each time a chunk of the data is read and processed.

DBMS_LOB.FILE_READONLY constant is used to specify that the file is to be opened file read-only.

Summary

Oracle8 provides a new set of datatypes called LOB data types. These data types can support up to 4GB of data and do not have restrictions that constrain LONG and LONG RAW datatypes. LOB types like BLOB, CLOB and NCLOB store data in the database but BFILE type stores data out of database and maintains only a locator to the actually data.

Oracle8 enhanced its SQL to support LOB data types. Oracle also provided a new package DBMS_LOB, which contains a collection of procedures and functions that manipulates LOB values.

Exercises

♦ Create APPLICANT table with the following columns.

Column	**Description**
name	name of the applicant
resume	a column of CLOB type
photo	a column of BFILE to refer to the file that contains photo image.

♦ Insert a row into APPLICANT table with the following details.

NAME - 'Nike', RESUME - 'Subjects : Oracle, Vb, WindowsNT, C++ ... ', and PHOTO - 'nike.bmp' which is in a directory referred by 'IMAGES' directory alias.

- Write a PL/SQL block to find out whether the pattern 'WindowsNT' is existing in the RESUME column of applicant 'Nike'. If found display the starting position otherwise display error message using DBMS_OUTPUT package.

- Check whether the file , which is referred by Nike's record, is existing on the disk.

- Insert a new row into APPLICANT with the following details.

  NAME - 'Ditchi', RESUME - Empty , PHOTO - Empty.

- Create IMAGES directory to point to 'c:\images'. And change the value of PHOTO column of 'Ditchi' to 'ditchi.bmp' in IMAGES directory.

- Recreate IMAGES directory to point to 'd:\images'.

- Display the length of RESUME column of applicant 'Nike'.

22. OBJECT TYPES

- Introduction to object types

- Creating object type and object

- Using object type

- Creating methods

- Accessing objects using SQL

- Object Type Dependencies

- Object Tables

- Using objects in PL/SQL

❑ MAP and ORDER MEMBER functions

Introduction to Object Types

Object type is composite data type defined by the user. Object type is a user-defined data type that contains the data and code for a particular entity.

An object type is used to model real world entities. For example, using object type you can design a data type to model an account in the bank, or an address of the customer etc.

An instance of the Object Type is called as **Object.**

An object type is consisting of data attributes and methods. Data attributes store the data of the object type and methods are used to perform operations on the data attributes.

Creating Object Type and Object

An object type is created using SQL command CREATE TYPE.

To create an object type called PROJECT_TYPE, enter:

```
create or replace type  project_type  as object
( name  varchar2(20),
  stdate date
);
/
```

PROJECT_TYPE object type has two attributes – NAME and STDATE.

An object type is a template. It doesn't occupy any space. You can now use object type just like how you use any of the scalar data types like NUMBER or CHAR in SQL statements.

Here is the syntax of CREATE TYPE command.

Create type object_type as object

  (Attribute   data type,

   [attribute   data_type] ...

   [MEMBER {procedure | function} specification] ...

   [{MAP | ORDER} MEMBER function specification]

  );

ATTRIBUTE	An attribute of an object type and its associated data type.
MEMBER {PROCEDURE | FUNCTION}	Member procedure or function of the object type. A member procedure or function can access the data of the object type and must be defined using CREATE TYPE BODY command.
{MAP|ORDER} MEMBER	MAP MEMBER and ORDER MEMBER functions are used to return a value, which is used in comparison of objects. More on this later.

Related Data Dictionary Views

The following are the data dictionary views that provide information about Object type.

Table	Description
USER_TYPES	Contains details of user defined data types.
USER_TYPE_A TTRS	Provides detailed information about each data type listed in USER_TYPES.

Table 1: Data dictionary views related to object types.

Using Object Type

After an object type is created, you can use it just like a predefined data type in SQL commands.

The following example will illustrate how to use object type PROJECT_TYPE to define a column of EMP table.


```
create table emp
( empno number(5),
  ename varchar2(20),
  project project_type
);
```


In the above example, column PROJECT is of type PROJECT_TYPE. Each row of the table contains an object of type PROJECT_TYPE.

You can use object type to define the following:

- ❏ Columns of relational table

- ❏ Variable in PL/SQL block

- ❏ Parameters of PL/SQL Sub programs

- ❏ Data attributes of another object type (nested objects)

- ❏ An object table

It is possible to get the structure of an object using DESCRIBE command as follows:

SQL> desc project_type

Name	Null?	Type
---	--------	--------------- NAME
VARCHAR2(20)		
STDATE		DATE

EXECUTE privilege on Object Types

By default only the owner of the object type can refer to it. However, owner of the object type can grant EXECUTE privilege on object type to allow others to access the object type.

If user SRIKANTH owns PROJECT_TYPE and user PRANEETH has to access the object, then the following GRANT command is to be given by SRIKANTH..

grant execute on project_type to praneeth;

Then user PRANEETH can use object type PROJECT_TYPE by using the schema prefix as follows:

create table company

(name number(5),

  project srikanth.project_type

);

Inserting data into objects

Every object type contains a constructor created by Oracle. The constructor is a procedure with the same name as the object type. It is used to initialize attributes of the object type.

The constructor should be passed as many parameters as attributes of the object type.

The following example inserts a row into EMP table. As EMP table contains PROJECT column, which is of type PROJECT_TYPE, we have to use constructor of the object type to put data into that column as follows.

insert into emp values

    (1,'Larry', project_type('Billing system','12-dec-2000'));

Values 1 and Larry will go into relational columns EMPNO and ENAME. Attributes NAME and STDATE of PROJECT are set to *Billing System* and *12-dec-2000*.

Note: You must give a value for each data attribute of the object type. If you ever want to set an attribute of the object to null then give NULL explicitly in the constructor.

Displaying object data

It is possible to display the data of an object using simple SELECT command. The following SELECT displays the data of PROJECT object from EMP table.

SQL> select project from emp;

PROJECT(NAME, STDATE)

PROJECT_TYPE('Billing system', '12-DEC-00')

PROJECT_TYPE('Taxing', '10-JAN-01')

When a column of the table is of an object type then the column is called as *Column Object.*

Creating methods

An object type can also contain methods apart from data attributes. Let us now add a method to PROJECT_TYPE.

A method is first declared in CREATE TYPE command using MEMBER option and defined using CREATE TYPE BODY command. The following example demonstrates it.

create or replace type project_type as object

(

```
    name varchar2(20),

    stdate date,

    member function  GetAge return number,

    member procedure change_stdate(newstdate date)
);
/
```

PROJECT_TYPE is created with two attributes and two methods. First method, GETAGE, returns the number of days between system date and project starting date. Second method takes new starting date and changes the starting date of the project to the given date if the given date is not after system date.

The following CREATE TYPE BODY command is used to create body for methods declared in PROJECT_TYPE.

```
create or replace type body project_type is

  member function  GetAge return number is
  begin
        return  sysdate - stdate;
  end;
  member procedure change_stdate(newstdate date)
  is
  begin
        -- make sure new date is not after sysdate
        if newstdate > sysdate then
```

```
        raise_application_error(-20011, 'Invalid starting date');
    else
        stdate := newstdate;
    end if;
  end;
end;
/
```

SELF

Inside the methods, data attributes are accessed without any qualifier. This is because each method is implicitly passed a reference to the object that is invoking the method. This reference is called as **self**.

So, there is no difference between directly accessing an attribute and using SELF reference, as shown below.

```
member function getage return number
begin
    return sysdate - self.stdate;
end;
```

Note: CREATE TYPE BODY command is required only when object type contains methods.

Accessing attributes and methods

You can access attributes and method using object and dot as follows:

<ObjectName>.<Method> [(ParametersList)]

Objectname	is	a valid object
Method		is a method of the object type
ParametersL ist	is	list of parameters, if method takes parameters

The following PL/SQL program displays the age of the project which employee 2 is dealing with.

```
declare
    pt   project_type;
begin
    select  project into pt
    from  emp where empno = 2;

    dbms_output.put_line (pt.getage);

    -- change stdate of the project
    pt.change_stdate( '15-jan-2001');

    dbms_output.put_line( pt.getage);
end;
```

Accessing objects using SQL

461

You can use SQL commands to access attributes of the objects and manipulate them. When you access attributes of an object you have to use dot (.) operator. When you are referring to an object in SQL you also have to prefix the object with table alias otherwise SQL doesn't recognize the attribute.

```
SQL> Select project.name
  2 From emp;
Select project.name
                *
ERROR at line 1:
ORA-00904: invalid column name
```

To correct the above command, use alias for the table and use that alias as the prefix for column PROJECT.

```
Select e.project.name
From emp e;

PROJECT.NAME
--------------------
Billing system
Billing system
Taxing
```

The following command is used to change the name of the project of employee 1.

update emp e set e.project.name = 'offers.com'

where empno = 1

Calling methods from SQL

It is also possible to call methods of object type from SQL by using dot operator and table alias.

SQL> select ename, e.project.getage() from emp e;

ENAME   E.PROJECT.GETAGE()

------------------- -------------------

Larry   362.27047

Scott   333.27047

The expression e.project.getage() is calling GETAGE function of PROJECT column. The table alias is required to access an attribute or a method of the object type.

Object Type Dependencies

Object types have dependent objects. For example, if you create an object type and then define a column as of the object type then the table is dependent on the object type. In the same way if an attribute of an object type is of another object type then the first object type is said to be dependent on the second object type.

create type marks_type as object

(subject varchar2(10),

  marks   number(3)

);

create table student_type as object

(sno   number(4),

  markdet marks_type

);

Now object type STUDENTS_TYPE is dependent on object type MARKS_TYPE.

When an object type has dependents, it cannot be dropped. If you try to delete object type when it has dependents then it displays the following error.

ORA-02303: cannot drop or replace a type with type or table dependents

Note: However, you can drop an object type in spite of having dependencies using   FORCE option of DROP TYPE command and the dependent objects become invalid.

Object Tables

An object table is a table whose rows are objects. In other words, a table in which each row is an object is called as object table.

The following command creates an object table that contains details of projects. Each row of this table is of type PROJECT_TYPE.

create table projects of project_type;

Now, each row of the PROJECT table is an object of the type PROJECT_TYPE and the attributes of the object type map to the columns of the table.

The following insert command inserts a row into object table, using the default constructor of PROJECT_TYPE:

insert into projects values (project_type('Billing System',sysdate));

You can also insert row directly without using constructor as follows:

insert into projects values ('Hotel Management', '10-dec-2001')

The following SELECT command is used to retrieve the details:

SQL> select * from projects;

NAME   STDATE
-------------------- ---------
Billing System   09-DEC-01
Hotel Management   10-DEC-01

As the attributes of the objects are treated as columns in the table, it is very easy to use object table. You can also access attributes of objects in object table directly from SQL as shown below.

465

The following UPDATE command is used to change STDATE of a project.

```
update projects set stdate = sysdate where name= 'Billing System';
```

The following DELETE deletes all rows where STDATE is in the month of November,2001.

```
delete from projects
where stdate between '1-nov-2001' and '30-nov-2001';
```

Constraints on object table

You can define constraints on object table just like how you define constraints on relational table.

The following example create PROJECTS table with NAME begin the primary key.

```
create table projects of project_type( name primary key);
```

Object Identifiers and References

Each row in object table contains an object, which is also called as row object. Each row object is assigned an object identifier (OID) by Oracle.

The OID or row object is either system generated or the primary key of the table can server as OID of the row. Whether OID is system generated or derived from primary key of the table is defined in CREATE TABLE command used to create object table.

The following CREATE TABLE command creates PROJECTS table by specifying that the ODI is primary key.

create table projects as project_type (name primary key) object id primary key;

It is possible to reference a row object using OID of the row object. For this

The following example creates EMP_TYPE where attribute PROJECT is of reference type referencing PROJECT_TYPE object.

```
create type emp_type  as object
( empno number(5),
  ename varchar2(20),
  project ref project_type
);
```

Now let us create object table EMP_OBT for employees as follows.

create table emp_obt of emp_type;

Since first two attributes of the object table are normal type, we can input simple values. But third attribute is a reference to an object of PROJECT_TYPE and for this we need to use REF operator to get reference of an object of PROJECTS table.

```
insert into emp_obj
  select  1,'Praneeth',  ref(p)
```

from projects p where p.name = 'Billing System'

The above insert command takes a reference of the object of PROJECTS table where project name is 'Billing System' and places that value into PROJECT attribute of the object table. And the remaining two values are literals.

Now it is possible to get the details of employee along with details of project as follows.

select empno, ename, deref(project) from emp_obt

DEREF operator is used to de-reference a reference to get the object to which the reference is pointing.

Using Objects in PL/SQL

It is possible to create object in PL/SQL blocks and use attributes and methods of the object.

The following example creates an object of PROJECT_TYPE and calls its methods.

```
declare
  proj  project_type;
begin
  proj := project_type('seconds.com','12-jun-2001');
  dbms_output.put_line( proj.getage() );
end;
```

First we created a variable proj as of type PROJECT_TYPE. Then we initialized the attributes of PROJECT_TYPE using the constructor. Project name is set to seconds.com and starting date is set to 12-jun-2001. Then we called GETAGE method of the object type and displayed the result on the screen.

The following example is used to get the number of days between the starting date of project of employee 1 and employee 2.

```
declare
    p1  project_type;
    p2  project_type;
begin
    select  project into p1
    from  emp where empno = 1;
    select  project into p2
    from emp where empno = 2;
    dbms_output.put_line( p1.stdate- p2.stdate);
end;
```

MAP and ORDER MEMBER functions

It is possible to compare two objects for we need to create a MAP function or ORDER function.

To use operators like >, < etc., you must provide either MAP MEMBER function or ORDER MEMEBR function.

469

MAP MEMBER function returns the relative position of a given instance in the ordering of all instances of the object. A map method is called implicitly and induces an ordering of object instances by mapping them to values of a predefined *scalar* type. PL/SQL uses the ordering to evaluate Boolean expressions and to perform comparisons.

ORDER MEMBER Function

Is a member function that takes an instance of an object as an explicit argument and returns either a negative, zero, or positive integer. The negative, positive, or zero indicates that the implicit SELF argument is less than, equal to, or greater than the explicit argument.

An object specification can contain only one ORDER method, which must be a function having the return type NUMBER.

You can define either a MAP method or an ORDER method in a type specification, but not both. If you declare either method, you can compare object instances in SQL.

If neither a MAP nor an ORDER method is specified, only comparisons for equality or inequality can be performed.

The following example shows MAP MEMBER function of PROJECT_TYPE.

create or replace type project_type as object

(

   name varchar2(20),

   stdate date,

```
...

    map member function map_stdate return date
);
/


create or replace type body project_type is
    . . .
    map member function map_stdate return date is
    begin
        return stdate;
    end;
end;
/
```

Since we created a MAP MEMBER function in PROJECT_TYPE it is possible to use objects of PROJECT_TYPE in comparison. For example, if we create EMP table (as shown previously) then it is possible to use PROJECT column in ORDER BY clause as follows.

```
select ename from emp order by project;
```

Rows of EMP table are sorted in the ascending order of STDATE of the project as MAP MEMBER function of PROJECT_TYPE returns STDATE.

The following example creates ORDER function in PROJECT_TYPE.

471

```
create or replace type project_type as object

(

  name varchar2(20),

  stdate date,

   ...

  order member function ord_function(obj project_type2) return number

);


create or replace type body project_type is

   ...

  order member function ord_function (obj project_type)  return number is

  begin

      return self.stdate - obj.stdate;

  end;

end;
```

Now also it is possible to use PROJECT column of EMP table in ORDER BY clause as follows.

```
select ename from emp order by project;
```

Summary

Oracle8 onwards users can create user-defined data types. A user defined data type is called as object type. Each object type is a collection of attributes and methods. Attributes contain the data part of object type and methods take actions. An instance of object type is called as an object.

Object type can be used to declare a column of the table or an attribute of another object type or a variable in PL/SQL.

You can define a table in such a way that each row of the table is an object. A table that contains row objects is called as object table. In this case, each row is uniquely identified by an object id, which is assigned to each row object by the system

In order to compare objects or use objects in clauses such as ORDER BY of SQL, the object type must have either MAP MEMBER function or ORDER MEMBER function.

Exercises

Fill in the blanks

♦ _____ command is used to define methods of an object type.

♦ _____ privilege is applicable to object types.

♦ What is the use of SELF keyword in methods of object type?

♦ What is the return type of ORDER MEMER function?

♦ Which command is used to get the list of attributes and methods of the object type.

♦ Create an object type called   JOB_TYPE with the following attributes and methods.

Attribute/Metho   Description

473

d

JOBDATE	date type
STTIME	Char
ENDTIME	Char
HOURRATE	Number
AMOUNT	Return amount to be paid for the time worked.
NOMIN	Return the number of minutes between STTIME and ENDTIME.

Create OVERTIME table with the following details.

ENO   - Employee Number.

JOB   -   JOB_TYPE.

Insert   a record into OVERTIME with the following details.

ENO- 20, JOBDATE - 28-Feb-98, STTIME- 10:20, ENDTIME-12:00,

HOURRATE-150.

For the above row calculate amount to be paid using AMOUNT   method and display the value on the screen.

Display the overtime details of   employee number 20.

Delete overtime record of employee number 20 with the following records.

STTIME - 10:10 and JOBDATE - 10-Mar-98.

23. VARRAY AND NESTED TABLE

- What is a collection?
- What is a VARRAY?
- Using VARRAY
- Nested Table
- Using DML commands with Nested Table
- Collection methods

What is a collection?

A collection is a group of values where all values are of the same type. Oracle provides three types of collections – Indexed Tables, Nested Tables, and VARRAYs. All these collections are like a single dimension array. A column of a table can be declared as of a collection type, an attribute of an object can be of collection type and a collection can also contain a collection of object types.

First let us see what is a VARRAY and how to use it.

What is a VARRAY?

VARRAY stands for variable-size array. It is an array that can be either manipulated as a whole or individually as elements. It has a maximum size and can contain 0 to any number of elements up to the maximum specified.

VARRAY is stored *in-line*. That means the data of a column of VARRAY type is stored along with the remaining data of the row.

You can use VARRAY data type for:

- A column in a relational table
- A PL/SQL variable
- A PL/SQL parameter of procedure or function
- A PL/SQL function return type
- A data attribute of an object type

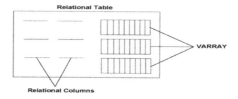

Relational Table

VARRAY

Relational Columns

Using VARRAY

The following procedure illustrates how to declare and use VARRAY.

The following is the syntax to create a data type of VARRAY.

CREATE TYPE array_name AS VARRAY (limit)

    OF data_type

Array_name   is the name of the VARRAY data type.

Limit   is the maximum number of elements that the array can have

Data_type   is the type of each element of the array. It can be any standard type or object type.

Example:

First create an object type called PROJECT_TYPE to store the name of a project and the role played by the employee in that project.

create type project_type as object

477

```
(
  name varchar2(50),
  role varchar2(20)
);
```

Create a VARRAY that can contain up to 5 elements of PROJECT_TYPE.

```
create type projectlist as VARRAY(5) of project_Type;
```

Then create EMP table where column PROJECTS is of type PROJECTLIST.

```
create table emp
( empno number(5),
  ename varchar2(30),
  projects  projectlist
);
```

The following INSERT command will insert a row into EMP table with data for PROJECTS column.

```
insert into emp
 values(1,'Ellison',
        projectlist
          (
```

project_type('Telephone Billing', 'System Analyst'),

project_type('Housing Loans','Oracle DBA')

)

  );

While inserting a row into EMP table use constructor of PROJECTLIST and then the constructor of PROJECT_TYPE for each project the employee is handling. The above INSERT command creates a single row in EMP table where employee is involved in two projects.

The following command displays the details of projects of employee with number 1.

SQL> select projects from emp where empno = 1;

PROJECTS(NAME, ROLE)

PROJECTLIST(PROJECT_TYPE('Telephone   Billing',   'System   Analyst'), PROJECT_TYPE('Housing Loans', 'Oracle DBA'))

However, it is not possible to access the details of a single project as follows:

SQL>select projects(1) from emp where empno= 1;

    *

ERROR at line 1:

ORA-00904: invalid column name

So, a VARRAY is always manipulated as a single value in SQL. The following update is used to change the role of employee 1 in Telephone Billing project to Project Leader.

```
update emp
set projects =
        projectlist
        (
            project_type('Telephone Billing','Project Leader'),
            project_type('Housing Loans','Oracle DBA')
        )
where empno = 1;
```

However, it is possible to handle individual elements using collection methods in PL/SQL. The following function is used to check whether an employee is in the part of the given project.

```
create or replace Function IsPartOfProject(p_empno number, p_projectname varchar2)
return  Boolean
is
  pl ProjectList;   -- VARRAY type to hold projects of an employee
begin
```

```
/* Get the VARRAY of projects */
select  projects  into   pl
from    emp
where   empno = p_empno;

/*check whether the given project name is existing
    in the list of projects*/

  for idx in  1 .. pl.count
  loop

    /* check whether project name is same as the parameter */

    if pl(idx).name = p_projectname then
      -- exit the function by returning true
      return  true;
    end if;

  end loop;

  /* Return false if project name is not found
        in the projects of the employee */

  return  false;
end;
```

The above function starts by declaring a variable – PL – as of type PROJECTLIST. Then we read value of column PROJECTS, which is of type PROJECTLIST, into variable PL.

COUNT method of collection is used to return the number of elements in the collection. We used it to set the loop that varies IDX from 1 to count of elements. As it possible to access individual elements in PL/SQL, we used IDX as subscript to access each element of array PL.

The expression *PL(IDX).NAME* returns the name of the project from the element at the given position. If it is equal to project name parameter then the function returns true and function is terminated. Otherwise after the loop is terminated the function return false.

Note: Currently, you cannot reference the individual elements of a varray in an INSERT, UPDATE, or DELETE statement. However, it is possible to add manipulate data using PL/SQL.

The following procedure is used to add a new project. It takes employee number, project name and role of the employee in the project.

create or replace procedure new_project

       (p_empno number, p_projname varchar2, p_role varchar2)

as

 pl projectlist;

begin

```
-- get varray of the employee
select projects into pl from emp2
   where empno = p_empno;


pl.extend;  -- make room for new project


-- place an object of project_type at the end of the varray
pl(pl.last) := project_type (p_projname, p_role);


-- change the data in the table
update emp2 set projects = pl
   where empno = p_empno;
end;
/
```

Nested Table

Nested table is a table that is stored in database as the data of a column of the table. Nested table is like an Index-By table, but the main difference is that a nested table can be stored in the database and an Index-by table cannot.

Nested table extends Index-by table by allowing the operations such as SELECT, DELETE, UPDATE and INSERT to be performed on nested table.

The following example illustrates steps related to creating and using nested table.

```
create type project_type as object
(
  name varchar2(50),
  role varchar2(20)
);
```

Now create a TABLE data type as follows:

```
create type ProjectTable as Table of Project_type;
```

Finally we use PROJECTTABLE type to create a column in EMP table as follows:

```
create table emp
( empno number(5),
  ename varchar2(30),
  projects projecttable
)
nested table projects store as projects_nt;
```

Table EMP contains PROJECTS, which contains a table of PROJECTTABLE type for each row.

NESTED TABLE option is required as we have a nested table column in the table. NESTED TABLE clause specifies the name of the table in which Oracle stores the data of the nested table. In this example PROJECTS_NT is created by Oracle and maintained by Oracle. It contains the data of PROJECTS column.

Note: The data of VARRAY is stored as part of the row, but the data of nested table is stored out-of-row in the table whose name is given in NESTED TABLE option.

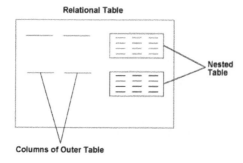

The following INSERT command inserts a row into EMP table. It stores two rows into nested table.

insert into emp

values(1,'Ellison',

    projecttable

    (

        project_type('Telephone Billing','System Analyst'),

        project_type('Housing Loans','Oracle DBA')

485

```
    )
  );
```

As you observed, the way we insert row into nested table and VARRAY is same. However there are many differences when it comes to data retrieval and updation.

Note: If the table constructor is called without any parameter then an empty table is created. An empty table is not equal to NULL.

Using DML commands with Nested Table

DML commands can treat a nested table as one of the following.

- ❏ As a table and deal with individual rows of the table.
- ❏ As an atomic value.

DML treating inner table as atomic value

The following DML commands operate on outer table treating inner table as a single value.

The following PL/SQL block will assign the projects of employee 1 to employee 3.

```
declare
    p1  projecttable;
begin
```

```
    select projects into  pl

    from   emp

    where  empno = 1;


    update emp set projects = pl

    where  empno = 3;


    commit;

end;
```

The following DELETE command will delete the details of where PROJECTS column is NULL.


```
delete from emp where projects is null;
```

DML treating nested table as table

In the previous section we have seen how to manipulate inner table by treating it as an atomic value. Now in this section we will see how to manipulate inner table as a table.

To manipulate the inner table we have to use a new operator TABLE. This operator takes a single operand that is of type nested table or varray.

The following command displays the details of projects of employee 1.


```
select * from table ( select projects from emp where empno =1);
```

NAME	ROLE
Telephone Billing	System Analyst
Housing Loans	Oracle DBA

Subquery retrieves PROJECTS column from EMP table. TABLE operator expects a Nested Table or VARRAY column. It then supplies the data of the column in the form a rows to outer query, which displays the data as it is.

In order to displays the names of the projects in which employee 1 is Oracle DBA:

select name from table (select projects from emp where empno =1)
where role = 'Oracle DBA';

NAME

Housing Loans

It is also possible to insert, delete and update individual rows of nested table. Remember that is not permitted for VARRAY.

The following INSERT command adds a new row to projects table of employee 1.

insert into table (select projects from emp where empno = 1) values ('BillsOnline.com', 'Web Developer');

Similarly, it is possible to change the role of employee 1 in project Telephone Billing to Project Leader.

update table (select projects from emp where empno = 1)

  Set role = 'Project Leader'

where name= 'Telephone Billing';

To delete the project BillsOnline.com from employee 1, enter:

delete from table (select projects from emp where empno = 1)

where name = 'BillsOnline.com'

Collection Methods

Oracle provides a set of methods that can be used with collections. These methods can be used only in PL/SQL and not in SQL.

The general syntax of these methods is:

collection_name.method_name[(parameters)]

Collection_name	Is the name of the collection object
Method_name	Is one of the methods listed in the table below
Parameters	Are the parameters that are to be sent to method (if required).

The following is the list of collection methods and their meaning.

Method	Meaning
EXISTS(n)	Returns true if n^{th} element is existing in the collection.
COUNT	Returns the number of elements that a collection currently contains.
LIMIT	For Nested table it returns NULL. For VARRAY it returns the maximum number of elements specified.
FIRST	Returns the smallest index of the collection. If collection is empty then return NULL. For VARRAY it always returns 1. But for nested table, it may return 1 or if first item is deleted then it will be more than 1.
LAST	Same as FIRST, but returns largest index. For VARRAY LAST and COUNT are same but for Nested Tables, it may be more than COUNT, if any items are deleted from Nested table.
PRIOR(n)	Returns the index number that precedes the given index. If no index is available then it returns NULL. This method ignores null values.
NEXT(n)	Returns the index number that follows the given index. If no index is available then it returns NULL. This method ignores null values. PRIOR and NEXT are useful to traverse a nested table in which some items are deleted.
EXTEND	Appends one null element to collection.
EXTEND(n)	Appends specified number of items.
TRIM(n)	Removes one or more elements from the end of the collection.
DELETE	Removes all elements from the collection.
DELETE(n)	Removes n^{th} elements.

DELETE(m,n)	Removes elements between m and n.

The following examples will show you how to use collection methods on the collections.

```
declare
-- declare a variable of projecttable type
pl projecttable := projecttable ( project_type('payroll','designer'));

-- procedure to display the values of the table
procedure displist(pl projecttable)
is
begin
  dbms_output.put_line('Available items');
  -- set the loop to varray from first element to last element
  for i in  pl.first..pl.last
  loop
    if  pl.exists(i) then  -- if item exists then display
        dbms_output.put_line( i || ' - ' ||  pl(i).name);
    end if;
  end loop;
end;


begin  -- beginning of the main block
```

```
displist(pl);


-- add two new elements to the collection
pl.extend(2);


-- set values for two new elements
pl(2) := project_type('inventory','network adm');
pl(3) := project_type('law.com','web developer');


displist(pl);


pl.delete(2);  -- delete second  item


displist(pl);


pl.trim(1);   -- remove the last item


displist(pl);
end;
/
```

Summary

A collection is a set of value of same type. Oracle provides VARRAYS, Index-by tables and nested tables.

VARRAY (variable-size array) is used to an array that contains a maximum limit and contains varying number of elements. Oracle doesn't provide much flexibility on VARRAYS. For instance, it is not possible to manipulate individual elements of VARRAY.

Nested table is a table within another table It allows better control on the elements of the table. The data in the nested table is not stored as part of the main table and instead stored separately in a table created by Oracle.

TABLE operator is used to perform data manipulation on individual rows of nested table. It takes a column of nested table or VARRAY type and allows you to treat that as a collection of rows.

Collection methods are used to provide information and manage collections in PL/SQL. They cannot be used in SQL but a collection can be changed by these methods and the result can be put back to table.

Exercises

♦ _____ method is used to remove an item of the collection from the given position.

♦ _____ is the command used to VARRAY type.

♦ Is it possible to use VARRAY column as operand of TABLE operator.

♦ Is it possible for COUNT and LAST methods to return different values? If so why.

♦ What is the purpose of NESTED TABLE clause in CREATE TABLE command?

♦ What are the difference between VARRAY and Nested Table?

♦ Create a table to store the details of STUDENTS along with the marks obtained by students in 10 subjects. Assume that the subjects are having fixed order and may vary from 5 to 10.

♦ Write a function to take students number and subject number and return marks.

493

24. Native Dynamic SQL

- What is dynamic SQL?

- Why do we need dynamic SQL?

- An Example of Dynamic SQL

- Execute Immediate Statement

- Using Placeholders

- Execute a Query Dynamically

- Executing multi-row query dynamically

- Dynamic PL/SQL Blocks

What is Dynamic SQL?

Generally programmer knows the SQL statements that are to be executed at the time of writing program. However, in some cases the programmer may not precisely know the command that is to be executed at the time of writing program. Instead the command may vary from execution to execution and it is to be constructed dynamically (at runtime). An SQL statement that is constructed "on the fly" is dynamic SQL statement.

Until Oracle8 the only way to execute dynamic SQL was by using DBMS_SQL package. Oracle8i introduced native dynamic SQL, where you can directly place dynamic SQL commands into PL/SQL blocks. Native dynamic SQL is faster then using DBMS_SQL package.

Dynamic SQL should be considered only when static SQL is not possible. Dynamic SQL will impact performance.

Why do we need dynamic SQL?

We should use dynamic SQL where static SQL doesn't support the operation that we want to perform.

495

The following are the situations where you may want to use Dynamic SQL:

- You want to execute an SQL DDL or DCL command that cannot be executed statically. That means the command is not allowed in the PL/SQL block. For example, you cannot execute DROP TABLE command from a PL/SQL block.

- You want to access a table or a view but do not know the name of the object until you run the program.

An Example of Dynamic SQL

Let's look at an example. Assume we have to drop a table. But the name of the table to be dropped is not known. The name of the table is formed using the word SALES and four digits year. For example, it the current year is 2000 then table name would be SALES2000.

That means depending upon the current year the name of the table changes. So the DROP TABLE command should drop the table of the current year and the current year is to be taken from the system date.

The solution to this problem is to construct DROP TABLE command as follows:

```
cmd := 'DROP TABLE  sales' || to_char(sysdate,'yyyy');
```

The above statement will put the required command into a char variable and then the command in the char variable is to be executed with EXECUTE IMMEDIATE command.

Execute Immediate Statement

This statement is used to execute a command that is a char variable. In the above example we put the required command in a variable called *cmd*. Now, we can execute the command as follows:

EXECUTE IMMEDIATE cmd;

Now let us examine the complete syntax of Execute Immediate statement.

EXECUTE IMMEDIATE dynamic_string

[INTO {variable[, variable]... | record}]

[USING [IN | OUT | IN OUT] bind_argument

  [, [IN | OUT | IN OUT] bind_argument]...];

Dynamic_string	Is the string that contains the command to be executed.
Variable | record	Is a variable into which values retrieved by SELECT command are to be copied. If a record is given then complete row is copied into the record. Record must be a variable of user-defined data type or %ROWTYPE% record.
Bind_argument	Is the value that is to be passed to SQL statement that is being executed. This value will replace a placeholder in the command (more on this later).

The following stored procedure takes the name of the table and drops the table.

create or replace procedure droptable (tablename varchar2) is
  cmd varchar2(100);

497

```
begin

   cmd := 'drop table ' || tablename;

   execute immediate cmd;

end;
```

You can now call the above procedure to drop a table. You have to supply the name of the table to be dropped. Remember that in PL/SQL DDL commands are not allowed in static SQL, so dynamic SQL is required.

```
execute droptable('oldsales');
```

The following is another stored function that takes the year and deletes all rows from the tables whose name is formed as *SALESyear*. Where *year* is the value passed to the procedure.

```
create or replace function deletesalesrows (year number)

return number is

cmd  varchar2(100);

begin

   cmd := 'delete from sales' || year;

   execute immediate cmd;

   return  sql%rowcount;

end;
```

The function takes year number and deletes all rows from sales table of that year. It also returns the number of rows deleted from the table.

You can invoke the function to delete rows of 2000 sales table and display the number of rows deleted as follows:

```
begin
   dbms_output.put_line( deletesalesrows(2000));
end;
```

Using Placeholders

Placeholders can be used to replace a missing value at runtime. A placeholder is a name preceded by : (colon). The placeholder is to be replaced with a value through USING clause of EXECUTE IMMEDIATE statement.

The following example deletes all rows of the given table where PRODID is equal to the product id passed.

```
create or replace procedure DeleteSalesRows
      (tablename varchar2, prodid number) is
cmd varchar2(100);
begin
   cmd := 'delete rows from ' || tablename || ' where prodid = :prodid';
   execute immediate cmd using  prodid;
end;
/
```

At the time of executing a command that has placeholders, we must pass values that replace placeholders through USING clause of EXECUTE

IMMEDIATE command. In the above example, the value of variable PRODID will replace the placeholder :PRODID and then the command is executed.

Note: The number of placeholders and the number of values passed by USING clause must be equal.

Placeholders and parameters are matched by the position and not by name. That means if the same placeholder is used for twice or more then for each occurrence the value is to be passed by USING clause as show below.

cmd := 'INSERT INTO sometable VALUES (:x, :x, :y, :x)';

EXECUTE IMMEDIATE sql_stmt USING a, a, b, a;

You have to pass four values to the above command although there are only two placeholders – X and Y. This is because of the fact that bind arguments are associated with placeholders by position and not by name. That means the first bind argument is associated with first placeholder and second bind argument with second placeholder and so on.

Note: Placeholders cannot be used for names of schema objects.

The following dynamic SQL statement is INVALID.

cmd := 'drop table :table_name';

execute immediate cmd using tablename;

500

Execute a Query Dynamically

So far whatever we have seen is related to non-query SQL statements. Now, let us see how to execute an SQL query dynamically. The difference between executing a non-query and a query is; a query returns one or more rows. In the beginning we will confine our examples to executing single-row query statements.

When a query in executed dynamically using EXECUTE IMMEDIATE command then we have to supply INTO clause to catch the values retrieved by the query. The following example shows how to use SELECT command with dynamic SQL to retrieve highest and lowest prices at which the given product is sold in the current year.

```
declare

    cmd  varchar2(100);

    prodid  number(5)  :=  10;

    lprice  number(5);

    hprice  number(5);

begin

    cmd := 'select  min(price), max(price) from sales';

    cmd := cmd  | |  to_char(sysdate,'yyyy')  | |  ' where prodid = :1';


    -- execute the command by sending product id


    execute immediate cmd into lprice, hprice using  prodid;


    dbms_output.put_line( 'lowest price is : '  | |   lprice);
```

dbms_output.put_line('highest price is : ' || hprice);

end;

While a query is executed using EXECUTE IMMEDIATE command   the following rules will apply:

- ❑ The number of columns to be retrieved should be known at the time of writing program.
- ❑ Only one record can be retrieved as only one set of variable can be passed using INTO.

The following function is used to return salary of the employee from the given table.


```
create or replace function GetSalary(tablename varchar2, empno number)
return number is
  cmd varchar2(100);
  v_sal number(5);
begin
  cmd := 'select sal from ' || tablename || ' where empno = :empno';
  execute immediate cmd  into v_sal using  empno;


  return v_sal;


exception
```

```
when no_data_found then

   return null;

end;
```

The above function returns NULL if the given employee number is not found in the given table.

Executing multi-row query dynamically

Using simple EXECUTE IMMEDIATE statement we can execute a query that retrieves only one row. However, when we need to execute a query that has the potential to retrieve multiple rows, we need to follow a different process.

To deal with multi-row query dynamically, we have to use a Cursor. All the rows retrieved by the query are copied into cursor. And then using FETCH statement each row will be fetched and processed.

The following are the statements used to execute a multi-row query dynamically.

Open-For statement to open the cursor

The first step is to open a cursor with the query statement. This statement associates a cursor variable with the given query and executes the query. This statement has USING option to pass values to placeholders.

The complete syntax of OPEN-FOR statement is as follows:

OPEN {cursor_variable}

  FOR dynamic_string

  [USING bind_argument[, bind_argument]...];

Cursor_variable   Is a weakly typed cursor variable, i.e. a variable that doesn't have any return type.

Dynamic_string   The SELECT command to be executed.

Bind_argument   Is the value to be passed to placeholders of the command.

The following is an example where all rows of SALES table of the current year are retrieved.

```
DECLARE

    TYPE SalesCursorType IS REF CURSOR; -- define weak REF CURSOR type

    salescursor  SalesCursorType; -- declare cursor variable

BEGIN

    OPEN salescursor FOR -- open cursor variable

        'SELECT  proid, qty, price from sales' || to_char(sysdate,'yyyy');

    .

    .

    .

END;
```

Fetching row from cursor

Fetches one row from the cursor and copies the values of the columns into corresponding variables.

FETCH {cursor_variable } INTO {define_variable[, define_variable] ... | record};

Cursor_variable	is the cursor variable with which the result of the query is associated.
Define_variable	is the variable into which the value the corresponding columns should be copied.
Record	is the variable of a user-defined record type or %ROWTYPE%.

To fetch rows from SALESCURSOR that we have defined in the previous step, we have to use Fetch statement as follows:

Loop

    Fetch salescursor into prodid, qty, price;

    Exit when sales_cursor%notfound;   --exit when no more records exist

    -- process the record here

End loop

Closing the cursor

The last step in the process is closing the cursor after it is processed.

CLOSE {cursor_variable};

A sample program

The following program is consolidating all that we have seen regarding how to execute a multi-row query dynamically.

```
declare

    type salescursortype is ref cursor; -- define weak ref cursor type

    salescursor  salescursortype; -- declare cursor variable


    prodid  number(5);

    qty    number(5);

    price  number(5);


begin


    open salescursor for -- open cursor variable

      'select  proid, qty, price from sales' || to_char(sysdate,'yyyy');


loop

    fetch salescursor into prodid, qty, price;

    exit when sales_cursor%notfound;  --exit when no more records exist

    -- process the record here

end loop


close salescursor;  -- close the cursor after it is processed.
```

end; -- end of the block

Dynamic PL/SQL Blocks

You can execute an anonymous PL/SQL block dynamically using EXECUTE IMMEDIATE statement. It is useful in cases where the procedure to be invoked is known only at runtime.

The following procedure invokes one of the two procedure based on the name of the company. For this we assume we already have two procedures with names HIKESAL_A and HIKESAL_B where A and B are company names.

```
create or replace procedure callhikesal(company varchar2)is
begin
  execute immediate
    'begin
    hikesal_' || company;
    'end;'
end;
```

The above procedure calls the procedure with the name HIKESAL_A or HIKESAL_B depending on the name of the company – A or B – passed to the procedure.

The same can be done without dynamic SQL but it becomes length and needs to be updated if more there is any change in number of companies.

The following is non-dynamic SQL version of the same procedure.

```
create or replace procedure callhikesal(company varchar2)is
begin
  if  company = 'A' then
      hikesal_a;
  else
      hikesal_b;
  end if;
end;
```

But as you can notice, if we add one more company to the list then the procedure is to be modified to accommodate another company.

Summary

Dynamic SQL is the process of constructing SQL commands dynamically and executing them. This was done using DBMS_SQL package prior to Oracle8i but in Oracle8i Native Dynamic SQL was introduced making dynamic SQL less cumbersome and faster.

EXECUTE IMMEDIATE statement is used to execute an SQL command that is constructed at runtime. You can execute DML, single-row SELECT and even multi-row SELECT.

While executing multi-row query, we have to use a cursor to retrieve the data into cursor and then fetch one row at a time from user.

It is also possible to execute a PL/SQL block dynamically.

Exercises

+ _____ option is used to pass bind arguments to placeholders.

+ When there are 2 placeholders used three times in the command then how many bind arguments are to be passed?

+ Create a function that takes table name and a condition and returns the number of rows in the table that satisfy the given condition.

USER-DEFINED FUNCTIONS

Functions are building blocks of a C program. In this chapter, we will understand what is a function, how to create and use functions. Understanding functions is one of the most important steps in C language.

◻ What is a function?

◻ Standard functions

◻ User-defined functions

◻ Passing parameters

◻ Returning value

◻ Function declaration and definition

◻ Recursion

◻ Summary

◻ Exercises

What is a function?

A function is a collection of instructions that performs a specific task. Every function is given a name. The name of the function is used to invoke (call) the function. A function may also take parameters (arguments). If a function takes parameters, parameters are to be passed within parentheses at the time of invoking function.

A function theoretically also returns a value, but you can ignore the return value of the function in C language.

Following are a few examples of using functions in C language. C is a function-oriented language. Many operations in C language are done through functions. For example, we have used printf() function to display values, scanf() function to read values from keyboard, strlen() function to get the length of the string etc.

Functions are of four types:

- Functions that take nothing and return nothing.

- Functions that take nothing but return a value.

- Functions that take something but return nothing.

- Functions that take something and return a value.

Here are a few examples of types of functions.

```
/* passing a single value and ignoring the return value */
printf("We are ignoring return value ");
```

```
/* not passing any value but taking the return value of the function*/
ch =  getchar();
```


```
/* passing the value and taking the return value */
len = strlen(st);
```

As you can see, almost everything in C language is done through functions.

A function can be defined as A set of instructions meant to perform a task and return a value. A function returns *one and only one* value. A function may also take one or more values, but that is optional.

In C a function is also used as a procedure since C doesn't support procedures. The difference between a function and a procedure is, procedure doesn't return a value and function always returns a value.

Functions in C language are divided into standard functions and user-defined functions.

Standard functions

Every C compiler provides good number of functions. All that a programmer has to do is use them straight away. For example, if you have to find length of a string , use strlen() without having to write the required code.

A function which is made available to programmer by compiler is called as standard function or pre-defined function. The code for all standard functions is available in library files, like cs.lib, and graphics.lib. These library files are supplied by the vendor of compiler. Where these libraries are stored in the system depends on the compiler. For example, if you are using Turbo C, you find libraries in LIB directory under directory where Turbo C is installed.

Declarations about standard functions are available in header files such as stdio.h, and string.h.

We will discuss more about function declaration and function definition later in this chapter.

513

Turbo C provides around 400 functions covering various areas like Screen IO, graphics, disk IO etc.

Compiler dependent functions

Out of standard functions, some functions are compiler dependent. That means these function are not available in all compilers. For example, Turbo C comes with functions like clrscr(), and gotoxy(). But these functions will not be found on UNIX C compiler and instead some other functions doing similar task will be available.

ANSI C functions

Some functions such as printf(), isupper() etc. are ANSI C functions. That means these functions are to be made available by every C compiler. So, if you are planning to compile your C program with different compilers then you better stick to these functions only as these functions are standard.

User-defined functions

User-defined function is a function that is defined by user. That means, the code for the function is written by user (programmer). User-defined functions are similar to standard functions in the way you call. The only difference is instead of C language providing the function, programmer creates the function.

User-defined functions are used mainly for two purposes:

To avoid repetition of code

In programming you often come across the need to execute the same code in different places in the program. For example, assume you have to print an array at the beginning of the program and at the end of the program. Without a function you have to write the code to display the array twice (see figure 1).

If you create a function to display the array, then you have to call the function once at the beginning of the program and once at the end of the program. That means, the source code need not be written for multiple times. It is written only for once and called for multiple times (see figure 2).

In nutshell, a function created by user is called as **user-defined function**.

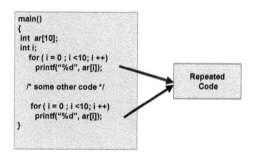

Figure 1: Program without user-defined function

```
main()
{
int ar[10];
int i;

    printarray(ar);

    /* some other code */

    printarray(ar);
}
printarray(int ar[])
{
    int i;
    for ( i = 0;  i < 10 ; i++)
    printf("%d",  ar[i]);
}
```

Figure 2: Program with user-defined function

To break large program into smaller units

It is never a good idea to have a single large code block. If you write entire C program as one block, the entire blocks ends up in main() function. It becomes very difficult to understand and manage.

If you can break a large code block into multiple smaller blocks, called functions, then it is much easier to manage the program. In the following example, instead of taking input, processing and displaying output in main() function, if you can divide it into three separate functions, it will be much easier to understand and manage.

```
main()
{

    /* take input here */
    ...

    /* process the input here */
    ...

    /* display output here */
    ...

}
```

Figure 3: A single large main() function.

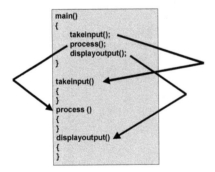

516

Figure 4: main() function calling other functions

Creating user-defined function

A user-defined function is identical to main() function in creation. However, there are two differences between main function and a user-defined function.

- **Name of main() function is standard, whereas a user-defined function can have any name.**

- **main() function is automatically called when you run the program, whereas a user-defined function is to be explicitly called.**

The following is an example of a user-defined function. This is a very simple function to display the name of the person and company name.

```
/* main function */

main()
{
    /* call user-defined function */
    print();

}

/* user-defined function */

print()
{
```

517

```c
    printf("P.Srikanth\n");
    printf("Srikanth Technologies");
}
```

Here is another user-defined function to draw a line.

```c
/* program to call a user-defined function called line
   to draw a line */


main()
{

    line ();  /* call function line */
    printf("Srikanth Technologies");
    line ();  /* call line function again */
}


/* user defined function line to draw a line across the screen */
line()
{
    int l;

    for ( l = 1 ; l <= 79 ; l ++ )
        putch( '-');
```

}

In main function we called line function. To call a function, use function name followed by parenthesis. If function takes any values then send values by giving them in parenthesis. In fact, there is nothing new about it. We have been doing it since our first C program. The only new thing is; we are writing code for function instead of calling prewritten code. We will see more about passing parameters later in this chapter. As you see in figure 5, when main function calls line() function, control is transferred to line() function. After the code in line() function is executed, control returns to next statement following the statement that called the function.

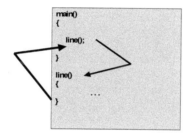

Figure 5: Transfer of control when function is called.

Passing parameters

Though line function is useful, it always does the same thing. I mean, it always displays a line of 79 hyphens. But what if we want to have a line of only 30 characters and not 79 characters. It would be far more flexible and versatile if line function were to take length and draw line of that length.

For this line function is to be slightly modified to take a parameter and use that parameter. A *parameter* or *argument* is a value passed to function so that function can use that value while performing task. A function may take none , one or more parameters depending upon the need.

Here is the modified version of line function.

```
#include <conio.h>

main()

{

    /* call function line with different values */

    line ( 10 );

    line ( 40);

    line ( 20);

}


/* len contains  whatever value  is passed  to this function */

line(int  len)

{

  int  l;

    for ( l = 0 ; l < len  ; l ++ ) /* draw a line of len  length */
```

```
        putch( '-');


}
```

Whenever we call line function we have to pass a value in parentheses. The value passed is placed in variable declared in parentheses of function definition (int len). In the function, the passed value is referenced using parameter (len).

Actual Parameter

Is the value that is passed to function while calling the function.

For example, 10,40 and 20 values that we passed to line() function in the above program.

Formal Parameter

Variable that is used to receive actual parameter. In the above program len in function line().

Passing array as parameter

When an array is passed as parameter, only the name of the array is given at the time of calling function. The formal parameter is to be declared as an array. Here is an example to print the given array.

printarray(int ar[10])
```
{
    int i;
```

```
    for ( i = 0 ; i < 10 ; i ++)

        printf("%5d", ar[i]);

}


main()

{

    int a[10];


        printarray(a);

}
```

Returning Value

Normally after performing the task functions return a value. The return value may be of any type. But a function can return only one value. To return a value from the function, we have to first specify what type of value the function returns and then we have to use return statement in the code of the function to return the value.

When return type is not explicitly mentioned it defaults to int. If a function doesn't return any value then specify return type as void.

The following program illustrates it.

```
 /* declaration of the function */

 int   getsum( int  n);
```

```c
main()
{
    int v, sum;

        printf("Enter a  number : ");
        scanf("%d", &v);
        /* call function  getsum() to get sum of numbers  from 1 to v */
        sum =   getsum(v);
        printf(" Sum = %d ", sum);
}


/* function definition  or body */
int  getsum(int n)
{
    int  s = 0;

        for ( ; n > 0; n --)
              s += n;

        /*  return the value of s as return value of function  */
        return  s;
}
```

In the above example, function getsum() takes a single integer and returns the sum of all numbers from 1 to the given number. The function has specified that it intends to return an integer and returned the value using return statement. We will understand more about function declaration and function definition in the next section.

Function declaration and definition

A function may contain declaration and definition. Function declaration specifies function name, return type, and type of parameters. This is normally given at the beginning of the program. Though it is not mandatory in all cases , it is better to declare each function. In fact header files(*.h) contain declarations of all standard functions.

The following is the syntax for function declaration.
    return-type   functionname (parameters);

Function declaration is called as **Prototype declaration** . Though it is not necessary in majority of cases, it is needed in cases where the following conditions apply:

- **Call to function comes before definition of the function**

- **Function returns non-integer value.**

The following is an example where these two conditions are satisfied.

/*function without prototype declaration */

/*This results in compile time error */

main()

{

524

```
int a[10];

float  avg;

/* get values into array */

   ...

/* call function to get average of the array */


/* compiler doesn't know the return type.
   So it assumes it is an int */


avg =  getaverage(a);
}


float  getaverage(int a[])
{
float f;
int i;


   for( i=0; i < 10 ; i++)
      f += a[i];


   return   f / 10;  /* return average */
}
```

Look at the above example. Here we have a function called getaverage(), which takes an array of 10 integers and returns a float.

But as C compiler encounters call to function before definition of the function, C compiler assumes the return type as integer. But when compiler gets to function definition it understands that the function returns float. As the assumption of the compiler (function returning int) and the reality (function returning float) are not matching it returns an error *Type mismatch in redeclaration of 'getaverage'.*

The remedy to this is to declare the function before it is called using prototype declaration. This lets compiler know that function returns float type value and not int type (default type) and that will solve the problem.

/*function with prototype declaration */

/* prototype declaration for getaverage() function */

float getaverage(int a[]);

main()

{

   int a[10];

   float avg;

    /* get values into array */

     ...

    /* call function to get average of the array */

    /* compiler already knows the return type.

So it doesn't take it as int */

```
    avg = getaverage(a);

}


float  getaverage(int a[])
{
float f;
int i;

    for( i=0; i < 10 ; i++)
      f += a[i];

    return  f / 10;  /* return average */
}
```

Note: It is always better you declare functions and then define them.

Function definition

Function definition is where the statements to be executed are given. When the function is called the statements given here are executed.

```
    return-type  functionname ( parameters )
```

```
{
    statements;
    return  value;
}
```

Return type specifies the type of value function returns. If function doesn't return any value then it must be void.

Parameters are formal parameters of the function.

Statements are the statements to be executed when function is called.

Return statement is used to return a value from function.

Recursion

When a function calls itself it is called as recursion. Recursion is natural way of writing certain functions. Though it sounds a bit intimidating in the beginning, once you get used to it, it becomes easy and natural.

The following program displays the given number in reverse order using function reverse(), which is recursively called. Every recursive function should have a way to terminate the function. That means, at one point it should stop calling itself. Otherwise, it becomes never ending recursion and program will be terminated with an error saying "out of stack space".

If you are wondering what stack has got to do with recursion then here is the connection. Whenever you call a function, certain information about the function, parameters and local variables are placed in a memory structure called stack. If you call a function several times (which will be the case with improperly written recursive function) then the stack may be filled and may stop the program. So that is the reason for stack overflow error.

```
/* program to display the given number in reverse */
main()
{
  int n;
```

```c
    printf("Enter a number :");
    scanf("%d",&n);

    reverse(n);

}

reverse(int n)
{
    if( n == 0 ) return;   /* stop calling it self */

    /* print last digit of the given number */
    printf("%d", n % 10);

    /* call function recursively by removing last digit */
    reverse( n /10);
}
```

If you find recursion difficult to understand, no need to panic. Because every function that is written using recursion can be written even without using recursion. However, in certain cases writing recursive version is easier than non-recursive version.

Summary

A function is a collection of statements to do a task. A function may or may not take parameters but it always returns a single value . Functions may be predefined or user-defined. User-defined functions are the ones that user created by writing the code. A user-defined function may contain function declaration, where information about function is supplied to compiler, and function definition, where code of the function is written. Function returns a value using return statement. When a function calls itself it is called as recursion.

Exercises

I. Fill in the blanks

1. A function can return _____ number of values.

2. _____ statement is used to terminate a function.

3. _____ is the default return type of function.

4. Out of function declaration and function definition which is optional ?
   _____

5. In which order function declaration and function definition should be given.

6. When a function calls itself it is called as _____

7. What are the differences between a user-defined function and main() function.

Write functions.

1. Write a function that takes a number as parameter and returns the next odd number.

2. Write a function to take a string as parameter and display it in lowercase.

3. Write a function to take a number and return 1 if it is a prime number otherwise 0.

4. Write a function to take a string and return the number of digits the string contains.

5. Write a function to take a number and return factorial of the given number. Use recursion.

BIBLIOGRAPHY

1. Advanced Micro Devices. *AMD Processor Recognition - Application Note*, January 2002.
2. Rakesh Agrawal and Arun Swami. A One-Pass Space-Efficient Algorithm for Finding Quintiles. In *Proc of the Int'l. Conference on Management of Data*, December 1995.
3. Anastassia Ailamaki, David J. DeWitt, Mark D. Hill, and David A. Wood. DBMSs On A Modern Processor: Where Does Time Go? 1999.
4. Gene M. Amdahl. Validity of the single-processor approach to achieving large scale computing capabilities. In *AFIPS Conference Proceedings*, pages 483-485, April 1967.
5. American National Standard for Information Systems. Database language SQL. ANSI X3.135-1992, November 1992.
6. Peter M.G. Apers, Carel A. van den Berg, Jan Flokstra, Paul W. P. J. Grefen, Martin L. Kersten, and Annita N. Wilschut. PRISMA/DB: A Parallel Main Memory Relational DBMS. *IEEE Trans. on Knowledge and Data Eng.*, 4(6):541-554, December 1992.
7. 7 Nanette J. Boden, Danny Cohen, Robert E. Felderman, Alan E. Kulawik, Charles L. Seitz, Jakov N. Seizovic, and Wen-King Su. Myrinet: A gigabit-per-second local area network. *IEEE Micro*, 15(1):29-36, May 1995.
8. Peter A. Boncz. *Monet. A Next-Generation DBMS Kernel For Query Intensive Applications.* PhD Thesis, Universiteit van Amsterdam, Amsterdam, The Netherlands, May 2002.
9. Peter A. Boncz and Martin L. Kersten. Monet. An Impressionist Sketch of an Advanced Database Systems. 1994.
10. Peter A. Boncz and Martin L. Kersten. MIL Primitives For Querying a Fragmented World. *The VLDB Journal*, 8(2), October 1999.

11. Trishul M. Chilimbi, Mark D. Hill, and James R. Larus. Cache-conscious structure layout. In *SIGPLAN Conference on Programming Language Design and Implementation*, pages 1-12, 1999.

12. Edgar F. Codd. Relational database: a practical foundation for productivity. *Communications of the ACM*, 25(2):109-117, 1982.

13. George P. Copeland and Setrag Khoshafian. A Decomposition Storage Model. In *Proc. of the ACM SIGMOD Int'l. Conf. on Management of Data*, pages 268-279, May 1985.

14. David J. DeWitt. DIRECT - A Multiprocessor Organization for Supporting Relational Database Management Systems. *IEEE Trans. on Computers*, 28(6):395, June 1979.

15. David J. DeWitt. Multiprocessor Hash-Based Join Algorithms. In *Proc. of the Int'l. Conf. on Very Large Data Bases*, 1985.

16. Xing Du, Xiaodong Zhang, Yingfei Dong, and Lin Zhang. Architectural Effects of Symmetric Multiprocessors on TPC-C Commercial Workload. *Journal of Parallel and Distributed Computing*, 61:609-640, 2001.

17. Michael J. Flynn. Some Computer Organizations and Their Effectiveness. *IEEE Transactions on Computing*, C(21):948-960, September 1972.

18. Ian T. Foster and Carl Kesselman. *The GRID: Blueprint for a New Computing Infrastructure*. Morgan Kaufmann, San Mateo, CA, USA, 1998.

19. Jim Gray, Adam Bosworth, Andrew Layman, and Hamid Pirahesh. Data Cube: A Relational Aggregation Operator Generalizing Group-By, Cross Tab, and Sub-Total. In *Proc. of the IEEE Int'l. Conf. on Data Engineering*, pages 152-159, New Orleans, LS, USA, February 1996.

20. David R. Helman and Joseph JáJá. Sorting on Clusters of SMPs. August 1997.

21. Jonas S. Karlsson and Martin L. Kersten. Scalable Storage for a DBMS using Transparent Distribution. Technical Report INS-R9710, Centrum voor Wiskunde en Informatica, Amsterdam, The Netherlands, December 1997.

22. Kimberly Keeton, David A. Patterson, Yong Q. He, Roger C. Raphael, and Walter E. Baker. Performance Characterization of a quad Pentium Pro SMP using OLTP workloads. In *Proc. of the Int'l Symp. on Computer Architecture*, Barcelona, Spain, July 1998.

23. Martin L. Kersten, Frans H. Schippers, Carel A. van den Berg, and Peter A. Boncz. Mx documentation tool. 1996.

24. Donald E. Knuth. *The Art of Computer Programming. Volume 3 - Sorting and Searching*. Addison-Wesley, Reading, MA, USA, 2 edition, 1997.

25. 25 Jack L. Lo, Luiz Andr Barroso, Susan J. Eggers, Kourosh Gharachorloo, Henry M. Levy, and Sujay S. Parekh. An analysis of database workload performance on simultaneous multithreaded processors. In *Proc. of the Int'l Symp. on Computer Architecture*, pages 39-50, July 1998.

26. H. Lu, B. Ooi, and K. Tan. *Query Processing in Parallel Relational Database Systems*. IEEE Computer Society Press, Los Alamitos, CA, USA, 1994.

27. Stefan Manegold, Peter A. Boncz, and Martin L. Kersten. Optimizing database architecture for the new bottleneck: memory access. *The VLDB Journal*, 9(3):231-246, December 2000.

28. Stefan Manegold, Peter A. Boncz, and Martin L. Kersten. Optimizing Main-Memory Join On Modern Hardware. *IEEE Trans. on Knowledge and Data Eng.*, 14(3), 2002.

29. Stefan Manegold, Arjen Pellenkoft, and Martin L. Kersten. A Multi-Query Optimizer for Monet. In *Proc. of the British National Conference on Databases*, Exeter, United Kingdom, July 2000.

30. Gurmeet S. Manku, Sridhar Rajagopalan, and Bruce G. Lindsay.Approximate Medians and other Quantiles in One Pass and withLimited Memory. 1999.

31. Gordon E. Moore. Cramming more components onto integrated circuits. *Electronics*, 38(8), April 1965.

32. M.Tamer Özsu and Patrick Valduriez. *Principles of Distributed Database Systems.* Prentice Hall, Englewood Cliffs, NJ, USA, 2 edition, 1999.

33. Donovan A. Schneider and David J. DeWitt. Tradeoffs in Processing Complex Join Queries via Hashing in Multiprocessor Database Machines. In *Proc. of the Int'l. Conf. on Very Large Data Bases*, August 1990.

34. S. Shekhar, S. Ravada, V. Kumar, and D. Chubb. Load-Balancing in High Performance GIS: Declustering Polygonal Maps. *Lecture Notes in Computer Science*, 951:196-206, 1995.

35. Abraham Silberschatz, Henry F. Korth, and S. Sudarshan. *Database System Concepts.* McGraw-Hill, Inc., New York, San Francisco, Washington, DC, USA, 4th edition, 2002.

36. Leonid B. Sokolinsky. Choosing multiprocessor system architecture for parallel database systems. 2000.

37. Pedro Trancoso, Josep-Lluis Larriba-Pey, Zheng Zhang, and Joseph Torellas. The Memory Performance of DSS Commericial Workloads in Shared-Memory Multiprocessors. In *Int'l. Symp. on High Performance Computer Architecture*, San Antonio, TX, USA, January 1997.

38. Transaction Processing Performance Council. *TPC Benchmark H version 1.4.0*, 2002.

39. Dean M. Tullsen, Susan J. Eggers, and Henry M. Levy. Simultaneous Multithreading: Maximizing On-Chip Parallelism, June 1995.

40. Annita N. Wilschut, Jan Flokstra, and Peter M. G. Apers. Parallel Evaluation of Multi-Join Queries. In *Proc. of the ACM SIGMOD Int'l. Conf. on Management of Data*, May 1995.

41. Mohammed J. Zaki and Ching-Tien Ho. *Large-Scale Parallel Data Mining.* Springer-Verlag, Berlin, New York, etc., August 2000.

42. McKenzie, E. Bibliography: Temporal Databases, ACM SIGMOD Record, 15, No. 4, Dec. 1986, pp. 40-52.

43. Stam, R. and R. Snodgrass, A Bibliography on Temporal Databases, Database Engineering, 7, No. 4, Dec. 1988, pp. 231-239.

44. Soo. M. Bibliography on Temporal Databases. ACM SIGMOD Record, 20, No. 1, March, 1991.

45. Kline, N. An Update of the Temporal Database Bibliography, ACM SIGMOD Record, 22, 4, Dec. 1993.

46. Tsotras, V. J. and A. Kumar, Temporal Database Bibliography Update, ACM SIGMOD Record 25, 1, Mar. 1996.

47. Ozsoyoglu, G. and R.T. Snodgrass, Temporal and Real-Time Databases: A Survey, IEEE Transaction on Knowledge and Data Engineering, 7, No. 4, Aug. 1995, pp. 513-532.

48. Xbase File Format Description / Erik Bachman, Roskilde, Denmark: Clickety Click Software, 1996-1998,44pages

49. Loomis, Mary:The Database Book, Macmillan Publishing Company, 1987, New York, New York: ISBN 0-02-371760-2

50. Dorfman, Len: Building C Libraries, Windcrest, 1990, Blue Ridge Summit, PA: ISBN 0-8306-3418-5

51. Eckel, Bruce:Using C++, Osborne, McGraw-Hill, 1990, Berkeley, CA: ISBN 0-07-881522-3

52. Aho, Alfred: Hopcroft, John: Ullman, Jeffrey:Data Structures and Algorithms, Addison-Wesley Publishing, 1983, Reading Massachusetts: ISBN 0-201-00023-7

53. Stevens, C Database Development, MIS Press, 1991, Portland Oregon: ISBN 1-55828-136-3

54. Pressman, Roger: Software Engineering: A Practitioner's Approach, McGraw-Hill, 1982, New York ISBN 0-07-050781-3

55. Chou, George Tsu-der:2nd Edition dBase III Plus Handbook: Que Corporation, 1986, Indianapolis, Indiana ISBN 0-88022-269-7

56. Krumm, Rob:Understanding and Using dBase II & III, Brady Communications Company, Inc, 1985, Bowie MD ISBN 0-89303-917-9

57. Hursch, Jack: Hursch, Carulyn:dBase IV Essentials, Windcrest, 1988, Blue Ridge Summit, PA ISBN 0-8306-9616-4

58. Borland:Turbo C++, Programmer's Guide, Borland International, 1990, Scotts Valley CA

59. Borland:Turbo C++, Library Reference, Borland International 1990, Scotts Valley CA

60. The Draft Standard C++ Library by P.J. Plauger, Prentice Hall, New Jersey, 1995.

61. H.M Dietel/P.J. Deitel: C++ How To Program, Prentice Hall, Englewod Cliffs, New Jersey 07632